ZULUS

ZULUS

Black, White and Blue: The Story of The Zulu Warriors Football Firm

Caroline Gall

MILO BOOKS

MILO BOOKS
Published in November 2005 by Milo Books

Copyright © 2005 Caroline Gall

ISBN 1 903854 48 2

Typeset by Avon DataSet Ltd,
Bidford on Avon, Warwickshire, B50 4JH

Printed in Great Britain by CPD

MILO BOOKS LTD
The Old Weighbridge
Station Road
Wrea Green
Lancs PR4 2PH
info@milobooks.com

Contents

Introduction   1

PART ONE
1 Zulu Dawn   9
2 Black and Blue   29
3 The Apex   39
4 The Leader   63
5 Junior Business Boys   81
6 The Leeds Riot   97

PART TWO
7 Villa   107
8 The Smoke   120
9 The Frozen North   133
10 Cream of the South   144
11 Middle England   157

PART THREE
12 Operation Red Card   177
13 Rave On   191
14 Pleasure Beach   199
15 Fisticuffs   211
16 Moseley Road   226
17 Rocky Lane   243

Final Word   272

Acknowledgements

Cud: Special mentions to all the firms I stood side by side with, as well as those from manors around Birmingham that never get any credit.

From the mid-to-late Seventies: the B.U.G. (Billesley Urban Guerillas), big up to Rockarse, Lance, Smelly, Frog, Mong, Bear, Jed and the Jellies, Cranmore Boot Boys, Jammy, Ozzy, Sim, JJ, Kibs, Ize, Clive Worstock, Jimmy G, Tony G, Kellys, Dean M, Kev R, Johnny Mac, Tommy C, Blocko, Johnny and Steve H and Colin H.

From the late Seventies and into the Eighties, I want to mention the many firms within the Zulus which made us top five for many years: the original Happy Trooper Skins – enough said – Ladywood Apex, the Broadway lads with a special mention to the Krays, the Yardley boys, and Quinton lads with a special mention to the Dove.

Acocks Green gets the biggest mention from me because they were the first firm to have black and white geezers battling side by side in the day. Even though we never had numbers, nobody could come down the Green and get a result. Other firms in those early days had black geezers but A.G. weren't about colour, just about pals and sticking together, white or black. The white geezers got shit for hanging around with black guys back then but they stood and led the way for us and others to come through. Getting rid of racism down the Blues was mostly down to them.

Respect to: Rev, Dud, Coss, Twins, Fizza, Monkey, Swainy, Gary C, Murphys, Mel, Lonny, DT, Frainy, Cockney Lenny,

Beaseley, J Hayes and Psycho.

From the Nineties: Zulu Baby Face Assassins Town Crew, Daddy C, Big Hands, T, Buzz, DT, ST, Lerch, Jell, Twins, Brains, Bird, Psycho, Smoodie, Craig, Claude, Wrock, Zam, Shirley and QT.

Big T: in the twenty-five at Pompey and for holding the line at Rocky Lane.

Wally: A special mention to all those at Man City on November 20, 1982, the Broadway, Bordesley Green lads, Lea Hall, Kings Norton and original Apex lads and anyone else who stood side by side in major battles, especially the twenty-five at Pompey. Also, all the lads currently in HMP . . .

RIP:
Fat Ron
Steve Mooney
Carl Plumb
Paki Wally
H
Graham Bowen
Coxy
Terra
Jinksy aka Freddie Skuttle
Gerard Watson
Twin John
Ronnie Bennett
Derek
Tony Clancey
Patrick Duffy
Anthony Gardner

Introduction

THERE can be few less lady-like pursuits than kicking the crap out of each other after a football match on a Saturday afternoon. It's a strictly male pastime that would not normally interest women, who have much more important things to do come the weekend.

Or so most people told me when I first mentioned I was writing a book about the Zulu Warriors, one of the most feared and dangerous football hooligan firms in the country. Others missed the point entirely and politely inquired why I was so interested in a black warrior tribe from South Africa. "No, I mean the Birmingham Zulus," I told one puzzled girlfriend.

I don't know exactly what it was that first drew me towards the hidden world of terrace mayhem and machismo that the Zulus inhabit. I'd never been particularly interested in football, apart from having a schoolgirl crush on players like Ossie Ardiles and Dino Zoff, who I watched on telly during the 1982 World Cup in Spain.

Although the first football match I ever went to, in the late Eighties, was at Birmingham City, it was mainly because my friend's brother, Mark Yates, was playing for them.

My only other contact with any footballers was at Lilleshall National Sports Centre, where I was doing gymnastics, and I remember my excitement at bumping into Gary Lineker and the rest of the 1986 England World Cup squad who were training there.

1

ZULUS

So I suppose my interest in the beautiful game at the time was very lady-like; crushes on a couple of players and becoming aware of the glamour that surrounded the game. Football hooliganism hadn't even registered with me; the only inkling I had that it went on was regularly seeing Bar St Martin, a popular city centre pub near the Rotunda, being trashed when I walked past it while shopping on a Saturday afternoon.

People told me it was a Blues drinking den and the violence, as they said, was "football related".

It wasn't until I began working in a city centre clothes shop in the mid 1990s that I first fully became aware of the Zulu firm. Because the shop I worked in sold trendy, club-orientated gear, we'd get free passes to club nights and bar and restaurant openings all over town, the idea being that if the so-called trendy people came, the rest would follow. At the time, Birmingham's nightlife was mainly made up of a close-knit clubbing and bar-hopping community and I got to know others who worked in the shops and bars. There were only a handful of designer or independent clothes shops back then, nothing like the amount that have sprung up now, so it was easier and kind of natural that workers mingled and got to know one another.

There was already a "scene" in existence – older lads and girls who had been going out and working in town for years – and we just joined it. Looking back, I guess these older lads were part of the Zulus but I didn't realise it at the time. But seeing them out in town, I noticed that they always seemed to have an edge about them, a certain moody presence that I was instantly aware of.

It wasn't as if they were flash-git hard men showing off with loads of money and glamorous bitches in tow, or bad boys who had rushed the doors and were now moping around with fingers tucked in their waist belts pretending to toy with their imaginary guns. No, these guys exuded silent authority and appeared to be respected and feared in equal measure, a rare breed indeed in the nightlife scene that existed in Birmingham at that time.

I slowly got to know some of them and soon became aware that they were all part of a "firm" who supported Birmingham

City FC and were prepared to batter opposing hooligans to a pulp to prove it. And they weren't just content with representing Birmingham on the terraces. The Zulus also took it on themselves to literally police and defend the city centre from any out-of-town mobs that might want to chance their luck.

The more I got to know about them, the less they lived up to the kind of mindless thug image I would have equated with a typical football hooligan.

One Zulu character who was the complete antithesis of what I had imagined a football thug (he didn't even like football!) to be like was Garry George. He was the perfect gentleman, charismatic, charming, gentle and polite and he knew a lot of people who all seemed to like and respect him. It was Garry who first explained to me exactly what and who the Zulus were – football fans who take pride in their city and region and protect it from "foreign invasions", although now, he said, the Zulus name was bandied about far too much and used by prats who weren't anything to do with it.

By this time, I was working as a journalist for a city press agency, which in effect meant I was working for the national newspapers, providing them with stories from Birmingham. I'd always wanted to be a reporter; it quenched my thirst to be in the thick of things, to know what was going on, who were the movers and shakers, the fraudsters and the gangsters.

As I began to hear more and more about the Zulus, both in the press and from personal contact, my journalistic curiosity went into overdrive and I became intrigued to find out more. I discovered that what had begun as a tight-knit football firm was mushrooming into some kind of supergang with people using and abusing the legend for their own ends. And who could blame them? The Zulu name carries a lot of weight in the Midlands – and not just on the football terraces. The firm's sheer size, popularity and influence in the region means they are the one firm that even gun-toting street gangs will not take on. Its members come from all walks of life and its diverse ethnic make-up is a true reflection of the cosmopolitan city it represents. As one gangster from the city's notorious Burger Bar gang told me, "When they come mob-handed, it's like the United Nations has just arrived."

I wanted to make some sense of these guys and find out why they did what they did, how it all came about, who were the leaders, what was it all about? But then where does a young, middle-class, female reporter from the Shires start when trying to gain entry to such an alien world? And what was I going to do with the information anyway? I didn't want to write newspaper articles, which were bound to come across as sensationalist and would be based on titbits of information that may or may not be right – and there was no friendly Zulu press office.

It was a colleague at work who first suggested that I should write a book about my chosen subject. He was a Birmingham City fan himself and had read a lot of the numerous football hoolie books doing the rounds, which he derided for "all being the same". But, he said, "every footy fan in the country would want to read about the Zulus, there's just something about them and that name."

Garry was always going to be my first port of call, and when I told him what I wanted to do he duly arranged a meeting with the main man at a bar in town. I really didn't know what to expect. I had only ever heard the name Cud being whispered in hushed tones; people spoke of him like some modern day Genghis Khan. Some even doubted he existed which just added to the mystique. I sat there waiting and wondering whether he would take to me or laugh at the idea of a woman writing the Zulu story. Personally I was confident I could do the guys justice and the fact I was about to meet one of the hardest and most respected men in the city just washed over me completely.

When he did arrive with a couple of mates, his measured manner and the deference the others showed around him made it clear to me that he was the leader.

So this is the man, I thought to myself. No grand entry or an entourage of flunkeys in sight. In fact the first thing that struck me about him was his humility and almost timid nature. Garry introduced us and I immediately explained what I did and what I thought would work as a book, while he listened intently. He seemed keen and said they (he never spoke in the singular, it was always "we") had thought about the idea of a book already but had just never got round to it.

We started off talking about the book, and his thoughts about the plethora of books by football firms – lots of rubbish written and not many honest accounts of rows. Cud made it clear he wanted the truth to be written. "When you have been done, say it because it has happened and no firm can honestly say they have never been turned over."

This observation hit an instant note with me. Critics of the burgeoning genre of football hooligan books argue that they glamorise violence and just serve as an ego trip for the writer. That may be true, to some extent, but there is also no denying the football hooligan his place in the annals of British social history. His exploits are a matter of public record, with reams of newspaper copy and sociological studies devoted to exploring the phenomenon. Football violence, as they say in journalistic circles, is sexy. It sells. People are interested by it and attracted to it.

I had no intention of glamorising the Zulus, I just wanted them to tell it as it was, no spin, no bullshit, no bravado. And that was Cud and the others all over. In the end we chatted for several hours discussing everything: Birmingham, racism locally and nationally, the police, the Government and how life has changed over the years. My being a woman never came into it. I believed Cud could see where I was coming from and I felt he trusted me to do it. If any of the others had any qualms about me, they certainly never said anything in front of him. We were on our way.

Since then, I have got to know the other main faces and interviewed them about their time in the first mixed-race football firm. Nearly eighteen months on, I am proud to present the real story of Birmingham City FC's Zulu Warriors largely through the eyes of Cud and Wally, who was one of the founding fathers of the Apex – a smaller group from which the Zulus emerged. But thanks must also go to several lads who have been excellent at recalling days gone by to provide as accurate an account of events as possible – and as we start as far back as the early Seventies, I am impressed. In no particular order: CC, Glenroy, Casey, Bala, Cockney Al, JJ, the General, Morris, Norman, Big Willie, Fizza, David George and Big C plus all the others that were there throughout the Seventies, Eighties, Nineties, and those who are still active today.

Caroline Gall, November 2005

PART ONE

Chapter One

Zulu Dawn

THE SOUND ECHOED around the Manchester streets.

"Zulu, Zulu, Zulu."

It was November 20, 1982, and the first time the chant had been heard on the football battlefield. A new football firm was born.

Hours earlier, a gang of "lads" – hooligans – who followed Birmingham City had caught a train for their team's match against Manchester City at Maine Road. They arrived in the vicinity of the ground, a grid of seemingly endless terraced streets in the infamous Moss Side district, in drizzling rain, only to encounter a rival gang of equal ferocity: the Young Guvnors.

The thirty Blues were outnumbered but one of them, Lanks, shouted, "Make a line," so they spread out in a straight line and joined battle until the police appeared.

As they were escorted to the turnstiles, they talked about the fight they'd just had and the fact that there were, unusually, a lot of black faces on both sides. One lad, Bamo, said it was like the Michael Caine film *Zulu,* the way City's black lads kept pouring towards them, to which they all nodded, saying, "Yeah, the Zulus." The name registered.

During the match, someone started singing, for no obvious reason but possibly because he'd been involved in the earlier conversation, a chant heard occasionally at rugby matches. It went, "Get 'em down, you Zulu Warrior, get 'em down, you

Zulu chief, chief, chief." Before long, nearly everyone was joining in.

One of the original Zulus, Noggin, a former soldier from the Yardley area of Birmingham, had been introduced to the drinking song in the Army and it involved some typically boisterous behaviour by bored squaddies. One member of the group would bend over while toilet roll was inserted between the cheeks of his arse, leaving it to dangle like a tail. He then had to drink a pint of lager whilst the rest of the group sang the song. The catch was that the toilet paper was lit and the soldier had to down the pint before the toilet roll burned his butt.

There was no toilet roll on this occasion but the catchy song struck a chord, literally and figuratively, with many Blues that day. After the game, a goalless draw, they made their way back to the city centre and Piccadilly train station. The Guvnors were once more waiting to start things up. Again, there were more of them than Blues (never *the* Blues), but whenever they were outnumbered, these lads tended to rise to the occasion.

The Guvnors ambushed them as they walked past a bus station and came running out of several bus shelters. Blues stood and someone shouted, "Zulu!" Suddenly the chant was everywhere as Blues ran into City and forced them to back off.

Pockets of fighting carried on all the way back to the station, before Blues jumped on a train home with the events the subject of much debate. It was during that journey it was decided that the firm should be from then on known as the Zulu Warriors. The name stuck, and would eventually unite hundreds of like-minded lads from all over Birmingham. That was the start of the legend.

The Zulus would soon make waves up and down the country, travelling to different grounds in large numbers in search of confrontations. The home lads would seek to defend their territory with equally big turnouts, upping the ante and making it even more important to perform.

Other firms had already adopted monikers, West Ham's Inter City Firm being perhaps the most famous at the time. It was becoming important for the hooligans to have a name under which they could unite, producing one large outfit that would stick together, rather than a loose collection of smaller firms.

To others, the Zulu name appeared natural because of the large contingent of black youths who helped establish their reputation, but the truth is that in the early days the number of black lads was relatively small. Colour was in fact irrelevant; as one lad, Fizza, put it, "We weren't black or white, we were Blues."

There was later a suggestion that the "Warrior" part of the name was adopted from the popular American movie out at the time called *The Warriors,* but Fizza said this was not the case. "We went to see it and we were blown away by it, because it was us. A gang from Coney Island go to a big meeting in central New York with all the other gangs, get blamed for a shooting they never did and then have to get back to Coney Island with every other gang in New York trying to stop them. It was so similar to what we were doing every Saturday along with a large portion of the young male population of the UK, going on other manors and having it with the local gangs.

"Anyway, this Coney Island gang were called the Warriors and they were, just like us, a mixture of different races. The only major difference between them and us was that they were twelve fictional characters and we were two hundred and for real. The thought of our name coming from this source is a natural one but inaccurate.

"Also wrong is the perception of the name coming from the large groups of Rastas who used to congregate around the Bullring shopping centre. It was suggested that London firms referred to these lads as Zulus and that these same lads joined up with the hardcore Birmingham hooligans to form the Zulu Warriors. It's a nice story but total fabrication. We didn't even know that the city centre Rastas were called Zulus until very recently, and although we all appreciate Bob Marley's contribution to music, I'm afraid his contribution to football violence was rather less influential.

"The name came out of Maine Road and it stuck because it was made-to-measure and fitted our persona like a glove."

The Zulu chant has now been taken on by normal Blues fans, and even among Brummies who don't know that much about football, most have heard of the Zulus.

Wally, from Bordesley Green, another of the main lads on the firm, confirmed, "November 20, 1982, at Maine Road, that's where the Zulus started. We always made a point from then on of turning out at Man City to mark the fact that's where it began. Things were starting to look up for Blues now the firm was getting well organised with good numbers. The future was looking good.

"When it's about to go off, you hear it, that shout, and it still feels the same now as it did years ago. I feel proud but you get a lot of lads using the name in town nowadays, jumping on the bandwagon when they have never really been part of it. A mate who is a Villa fan once got talking to Frank Bruno at a boxing match and when he said he was from Birmingham, Bruno asked, 'Are you a Zulu?' Younger lads have said to me that if they go down to the football, they'll be singing it. Other firms sing their songs but the whole crowd in St Andrew's sing ours, and when some big teams come down you can hear 'Zulus gonna get ya' coming from the normal fans."

As the Zulus rose to become one of the top five firms in the country, the police and the media also became more aware of their existence and of their chant. In 1985, a senior officer with West Midlands Police said, "They chant a war cry at Blues games which they attend faithfully, both home and away. The group takes its nickname from the well-known film *Zulu*, and they mime the warrior chant to try and instil fear in their opponents. There must be hundreds of them in the faction but our trouble lies in identifying the lads because they have no badge or insignia."

Cud, their leader, agrees. "It is like a war cry. At first it was a bit of fun but it gradually went deeper than that and meant a lot more as the firm grew and grew. Once you hear it, you know you can't run. We'd never got to London in the early 1980s, although we dominated the Midlands, but when we became Zulus we started going south and taking on the London firms. It put us on another level."

BIRMINGHAM CITY FC began life in 1875 as Small Heath Alliance, an amateur football team founded, oddly enough, by a group of cricketers from Bordesley Green. In 1905, it became known as Birmingham City and the following year it moved to the current St Andrew's stadium site. Around 32,000 people turned out to watch the first game there, a draw with Middlesbrough. The first goal at St Andrew's was scored three days later by Benny Green, who was allegedly rewarded for his effort with a piano.

Yet success was always elusive; Blues have never won either the League Championship or the FA Cup. The ground was bombed during the Second World War, the Railway End and the Main Stand were ruined and the Spion Kop roof collapsed, preventing any more games there until 1943. In the meantime they played at Aston Villa's ground after their neighbours offered to help out.

One of the best teams to play at St Andrew's was Arthur Turner's side of the mid 1950s. They were promoted to the top flight in 1955 and the following year achieved their highest-ever league position, finishing sixth. They also reached the FA Cup Final, only to be thwarted by Manchester City's goalkeeper, Bert Trautmann, who famously played with a broken neck. In May 1956, Birmingham also became the first English League club to play in Europe, when they drew 0–0 with Internazionale in the Inter Cities Fairs Cup, now the UEFA Cup.

In the mid Sixties, they fell from the First to the Second Division, and in 1970 manager Stan Cullis called it a day. Freddie Goodwin replaced him. Signing four players in six months, he was responsible for introducing sixteen-year-old Trevor Francis as a substitute at Cardiff in September 1970. Francis went on to score 133 goals for the club in 328 appearances. He hit the ground running and scored sixteen league goals in his first season. A fourteen-game unbeaten run from mid-December until March saw the club finish ninth in the Second Division.

Fans believed promotion to the First Division in the 1971/72 season was now tangible. A successful FA Cup run to the semi-finals also bolstered support for the team. Losing only one match between January and the end of the season, Blues clinched promotion for the first time in seven years with a 1–0 win against Orient, in front of 15,000 away fans, thanks to Bob Latchford.

After finishing nineteenth in the 1973/74 season and seventeenth the following year, Freddie Goodwin departed and former Leeds United full-back Willie Bell took over a rather dejected team. During his first season in charge, 1975/76, they only managed to finish nineteenth, narrowly avoiding relegation. Mid-table finishes in the following two seasons were an improvement but the team went out of both cup competitions and the manager lost his job in 1977. There was a brief liaison with Sir Alf Ramsey, but he was replaced in 1978 by Jim Smith. Relegation beckoned and the team dropped to Division Two in 1979. Players came and went. Among those to go was Trevor Francis, who became English football's first £1 million player when he joined Nottingham Forest in 1979. He was to return two decades later to take the club to the brink of the top flight as manager.

Things began to improve and the club was tipped as one of the favourites to win promotion. A point at Burnley in their penultimate game meant they needed just one more point at home to Notts County in their final match to secure promotion. It was a close run thing. Blues led 2–0 after twenty minutes, only for County to claw back, but Birmingham managed to hold on, the match finishing 3–3 in front of a whopping 34,000 gate.

On the terraces, St Andrew's was, by the 1970s, an aggressive, racist and intimidating place to visit. Football hooliganism was on the rise, and skinheads ruled the roost. A sea of lads dressed in white skinners, ox-blood Dr Martens and, at the end of the decade, Sham 69 or Angelic Upstarts tee-shirts, showed up on the terraces week in, week out.

The Happy Trooper Boot Boys were the best-known "firm" at the ground and led the way from the mid-70s. They were predominantly skins and took their name from the Happy Trooper pub in Chelmsley Wood, an area directly to the east of Birmingham which was dominated by Blues. The "Trooper Mob" consisted of the Town Centre Boot Boys, who were older and not all involved in the football scene, the Friendly Inn, which had a large Irish contingent, and lads who drank in the Yeoman, the Hiker and the Greenwood pubs. The Happy Trooper itself was in the southern area of the Wood and in the north there were lads who drank in the Woodman and Centurion, who rarely associated with the rest.

Chelmsley Wood started life in 1963 as an overspill town for Birmingham, as demand for new housing increased, and at one time was one of the largest housing estates in Britain. A vast area filled with several high-rises, rabbit-warren paths and roads and faceless concrete buildings, it is a testament to 1960s architecture for which Birmingham is infamous.

Not surprisingly, it produced some of the hardest lads in and around the city. On a match day these lads would get the train from nearby Marston Green and, depending on the game, there would be anywhere between twenty and 200 of them. One, Cockney Al, so called because he had moved to Birmingham from London when he was young, drove a Cortina Mark Two with a bright red sticker on the top of his windscreen that said "Chelmsley Wood Skins" in white lettering.

GG: I'm from Chelmsley Wood and most of our lot went to the same schools and grew up together. We loved going to the football and we'd wag school to go to away matches. Me and my mates would climb into the ground over the barbed wire by the toilets, and the adults would watch and laugh at us. It's not like that now. Money was tight when we were young and we'd do what we could to get money, like collect empty beer bottles and get cash for them. I can remember paying 65p to travel on the coach to matches and not being able to afford the extra 5p to enable me to go on the train.

I eventually went into the Army and there were lots of football lads in there. I did some bad things with Blues but I did some bad things with the Army too – back then you were encouraged to do it. We had a lot of good lads in the firm. I can go anywhere in Brum now and I will know someone and they will know me. Birmingham is our town, we love it too much and we are not going to let people come in and take the piss.

Although skinheads dominated the St Andrew's terraces, as they did across the country, the area did not divide black and white; rather it united, and led to the firm becoming one of the first mixed-race outfits in the country. In this era of Docs, drainpipe jeans and shaved heads, it was natural that the black lads dressed the same way – and sixty of them did indeed dress exactly the same for a match at Manchester United in August 1978. Blue drainpipe jeans with turn-ups, red twelve-hole Doc Martens, red check lumberjack shirts and black Harringtons with a red check on the inside was the look. No-one bothered them *en route*, no doubt due to the way they looked and the fact they were singing songs about Chelmsley Wood.

While racism was not an issue for the Trooper Mob, with black and white drinking together, fighting together and watching football together, it was a problem at Birmingham City, the club they all passionately followed. The years 1976 to 1979 were hardcore skinhead times at Blues at the same time far-right groups were rising to prominence. In the mid-70s you could count on one hand the number of black guys at a match: Junior, Garry (aka the General), Tony Austin and a couple of others.

Later, when the racist songs and chants started up, it was hard for the white lads to stand with their black friends like DG,

Bobby Fuller and Glenroy and have to hear "Nigger, Nigger lick my boots" and "Lick them lips and stick 'em to the windows." When black players like Cyrille Regis – one third, with Brendan Batson and Laurie Cunningham, of the so-called "Three Degrees" at West Bromwich Albion – were playing, songs like "Gimme dat, gimme dat, gimme dat banana, Cyrille Regis, Cyrille Regis" would belt out from the terraces, while bananas rained on to the pitch. But it was the norm and the white lads stood there, unable to do anything, feeling as awkward and embarrassed as their black friends. However, the black lads were never on the receiving end of any direct racist comments, always reassuringly told, "You're alright though."

Although Brazil had long been the best team in the world, there were hardly any black footballers playing in English teams in the late 1960s and 1970s. The pioneers were players like Albert Johansson at Leeds, Clyde Best at West Ham – two clubs noted for the racist element among their supporters – and Regis at West Bromwich, the area where Enoch Powell had made his notorious Rivers of Blood speech a few years earlier. There were just as few black fans, but the black and white lads in Chelmsley had grown up together, knew no different and didn't want it any other way, despite efforts by heavy-handed West Midlands Police and the National Front to create tension.

The NF held a march one Saturday in Birmingham city centre in the mid-70s. It coincided with a Birmingham City home match, so it was perhaps inevitable that they would encounter a bunch of football-loving skinheads walking through town. But this particular group was made up of black and white.

The NF marched along the middle of the main road in Digbeth, walking distance from the city centre, with a smattering of police surrounding them. At the same time, a sizeable group of Blues, having enjoyed a few beers, walked down a side street, past the old Outrigger pub and out on to the top of the main road, where they saw the right-wingers heading towards them, singing, shouting and brandishing England flags.

The black guys in the group were mostly at the back and were told to stay there while the march got nearer. The marchers thought they had encountered some like-minded people and acknowledged them – until they were hit with a barrage of beer cans and debris. Blues let rip, with the black lads laying into whoever they could get their hands on. At the same time, counter-demonstrators from the Anti-Nazi League attacked the marchers from behind. The police were overwhelmed at first as casualties littered the ground. The marchers scattered under the onslaught and brawling spread across the road. It lasted only a few minutes before the police started to restore order, which signalled time for Blues to scarper and continue on their way to St Andrew's relatively unscathed.

West Midlands Police generally had a bad reputation in this period, and were particularly disliked on the Wood. Reggae poet Linton Kwesi Johnson was a big influence on a generation of youths soured by the treatment they received. His song "Sonny's Lettah", about police brutality, made sense as did the Angelic Upstarts' "We're not anti-police, we're anti police oppression" and "Who Killed Liddle Towers?"

The fiercest reputation was held by the Special Patrol Group (SPG) of officers, who patrolled the city by van. They were known not just for their height and build but for their infamous black gloves. Like many police units, at first they didn't know what they were dealing with at matches, and most lads causing trouble just got a slap and were told in no uncertain terms to "piss off". There were no organised operations targeting groups, but as each firm improved and became better known, the more unwanted police attention they got. Officers would later pick up some names of Blues lads and would shout them out as they recognised them walking past on their way to grounds, which was a bit of a shock to some. The SPG van was usually present at home matches and if lads were carted away and put in the back they knew what was coming – a reminder of who was boss.

The SPG seemed to pick off black lads, whether they were at a match or not, to make sure they knew who called the shots.

Cud, the Zulus' main man from the 1980s onwards, was followed by them as he walked home one day.

Cud: I was only a teenager walking home from Solihull. I hadn't been to a match but as I walked down the road I was aware of the SPG van behind me. I turned and saw it slowly driving along with several police officers inside and I could see their black gloves. They were deliberately following me and carried on creeping behind me. I kept my head down and continued walking, ignoring them but shitting myself about what would come next.

Then one of them shouted at me, "Been robbing houses have we?" and they laughed. "I've been to Solihull, that's all," I said as I carried on walking, getting more worried that a beating wasn't far away, but they pulled in front of me and kept driving for a bit before driving off laughing.

It was hard enough walking around estates after matches or just generally when you were out and about. I used to make sure I had a couple of bottles up my sleeves most times, because there were cars full of skinheads driving about, and sometimes if they saw you and you retaliated to their abuse, you'd hear the all-too-familiar sound of brakes being slammed on and off it would go.

———————

The early Seventies were also a period when many football fans started travelling to away games in large numbers for the first time. The violent exploits of some of the bigger followings, in particular the notorious Red Army of Manchester United, influenced others, and soon fighting at games, and in particular the taking of "ends", was a regular weekend occurrence. Segregation at the time was poor or non-existent in most stadia, so it was easy for a crew of visitors to infiltrate the area normally occupied by home fans. Maine Road, a place with which Blues now have many links, provided at least two memorable occasions: once when Blues "took" the Kippax, and an FA Cup match against Fulham.

Blues were at Maine Road for the first game of the 1973/74 season. Around 450 lads headed to the Parasol pub in Birmingham city centre in the morning and began drinking and singing before stocking up on food and more beer and getting the train to Piccadilly Station about midday. Surprisingly, no City fans were waiting for them when they arrived; instead the police rounded them up and escorted them to the ground, where they met many more Blues fans who had driven up in cars and on coaches. They went to the away end and the police left them to it.

Well before kick-off, some of the lads decided they wanted to go into the Kippax, the side of the ground that was considered City's end, where the home singers and bootboys gathered; a terrace that would be defended at all costs from intruders. It was only about a quarter full with lads, probably not City's main hooligan mob. A group of mainly older Blues made their way to the gates and then ran in shouting, "The Brummies are here."

City surged forward but their response was brief. The Birmingham mob punched and kicked them backwards and soon took control of the terrace, goading the furious Mancunians. The police came in and broke it up, pushing Blues into one corner and holding them there until more and more City came in and they decided they had better get them out.

Retribution came after the game. "I was a teenager, and after the game me and my mate got chased," remembered Norman from Acocks Green. "A big mob of City were waiting outside and Blues were scattered all over. Blues lads were saying, 'We took your end,' and shouting abuse but we knew we had to get away. As we walked towards the station we encountered about thirty City who singled me out because I am black. I heard, 'We want the nigger.' I told my mate we had to run but he was quite big and reckoned he couldn't so I ran ahead, thinking they wouldn't get him because he was white.

"Up ahead I saw some 'Daddies' – a name we used for the

older lot – and they asked why I was running. I told them and they said to stay with them. They then ripped up part of a fence and went after them. City were no longer interested in me. The Kippax had never been taken before, not even by United, so we were pleased with the result."

The mid-week FA Cup match against Fulham in April 1975 was particularly violent. Around 35,000 Blues fans had watched Joe Gallagher equalize late on at Hillsborough a week before, forcing a replay at Maine Road. With London, Birmingham and Manchester involved, it was a given that it would be one of those nights. Everyone met up in various pubs in Brum in the afternoon and started drinking before heading up to Manchester on coaches. The lads arrived at 5pm and joined the 20,000-odd Blues supporters who had made the trip. As soon as they got off the coaches they ran amok, buzzing, shouting and robbing practically all the alcohol the local shops stocked, much to the astonishment of the Indian shopkeepers.

Inside the ground, Fulham were behind one of the goals while Blues were given the Kippax. Much to the surprise of Blues, it emerged that Manchester City and United had joined up for the evening's entertainment and were singing loudly from the corner of the stand, letting Blues know they were a force to be reckoned with. Fights and scuffles between the three firms kicked off straight away – with not much going on with Fulham – before the match started. Everyone was tanked up thanks to the crates of beer and hurling abuse, jeering their rivals. The police surrounded a very drunken Norman and threw him out of the ground because of the level of abuse he was spouting. He was promptly chased by some locals and had to hide in a nearby shop until the match ended and it was relatively safe to walk, or stumble, back to the coaches with everyone else.

After the game, it went off between London, Birmingham and Manchester in many of the narrow terraced streets in Moss Side. No-one had ever known City and United to link up and Blues were amazed, as they would never have done the same with Villa, no matter who the opposition. No-one was coming out on top; it was just a case of chasing, fighting, getting chased and then fighting again. Dustbins and other street debris were hurled and pockets of fans fought running battles down the ginnels and alleyways.

When Norman made it back to the car park, he found every window of his coach bar the windscreen had been smashed. Blues had lost 1–0 after extra time and were out of the Cup, it was freezing cold and there was the prospect of an even colder journey, but the driver was determined to get back, so they shivered all the way home, thoroughly pissed off.

Not long after, on a cold, rainy day in 1974, around 200 Brummies arrived at Stoke train station. There to greet them was a similar-sized firm of locals dotted about the side streets and back-to-back houses. As Blues walked out of the station, a volley of bricks and cans flew towards them, prompting them immediately to retaliate. The two police officers on hand were powerless to stop the two groups charging into each other, shouting obscenities. The brawling spread to the side streets and gradually moved away from the station, with lads bouncing around each other, fighting one-on-one, and two large groups confronting each other in the road.

Not far away, one of the Blues lads spotted a delivery man slowly driving a lorry load of Alpine Pop out on his rounds. The home-delivery fizzy drinks firm was based in Chelmsley and he was surprised to see its produce being delivered as far away as Stoke, but he knew its large bottles, with a mottled effect around the neck, made good ammunition. A couple of lads broke away from the fight and jumped on the back of the wagon. They swiped bottle after bottle and hastily distributed them to the rest, who then flung them in the direction of Stoke, hitting their targets and smashing on the floor. Stoke were overpowered and scattered, leaving Blues to talk over the battle and swap stories as they carried on walking to the old Victoria Ground.

Inside, Stoke were settled in their partially covered Boothen End, facing up to 6,000 Blues fans in an open end behind the goal. Before the match started and amid the chanting and swaying on the terraces, there was time for some fun on the pitch.

Donkey, one of the older lads, decided to confront the Boothen End. He stepped over the knee-high hooped fence – the only barrier in place to prevent people from getting on the pitch – and with the rest of the lads eagerly cheering him on, ran all the way to Stoke's end with a huge Blues flag. When he got there he beckoned and shouted for their main man to join him on the pitch before running back to the centre circle, where he opened out the flag and lay down on it, flat on his back. It wasn't long before a solitary figure made his way on to the pitch from Stoke's end and headed towards the circle. As soon as the pair met in the middle of the pitch they began scrapping. The clapping and cheering from the Blues end, hugely entertained by Donkey's behaviour, grew louder as the kicks and punches continued and there was rapturous applause when the Stoke lad fell to the floor after Donkey landed a hefty punch. Victory complete, there was no need to do any more, so Donkey returned to the stand a hero. The Stoke lad was then helped off the pitch and went back into the Boothen.

Leeds, later that same season, was a different story. More than 50,000 people turned up for their visit to St Andrew's, with thousands being unable to get in. (Match attendances in the Seventies regularly topped 30,000 but declined towards the end of the decade and dropped to as low as 6,000 in the late 1980s.) Many of those that couldn't get in hung around outside after kick-off, and it wasn't long before the club made an announcement informing the crowd that they had received a bomb threat from the IRA and the ground had to be evacuated. Ground staff opened the gates expecting people to make their way out but, instead, the thousands outside poured in. The players, who were on the pitch, also didn't move and the game continued, trouble free, before ending in a 1–1 draw.

The following season, a hardy bunch of skinheads travelled to Leeds on a British Rail Special but soon found themselves in trouble. A firm of Leeds were waiting for them outside the station

23

and launched into Blues, sending them scattering in and around the station. Leeds were everywhere and overpowered their rivals with their strength of numbers. Once Blues had been split up, they were easier targets. Everybody got a good going over and had black eyes, ripped clothes and bruised egos. Leeds were the best team in the country in the mid-1970s and their firm was feared because of their countless victories. The beatings were so bad and numerous the lads decided to forget the game and go back to Brum on the train. They were home before the match had even kicked off.

Inside St Andrew's, the main areas adopted by Blues were the Tilton Road End, Railway End and the Kop. The Barmy Tilton Army, in the Tilton Road End, would often challenge the superior and larger Spion Kop mob in the neighbouring Kop stand. Some of the older lads stood on the right side of the Tilton End, and "Right Side" stuck as a nickname for them all. Around the same time, Bruce Lee and his kung fu films were making a huge impression and were avidly watched by the lads. A dull match was often the perfect opportunity to try out a few of his fighting techniques. The two groups in neighbouring terraces would sing at each other, getting more and more heated and abusive. The Kop would sing the well-known chant, "Come and have a go if you think you're hard enough," and the Tilton Army would chant back, "We're the Barmy Tilton Army," prompting several hundred of them to walk across and have a go. But after a couple of minutes of fighting the Tilton would run back, unable to overpower the Kop. They never managed it and the Kop reigned supreme.

Other firms tried to take the Kop over the years. Celtic got in because they arrived very early for Birmingham City's Centenary match in 1975. It was a night game and they had taken over several pubs near the ground, including the Greenway. Thousands of them drank and sang, but as more and more Blues turned up they were not too happy about them being in the Kop and set about removing them. Celtic put up a good battle for five to ten minutes, despite having cups of tea and beer thrown in their faces amid the punches and kicks, but Blues successfully got their area back. After that, the song, "Celtic tried to take the Kop but Rangers took the Holte," could be heard from time to time on the terraces.

The Rangers episode came when Celtic's great Glasgow rivals came down to play Aston Villa the same year. Blues linked up with the Rangers hordes to have a go at the team every Bluenose hates the most, and got into the massive Holte End at Villa Park with some Scottish lads. They quickly did over some Villa lads and chased them about, singing the "Rangers took the Holte" song. Villa would turn the tables in the early 1980s when some of them made it into the Birmingham Kop, but it was way before any Blues had arrived for the match and they went in the far corner, away from the adjoining Tilton End, knowing that no Blues lads ventured that far over. Instead of Villa being able to claim a psychological victory from that escapade, they have been ridiculed ever since.

Blues needed a point out of the last game of the 1975/76 season to be certain of staying in Division One. It was a night game against Sheffield United and about 100 of the main lads travelled to Bramall Lane on an afternoon train and settled in a pub near the station. Around an hour before the match, rival fans were spotted outside. The Birmingham mob emerged throwing bottles and glasses before fighting hand to hand with the Sheffield lads in the street. The police arrived and steamed in, arresting many from both sides and telling them it was for their own safety.

In the ground, Johnny H, one of the main Blues lads from Kings Norton, walked round to Sheffield's main end with Jayo and Gnocchi and kicked it off with some of their lads. The fighting attracted the attention of the police and prompted several mounted officers to enter the terraces and separate the fans. The lads were eventually walked back round to their end to the familiar sound of rapturous applause from the rest of the Blues firm. The game ended in a draw and Blues survived the drop.

A night game against Blackpool in August 1976 saw Blues let

rip in the seaside town. "It was the second round of the League Cup and two coaches of pure loons went up," recalled Cockney Al, one of the original members of the Trooper Mob. "We got there just as the fair was preparing to close for the night and we headed straight for the beach. We raced to see who could be the first person to make it into the sea. Then we hit the pubs and some got in but some were turned away for being too young – or too wet.

"We lost the game two-one, and as we made our way out, singing our songs, we met some local lads. Running battles ensued, lasting for three or four minutes underneath the old wooden ground. There were about 100 of us, all game lads, and although Blackpool weren't really known, there were sixty of seventy of them and they were up for it. I think they expected us to run but we didn't. I can't say no Blues fan has ever run when faced with a load of game lads but certainly none of the hardcore Zulus ever have. About 100 lads were also arrested that day after a car was chucked into the sea. They were charged with taking a vehicle without consent.

"I was also present in February 1977 for the FA Cup match with Derby. We went on the train and the minute we arrived it was pure carnage with their lads. They had a good firm and were making a name for themselves. The Old Bill tried to hold us back and separate us but we got away, and every chance we had on the way to the ground, we had a battle. At the back of the away end, behind the goal, was a burger bar and someone set it alight during the game, which was not good when you think of other similar well-known incidents at grounds where people died. The police arrived and tried to put the fire out. We fought them and one of them got a broken nose but there were so many of us he didn't know who had done it.

"We lost two-one and after the game we were charged up and hunting Derby lads. We walked round a corner past an off licence near the ground and bumped into some. One of them was promptly thrown through the window of the shop but he got up and ran off. We carried on and a bigger firm appeared, fronted by a guy I recognised from earlier as one of their main men. We confronted each other and I nutted him. He dropped to the floor and didn't move. It didn't look good so we dispersed and headed for the train station.

"We saw the Old Bill, who said they had witnesses to what had happened and arrested five of us and took us to the station. As we were put in the cells, I saw the copper whose nose had been broken. He was saying, 'If I ever catch who did this to me I'll bloody kill them.' But he never saw me. We sat in the cells and all shouted across to one another to say nothing. After a while I heard coppers letting a couple of the lads out, saying, 'Thanks lads, hope you get your train alright.' I was told the lad I'd butted was in a coma and I wasn't let out. Instead I was charged with GBH, appeared before magistrates in Leicester the next day and was remanded in custody for seven days. During that time he came out of the coma and I was released on bail. In December that year, nine months later, I pleaded guilty to GBH and got sentenced to seven days in jail, which I had already served, received an £800 fine and was ordered to pay the lad £1,400 in compensation. Since that day Derby is a firm we destroy every time we meet. I missed the next few games, as I didn't want to go back there really. And although I have been there since I've never seen that guy again.

"After the game, another group of about fifteen Blues lads who had travelled up in a Transit van were followed by about thirty Derby lads as they made their way back to it. Derby had clocked their van and the lads decided they would get some tools out of the back if it went off. It did, and one of the Blues lads, Jamie, got whacked round the head with a wheel brace by another Blues lad, Milko. It was a complete accident. After Derby got bashed, Jamie had twenty-six stitches in a Birmingham hospital. Derby weren't really rated by the older Blues lot but the lads remember their main man because he was a dead ringer for Elton John."

It was at a match at Derby that several of the lads wore surgical masks because of a chickenpox epidemic in the town.

One of the lads dished them out at New Street Station, much to the amusement of everyone, including the police.

When Nottingham Forest beat Blues 2–0 in December 1977, there was serious fighting afterwards along Garrison Lane, near St Andrew's. Forest's coaches were parked on one side of the main road by a scrapyard, and as they made their way there Blues launched a relentless attack. The front line stormed into them, sparking running battles in the middle of the road with debris being chucked in both directions. CC, one of the original Chelmsley lads, was at the front but was hit square in the face by a heavy, unidentified object. He stood dazed before falling to the ground in the middle of the battle. He was kicked along the ground, unable to get away until, out of nowhere, a Ford Capri pulled up nearby. Three lads jumped out, scooped him up off the floor, chucked him the back and sped away to the Blues' ground.

CC was in a bad way and came to in the changing rooms. An ambulance was called and he was taken to hospital, where he stayed for three months. He had no idea what hit him but he had a fractured skull, broken nose, jaw, cheek and collar bone and broken a rib. He recovered but his eyesight was permanently affected, as was his opinion of Forest, who became his pet hate. Regular hospital visits from the lads kept him abreast of their escapades, and he was determined to get back as soon as possible. He made it in time for a match against Villa around three months later. He was seventeen years old, feeling invincible and completely caught up in the era, so nothing would deter him, not even serious injury.

It was from lads like CC, young, committed and hardcore, that the Zulus would ultimately spring.

Chapter Two

Black and Blue

WHILE CHELMSLEY WOOD dominated on the St Andrew's terraces, other areas were also well represented, and this in itself brought problems. Throughout the decade there was no real organisation, nor one clear leader of the Blues hooligan firm. Lads like Ashford, Yeatesy, Noggin, Jayo, J. Sherry, Jamie Q, Johnny H and Gnocchi had been causing mayhem for several years and were at the forefront, but they all came from different towns in the city. Towards the end of the decade, in-fighting and scuffles between certain areas were common.

Cud, from Acocks Green, had been going to matches since the late 1970s and built up a reputation, as he knew lads from nearly all the areas and sometimes helped to defuse tension and potential rows. He had his work cut out. Chelmsley did not get on with the Shard End, Kingshurst, Sheldon and Lea Hall areas that were all nearby, and there were several disputes and fights amongst lads from Solihull, Billesley, Acocks Green, Maypole, Kings Norton, Small Heath, Northfield, Selly Oak and Warstock. Chelmsley was the main mixed firm, while the others were predominantly white. All these areas surround Birmingham and it wasn't until a group of around sixty black and white teenagers from areas like Ladywood, Highgate, Bordesley Green, Lee Bank and Sparkbrook formed a crew called the Apex – the forerunners of the Zulus – in the early 1980s that the city centre became officially involved.

The in-fighting wasn't about who wanted to be an overall leader, it was general rivalry between different areas which, for the most part, was kept away from the ground. As Chelmsley Wood had such a fierce reputation, other lads would go there on buses to have a look – but only if they were prepared to fight. The Trooper Mob would often be sitting outside and would pelt the buses with bricks as they sang a chant about their home town. When a fair came to Chelmsley Wood one year, two bus loads of Northfield lads came over, it was assumed, for a row. Whatever their intentions, they were chased ragged before being beaten up and sent on their way.

Because of all the trouble at the Trooper over the years, the police finally got their wish when the pub was earmarked for demolition in the mid-1980s. But when the demolition workers came to knock it down they were met by angry mobs who didn't want it to happen. One of the workers, who knew a lad from the area, told him some years later it was the scariest job he'd ever had to do. It started with gangs of youngsters at first shouting abuse, chucking bricks and doing what they could to prevent the work getting under way. Eventually, a huge mob of adults and kids assembled and managed to stop the demolition. Despite this, it was eventually bulldozed a short time later.

Heading into the city centre on a train from the Wood could be hazardous, as lads were bound to encounter groups from rival areas. To get to Chelmsley, trains from Birmingham stop first at Stechford, Lea Hall and Marston Green. Once, after a match, around fifty Chelmsley were in two carriages and ten Lea Hall in another. Lea Hall were left alone until it was their stop, but when they got off the Chelmsley lads joined them on the platform and shouted at them to kick things off. Fights broke out immediately, but little did the Chelmsley lot know that reinforcements lay in wait at the top of a sloping path from the platform. Bricks and chunks of concrete rained down on the unsuspecting Chelmsley lads and bounced off the train. The women and children passengers on board watched in horror as more carriages were hit, smashing windows and denting metal before the train pulled away from the station, leaving the lads brawling on the platform. Lea Hall did well and Chelmsley acknowledge it was a victory for them.

The Chelmsley Wood lads would also often struggle to get home from night games, as there was no late bus service to the town; it was deemed to be too dangerous for the drivers. Instead the lads would have to take the number 14 bus to nearby Tile Cross, where the police would often appear, saying they wanted to search the group for drugs or on some other pretext. They'd search everyone and annoyingly remove the laces out of their Docs so they were rendered useless in terms of fighting anyone, and then leave.

As youths from all areas grew older and socialised more, some of the friction eased. In the close season, some from the Wood frequented a pool hall in the city centre and mingled with the various lads they bumped into there. Also, the hunt for women took several lads from Acocks Green, Solihull, Sheldon, Billesley and Chelmlsey to the Solihull Civic Hall, the Barn and Cinders nightclubs in Hockley Heath. The two clubs – favoured by "rich girls dropped off by their dads" – provided many with superb memories of going after them on the pull, so much so that several lads returned around 1995 to check out the disco one last time.

They arrived in three carloads, with one passenger, CC, being kept in the dark about where he was being taken until they hit the M42 motorway and he guessed. They pulled up and walked to the entrance, where they were confronted by two doormen who came out with the usual, "How can we help you lads?" When the lads said they had come for the disco, the doormen both smiled and told them to wait while they fetched someone. The manager then appeared and asked them what they wanted and when they explained he also smiled and told them to hold on before disappearing. He came back a few moments later with the chef kitted out in his whites, and the confused and slightly annoyed lads again asked about the disco. The chef said he was the manager of the disco back in the old days and informed them it had closed some fifteen years earlier. But he took them round the premises and bought them all drinks as they reminisced about the crazy nights they'd had there.

IN SEPTEMBER 1978, European Cup holders Liverpool came to St Andrew's. It was one of those balmy early autumn days: the sun was shining and the drink was flowing. In the ground, a few coins were thrown between rival fans, along with a bit of banter, then came bricks and, bizarrely, a jar of Colman's Mustard. One of the Scousers chucked the jar in amongst Blues, where it was caught and returned. A few moments later it was thrown back towards Blues, but was again caught and hurled back into the Liverpool crowd, where it landed on someone's head and broke.

Cud, who was aged sixteen at the time, had started the day in and around the pubs. "There were loads of people about," he said. "In the ground both Liverpool and Blues lads were in the Tilton, with a line of coppers dividing the firms. As the game wore on and the abuse and throwing competitions continued, some blokes working in a factory that backed right up to the Tilton End started passing stuff down to the lads to chuck at Liverpool. They gave out pipes, bolts, anything you could chuck, so that's what we did. During the game there was a pitch invasion and in the madness a punk called Potter, who was on the pitch, got a dart right in the middle of his forehead. He was nabbed by the Old Bill who walked him back round still with the dart in his head."

A lad called Jamie from Small Heath was also apprehended by the police before the game for fighting with some Welsh Liverpool fans. He was let out at 5.30pm but was back in the same police station two hours later for fighting the same lads again. Two police officers, Quinn and Nicholls, are remembered by many. They were in the Special Patrol Group and gave as good as they got when it came to catching lads.

Another character who deserves a mention is Bully Beef. He was seen on the terraces without fail throughout the 1970s and 1980s, with his trademark pipe in his mouth. After chinning someone, he would stop and have a smoke while his victim lay flat out on the floor or beat a hasty retreat. As well as plenty of beer, some were dabbling with drugs at the turn of the decade, just for a bit of extra mayhem on a match day. They favoured French Blueys, which contained strychnine and thinned your blood, and speed-based Dexedrine, or Dexys (hence Dexys Midnight Runners).

The next time Blues played Liverpool, in a mid-week League Cup match in December 1980, they knew it would be another eventful day. About forty Chelmsley Wood lads made the journey, including J. Sherry, Cockney Al, CC, DG and Bobby Fuller, with a tasty contingent from other areas, including Jayo and Gnocchi. The main guys were out in force once again. Quite a few lads were kitted up with rounders bats, lovingly made by one of the lads who worked as an engineer. He had fashioned several on a lathe at work and they fitted snugly in the inside pockets of Harringtons or flying jackets.

The lads caught a Special to Liverpool and decided to walk the several miles to Anfield. On the way they came to a two-lane dual carriageway and attempted to cross it, but J. Sherry was hit by a car in the middle of the road and the driver didn't bother to stop. His pals came to his rescue and called an ambulance, despite his protestations that he still wanted to go to the match, then carried on without him. As they walked through the town centre they encountered some locals drinking outside a pub. Although they had the wedge haircuts then popular on the Merseyside terraces, it wasn't clear if they were full-on Liverpool lads.

Because DG, an extremely fit guy who later went into the Marines, and Bobby Fuller were black, they were immediately singled out for abuse, with "Give it de darkie" comments as the locals came towards them. It kicked off in the street near the pub and out came the rounders bats, which were bounced off the heads and bodies of several Liverpool lads. The search for more weapons – in nearby bins – produced a bag of bottles which were wrapped around someone's head. Blues beat Liverpool up and down the road and "took the piss", in their parlance, but the police were soon there and started making arrests. Nearly twenty Blues lads were apprehended. Two of them had bats but managed to drop them in the police van on the way to the station. The lads had to laugh when the police guessed what area they were from when they said Birmingham.

"You're not from Chelmsley Wood are you?"

The others carried on to the ground, ready for more, and during the match there were several small outbreaks of fighting in the Anfield Road End, which was divided between home and away fans. The Liverpool police weighed in with their notorious "night sticks" – long baton-type weapons that allowed officers to hit troublemakers from a distance. After the game, which Blues lost 3–1, Liverpool gangs sought their revenge and picked lads off as they made their way back to the train station.

In September 1978, Chelsea, another of the big firms who dominated the decade, came to St Andrew's. Before the match, a load of Blues congregated near the Old Crown pub in Digbeth, opposite the coach station, while another firm drank in the Greenway pub on the Coventry Road, the last watering hole on the way to the ground, waiting for Chelsea to pass by. Numbers swelled to 200–300 at the Greenway as more and more arrived, eager to meet Chelsea.

Only a thin police presence guarded the 300-400 Chelsea in the escort to the ground, and as they passed the pub a glass landed in their midst, followed by shouting and a huge surge by Blues. Chelsea split up in the middle of the road as the two groups clashed, with the police powerless to stop it. Blues seemed to have the upper hand and beat Chelsea back down the road, even though they had the smaller numbers. A large number of Blues regrouped near the pub, waiting for Chelsea to make a second pass in a bid to get to the ground. The police managed to arrest a few lads and back-up arrived to walk Chelsea up the road a second time.

Prior to this, a far more serious incident had taken place in the city centre. TS and his younger brother, Les, were walking through Digbeth to the ground with CC and Cockney Al when they decided to stop for refreshments at a chip shop on the main road. Les went inside but came out a few moments later with his eye cut open. His older brother asked him what happened and he said a Chelsea fan had hit him in the face with a can of Coke. A few moments later a big, black guy came out and was identified as the perpetrator. He was immediately confronted and hit by TS. The guy took a few steps back on the pavement and fell into the road just as a bus was passing by. He was caught under the back wheel and killed.

The shocked lads panicked and left to go straight home. The deceased turned out to be a Chelsea fan from the Sparkbrook area of Birmingham. TS handed himself in a few days later, was convicted of manslaughter and went to jail for four years. When he came out, a party was held for him at the Trooper. It was the first time he had seen most of the lads for years, and he was a shadow of his former self. He had lost a lot of weight and his hair was falling out.

The death was a tragic accident which changed the lives of several people. Chelsea were also obviously angry at what had happened and Blues heard they were handing out cards which said, "Kill a Birmingham City fan." In the twisted way of football fans, some Blues responded by singing at Chelsea matches, "Ra, ra, Rasta man, thought he was a Chelsea fan, until he got pushed under a bus" to the tune of Boney M's "Rasputin".

The next time the two firms clashed saw another Chelsea fan on the receiving end of a terrible assault. Before the match, four Blues lads were walking through the bus station in Digbeth when they saw several Chelsea. Realising they had been spotted, the Chelsea lads turned on their toes and began walking out of the station. One of them tried to skulk away on his own, trying to blend in with the other people waiting at the station, doing his best to disassociate himself from the lads. Blues caught up with him and confronted him. After a bit of banter, one of the Blues lads, DM, grabbed a stick which had a nail in one end. He took a swing at the Chelsea lad and hit him in the face with the nail, catching his eye. The lad started screaming, holding his eye, and the Blues lads, realising what had happened, panicked and left the station. They ran off, but wanted to make sure the lad made it to hospital, so they hovered nervously down the road to see if an ambulance arrived. When it did they left the area, freaked out by what had happened. They never found out who it was or came across him again.

At the next game against Chelsea at St Andrew's, a hefty contingent of London skinheads got into the Kop, a Blues stronghold. It was a night game which drew one of the highest gates of the season and ended up being one of the biggest fights many had been involved in. Around 200 Chelsea, in Harringtons, flying jackets and Doc Martens, came in from the Clock entrance after paying to get in at the front of the stand along the halfway tier. Blues were in one corner of the Kop and decided they had to get Chelsea out of there. They moved across and a huge fight broke out.

Blues were winning on the pitch and when yet another goal went in Chelsea went berserk. It was a hectic scene of fists flying around, mad surges and battling by both firms vying for control. Chelsea had caught Blues out by coming into the Kop, but that just made Blues all the more determined to bash them. The front line waded in and the punches and kicks began. As with so many fights on the terraces, as soon as a punch was thrown a gap would appear so everyone could weigh up what had happened and what to do next. The need to know where everyone was stood, who had been hit and whether it was time to get stuck in or scatter was vital, but all that could be seen in one corner of the stand was mass brawling between hundreds of skinheads. Chelsea managed to clear a corner of the Kop but gradually Blues gained control and began chasing them out of the stand and on to the pitch, where fighting continued. Chelsea ended up being put in the Railway End by the police.

Wally, one of the lads who would help set up the fledgling "Apex" firm – forerunner of the Zulus – was with his schoolmates at the front of the Kop. They got out of the stand when the big lumps from Chelsea charged towards Blues at the back of the

Kop, and watched the violence unfold. They saw the corner get cleared and Blues retaliate, and said to one another, "Fucking hell, this is good!" That day contributed to Blues becoming more organised as a football gang, and was the culmination of several seasons of trouble between the two firms.

A week before the mayhem with Chelsea at St Andrew's, a match at Shrewsbury provided some light relief. Thousands made the short journey to Gay Meadow on the train and took over all the pubs in the medieval market town. Because so many had travelled, there was no way everyone would be allowed into the ground, which called for some improvisation. It wasn't long before someone suggested they make use of the roof on one side of the ground. Up to seventy lads hastily helped each other up before settling down to watch the match.

During the first half, thoughts turned to how they would get down again, as most thought they were too high to jump. As thousands of Blues stood below, they made a hole in the roof by ripping apart the covering and lowered themselves down inside. The first person went down and then supported the next person's feet, gently lowering them into the stand, followed by the next and so on. But they were in for a shock when they did get down. The stand had been occupied by Blues but the police had spotted them on the roof, followed their endeavours to get down and anticipated their arrival. They cordoned off an area directly below the hole and when anyone landed they immediately ushered them out of the ground – although most managed to sneak back in again for the second half. Later, some lads who had been in the stand said that they thought it had been raining during the game, but those on the roof knew better: it was because toilets were in short supply up there.

The following month, the lads travelled to Burnley who, for a small club, had a tidy firm. Inevitably little scuffles broke out in the ground when Burnley came round from their open end to where Blues were. During the fights some enterprising Burnley lads decided to use the fence rails that surrounded the pitch as spears. Lads began tugging at the 8ft fence and pulling it down and bending it to release the spikes. They started swinging them round their heads and bashing anyone they came across but the police broke it up before anyone was speared or seriously injured.

The youths who would form the Zulus were gradually coming together, but one more element was needed to cement the mix, a multi-racial musical movement in a region where black faces on the terraces were still a rarity. In the late 1960s, the bouncy dance sounds of Ska had become popular on the British Mod scene. A decade later came a revival, with a new sound incorporating elements of British reggae and punk rock, led by the first releases of Jerry Dammers' Coventry-based 2-Tone label in 1979. At a time when it seemed the National Front was on the rise, the infectious dancefloor sounds of 2-Tone united people of all races, colours and creeds. Two popular Birmingham punk bands, GBH and The Drongos, were also influential, while for others "Roxanne" by The Police ushered in the new ska/reggae/rocksteady era. Soon the city was bouncing to the vibe of The Beat, The Selecter, The Specials and Madness.

Chapter Three

The Apex

CUD: NEARLY ALL my mates in the late Seventies were punks. We all got on, went to matches and went out. I listened to the music they listened to and other stuff such as the Sex Pistols, Stranglers, Eddie Grant, The Whispers, Blondie and 2-Tone. A really memorable night was when we saw The Specials at Barberella's in 1978, before they were really major. We went to various bars, pubs and clubs in the city centre – the Rumrunner (where Duran Duran started), the Guilded Cage, Mr Bill's, the Glue Pot and the Parasol.

The Rude Boy look was around and somewhere between fifty and 100 of us went, all dressed in our Harringtons, Army coats and donkey jackets. In fact I was never even really into the later fashion scene; I was happiest wearing a donkey jacket or Harrington with jeans and Doc Martens. It was one of the best nights I've ever had. They were supported by some punk band, which were good, but there weren't many black lads there. When The Specials came on the crowd went mad and when they played "Too Much Too Young" the whole place was jumping. We surged to the front with pints in hands and one of the lads, Ryan, managed to get on the stage and started dancing, but not for long because the big black guy in the group, Neville Staple, grabbed hold of him and chucked him back into the crowd, where we caught him. Loads of people talked about the night for ages after.

2-Tone really took off after that and we got the suits to match. I got a granddad suit at the Rag Market for £8 and then a 2-Tone one which I liked wearing with Hush Puppies, a t-shirt and a Harrington. Different areas would have their own takes on the same sort of clothes and looks. We all wanted to look good and we also dressed like Dexys Midnight Runners at one point when we saw them at the Romulus bar by Birmingham library.

JJ: Choosing a club is a perilous business. Although I grew up and went to school in "Villa" areas, I had already made my choice. Reasoning was simple for a six-year-old – I lived in Birmingham, not Aston, and didn't much care for the name Villa. So Blues it was for better or worse. My first match was actually a pre-season friendly between Villa and Blues in 1970 which we lost 2–1. I remember those disgusting yellow and blue away colours Villa used to wear and some youth in flares running down the road with a scarf tied to his wrist. The first trouble I recall was against Millwall. There was some kind of altercation in the Railway End, which at that time was the away enclosure. It looked like knives drawn in the sunlight, but I was never really sure. The violence was always there somehow, but I guess parents and elders shielded you from it and it just lurked in the background, fascinating and frightening though it was.

I drifted out of it in my early teens when music and other stuff took over, but became re-acquainted through the punk-skin scene. Football or at least regionalism drifted in and out of the music scene in Birmingham. When Adam and the Ants played Digbeth Civic Hall in 1980 they brought along their famous "Ant Army" made up of relatively older punks from all over the country, but mostly Londoners. Clearly the Blues skinhead contingent had got wind of this, as had most of the local punks, though we turned out to be among only a dozen local punk rockers in attendance. The Birmingham skins were determined to put one over the Ants, but were overwhelmed inside the hall by sheer numbers. As was the way in those days, the Wolverhampton Hell's Angels were "bouncing" the gig, so it really was a recipe for mayhem. It put us in an odd position, we were supporting the same footie team but our leather jackets and spikes aligned us visually at least with the "outsiders".

The skins re-grouped and turned out a massive mob down Digbeth High Street. As I recall, there were about seventy treated in hospital that night. The Ant Army was well and truly routed. We did several major swerves to avoid getting the same, unsure any of the skins would have listened to our reasoning regarding the same team.

The most infamous musical-football interchange came with the Cockney Rejects a couple of years later, when their gig in Birmingham was greeted by a massive Blues Skin contingent singing "keep right on to the end of the road." The Rejects got trashed and the gig was abandoned. I actually heard that Blues had a "punk mob" from Villa fans at school although, by the time I started going down regularly again, it had morphed into a mix of Skins, Mods and Rude Boys. There was also a good, rowdy bunch of skins who'd come into the city on my bus from the north. They were young coal miners from Polesworth in Staffordshire.

This seemed like the order. Fearsome, shaven heads, big boots. Then all of a sudden the casual scene emerged. I was in Manchester (not for football) one evening and couldn't believe all these guys in legwarmers, wedge haircuts and puffa coats. They looked so "unscary" compared to what had gone before. It was Man City's crew heading for a night match at Stoke. No doubt they raised a few eyes in the Potteries that night too.

Then Villa's C-Crew got started and they probably had their best year in 1981/1982. They were doing well in the football, winning the Championship and the European Cup, and their "casual" tactics I think took Blues by surprise in that short era. I had first-hand accounts of their exploits from a close friend from school who became one of the original members of that group. He's respectable now, so won't mention his rank or service.

And you have to hand it to a guy who paints his name across the length of the wall of the railway station at Aston. "Danny James of Aston Villa" would greet you every time you passed through the station. "Black Danny", the talisman of the C-Crew, was jailed in about 1982. He was soon back on the scene though, I bashed him over the head with my telescopic brolly in a fight outside the said Aston station sometime after. But by the end of that season Blues had grabbed the Casual idea and it was all Patrick cagoules and Fila tracksuits. The Apex had emerged as a transition from the skinhead mobs that terrorised the Holte End for so many years, but faltered in the face of the new casual tactics of the firmed-up Zulus, who would take it to the whole country by the mid 1980s.

The demise of the skins, although of course there were black skins, also opened the door wider, I think, for the multi-racial picture that has marked Blues out for more than twenty years. The music was changing, nightlife was changing, soul and funk were becoming the music of the white boys too. It was no longer Barbarellas and the Cedar Club, by the mid-Eighties you could live out your own little Club Tropicana at Pagoda Park.

I finally joined the "movement" in 1982 at a pre-season friendly at Leamington Spa. There was about half a dozen Blues lads there, some of whom became Zulu stalwarts, and that was that. It was pleasing to now know more "Zulus" than C-Crew members. It snowballs. You meet more people, do your bit, get known, and on it goes. Season 1982/83 was transitional. Man United were still a big force, West Ham obviously were doing it, Leeds. So many of the lads were so young, yet you'd come face to face with some real adults. The hooligans were all called "boys" which led to one funny line I heard after someone came off worse against an older set of opponents, possibly Man U: "They weren't boys, they were blokes!"

We had a few "blokes" as well, legendary names, some now sadly deceased, and while they were rightly suspicious of the younger ones, they were less "cliquey" than the young casuals, many of whom still operated along the lines of postcodes – we're

Acocks Green, Chelmsley, Kings Norton, Warstock, Yardley and so on. I was not associated to a hardcore Blues area, and wasn't even living in the city by then. So I drifted between different sets, not least those who joined from the outlying towns and districts such as Redditch, Cannock, Telford, Corby, (The Royal Borough of) Sutton Coldfield – even Milton Keynes.

When Nottingham Forest came to St Andrew's at the start of the 1981/82 season they brought a bunch of lads ready to wreak havoc. The two firms hadn't really encountered one another until then, but the Forest left a lasting impression on Blues.

A rabble of about twenty Blues lads met in a pub near the ground before the match, most hailing from the Acocks Green area. After a few bevies, they were walking along the Coventry Road towards the ground when a coachload of Forest fans passed by. The customary exchange of abuse ensued, with Blues "lobbing the V's" and jeering, their faces squashed up against the window of the coach.

The fifty Forest lads looked slightly older than Cud and his crew, who were all about twenty years old or younger, and despite being dressed in club colours, they looked like a game bunch and not your normal supporters. As the coach headed towards the Spion Kop entrance, a brick was hurled through one of the windows, showering the occupants in glass and causing the startled driver to stop suddenly in the middle of the road. The lads descended on the vehicle, trying to force open the doors and soon succeeded. There was then a stand-off between the two firms in front of the bewildered and scared driver, rooted to his seat.

While the action was happening at the front of the coach, several of the feisty Forest fans had jumped through the smashed window and took the Blues lads by surprise from the back. A mad tear-up lasted two or three minutes before several truncheon-wielding police officers burst on the scene, grabbing and arresting those in their path. Order was soon restored and the lads from their respective firms were marched to the ground.

Not much more happened during the game, which Blues won 4–3, but afterwards, as hundreds of Blues lads poured out of the ground, several scuffles kicked off. After things calmed down, about ten lads, including Cud, went for a few beers before making their way into the city centre. As they walked through Digbeth, they ran into the Forest lads who had been on the coach. Their driver had fled without them, forcing them to head to New Street to get a train home. There were far more of them than there were Blues but the two firms faced each other for a few moments before both charged forwards, punching, kicking and throwing bricks.

Cud realised his lot were outnumbered and needed back-up, so he signalled for them to leave and find more lads. By the time they had reinforcements, the Forest lads couldn't be found despite a lengthy search of the station platforms. The two firms would meet again on several occasions, reminding Blues they were a good outfit who were prepared to stand and fight when it counted.

The first game of the season usually provided some action, and when 8,000 Blues fans travelled north to see the game against Manchester United on a hot August day in 1982, the hardcore Blues element didn't leave disappointed. Making use of the Specials put on by British Rail, the several hundred lads were all in neighbouring carriages. It was the club's third season in the top flight and Ron Saunders had been manager for around six months after a successful spell across town at Aston Villa.

As they pulled into Piccadilly the police were waiting and everyone was escorted to the ground. Once inside, Blues took their usual position behind the goal in the Scoreboard End. When United scored the first of their three goals that day, about fifteen of their lads jumped up and down, cheering, on the Blues side of the fence dividing the two sets of fans. Vexed, Cud spotted them and decided to wade through the crowd to confront them. He made it across and ran into them, fists flying. Once the Mancs realised what was happening they pummelled him back. The fracas immediately attracted the attention of nearby stewards, and police officers were despatched to break it up. They grabbed hold of a bedraggled Cud and promptly marched him out of the ground, ordering him not to return. He stood alone outside for the remainder of the match, waiting amongst the litter on the pavement.

When the game ended, he found himself among hundreds of United fans, as the police had decided to keep Blues tucked away inside for twenty minutes or so until the coast was clear. Cud hovered inconspicuously but was soon spotted and jeers and abuse came his way. He knew he was seconds away from getting battered, something the police had also realised, and suddenly some gates were opened and he was plucked to safety and able to rejoin the rest of the rabble inside the ground.

When it was the turn of the Blues supporters to vacate the stadium, the vast majority were singing despite nursing a heavy defeat. As they ambled out, the main lads soon noticed United waiting down a few side roads branching off the police escort. Most knew what to do next and fifty managed to slip away to indulge in running battles in and around the streets that led from Old Trafford. There was fierce fighting, with lads brawling on the pavements in front of houses and passers-by crossing over the road to avoid the mayhem.

As the mobs passed a school a few minutes later, Blues were in hot pursuit of about forty United but proceedings were halted when the Old Bill caught up with them and managed to get Blues back into the escort to the train station. That left unfinished business with one of the top five firms of all time, an outfit with huge numbers who could claim innumerable victories throughout the Seventies and Eighties.

By the early Eighties, every team in the Football League boasted a crew. While West Ham's ICF, Chelsea's Headhunters and the Leeds United Service Crew were making headlines most weekends, locally Aston Villa's C-Crew and Wolves' Subway Army were rated and getting results. While there was no doubt that Blues had caused untold mayhem throughout the previous decade, thanks to older lads like Ashford, Yatesy, Jamie Q, Jimmy Sherry and Noggin, the firm lacked real organisation as the casual era dawned.

The skinhead element that had dominated football hooliganism nationwide were overtaken by a younger, more organised and fashion-conscious breed of supporter. Lads wanted to look good and achieve a certain look with their latest sports gear, Farahs and trainers, and certain labels became much sought-after with the terraces providing the perfect catwalk.

But the in-fighting between lads from different areas in Birmingham continued and it was becoming clear something needed to happen to unite the large number of game black and white lads as life on the terraces began to change.

No one can recall the exact day it happened but the Apex became the first organised group to emerge within the firm. The main older lads, who had numerous victories under their belts, were still active and linked up with them. There are two versions of where the name Apex came from: it was either taken from a building firm of the same name owned by one of the lads, or from a cheap P&O Ferries route that sailed between Liverpool and Ireland in the early 1980s. No-one is quite sure.

It is fair to say the Apex weren't known or rated much nationally, and did not achieve the heights their successors, the Zulus, managed, but the internal scuffles began to decrease and a new, united firm evolved, ready to compete with local rivals who had built up hefty reputations. On the pitch, Leicester City, Coventry City and Wolverhampton Wanderers were all in the top flight, along with Aston Villa and Nottingham Forest who had both won the European Cup. Blues were up there, too, for seven consecutive seasons in the 1970s until a slight blip at the turn of the decade when they dropped down a division for one season before returning until the end of 1983/84.

Wally: I grew up in Bordesley Green and I suppose I started off on the wrong foot in some people's eyes by being one of those people who switched teams. But I went from Arsenal to Blues, so don't class me as one of those Man United glory hunters. When I was a kid, Arsenal was my team and I went to Highbury a fair bit as a teenager. I would meet up at New Street with some other Midlands-based Arsenal from West Brom and Walsall, who carried on going and became active members of the Gooners. I took some Blues lads with me – Brains or Tommy G – but at the same time I went to a lot of Blues matches.

Bordesley Green is a Blues area but at that time, around the start of the casual era, Blues didn't have much of a firm that stuck together, although there were loads of lads around. The problem was that the different areas in Birmingham were having rows with each other at the ground and not uniting as a single force to be reckoned with. There was no one organised mob, just loads of game lads.

In Bordesley Green, we should have had a good firm but we just kept fighting with others from our area as well as lads from outside. Going to school or to the shops you would always end up in a row with someone. But we had to get together and become one down the Blues. The Blues firms then were mainly skinheads but as the younger heads, black and white lads, got into the casual dress we began uniting and we called ourselves the Apex. Although we had a name, our little firm still wasn't completely organised but it was getting bigger and I was recruiting more lads from Bordesley, like Errol, Claz, Skinny E, John H, Balla, Pete D, the ginger brothers and the Twins.

The Bordesley firm was coming together really quickly and making a name for itself on the town, down the Blues and all over Brum. The main things we had in common was that, first, we were all violent, and second, we could thieve. We were always in two modes: fighting and earning.

We were having some good offs at matches. In one incident in town, we bumped into a firm of Villa lads. There were about five of us and twenty Villa at the top of the ramp at New Street, near McDonalds. They clocked me and it went off. We were fighting and it stopped suddenly when one of their lot, a guy called

Heathy, was thrown from the top of the ramp on to the road below. They all went to see him and we did one. One of our lot was pulled by the Old Bill but released.

We separated, I ended up in town on my own and not long after bumped into some Villa again. They blamed me for Heathy and six of them grabbed me and marched me round to the nearby Temple Bar, where the rest of their firm were. There were now about twenty of the cunts around me, screaming about their pal. One of them gave me a dig and I saw a little gap between them and had it up and escaped. I'm not afraid to admit when I've had to run. Why they didn't do me proper I'll never know, but I bet they wish they'd done me now.

The Apex tended to base their look on the fashion going on in the south, believing the Londoners – with West Ham's ICF leading the way – achieved a classier look than the Liverpool scallies, despite them being mainly responsible for starting the casual era.

Dressed in Fila, Burberry, Lacoste, Tacchini and Farah, the dapper-looking lads spent their days hanging around Birmingham's infamous Bullring shopping centre and at a nearby café called Ginos with some of the older Blues lot, just waiting for the next opportunity to bash some away supporters.

On match days the Nightrider pub, in the city centre, was a popular watering hole and the younger Apex element could also be found nearby or at New Street station waiting for those fans. The shift in dress from the 1970s trademark drainpipes, Levi Sta-press and donkey jackets to the slick designer labels and hard-to-find clobber couldn't have suited the light-fingered lads in the Apex more.

It was all about the look that put the humble trainer centre stage and several lads were pretty good at relieving numerous city centre stores of their latest gear. Most firms can boast a healthy contingent of lads with their own individual talents and Blues were no different. The Scousers had cornered the market in terms of cleaning shops out during their club's European escapades, and several trips were made to London to get the latest gear to then sell on to eager lads back in Brum. Visits were also made to Manchester and Cardiff in search of the latest clothing. Looking good was key and the Blues, as a whole, certainly managed that.

The shops in Birmingham that actually received money for their clothes were Austin Reed in the Pallasades Shopping Centre and Nicholls. Sought-after gear including Pringle jumpers, Farahs, Ellesse, Fila Borg, Sergio Tacchini, Dallas tracksuits and tops, Aquascutum blazers, Trim Trabb and Adidas Munchen trainers were bought and worn each week. Fashion was taken seriously and the desire to look good, yet different, even resulted in a penchant for leg warmers over tight jeans with strap-over trainers for a while as one lad, Glenroy, will vouch for when he went to Everton in 1981.

Glenroy: It was our time to cause problems, the first away game of the season at Everton. We had a firm of about 250 travelling by train and as we pulled into Lime Street Station, before the train had even stopped the doors were opening and the guys were jumping off. A couple of years earlier I had been chased out of Liverpool's ground because I was a nigger, but this time things were different. We were firmed up and going to give it to everyone that day.

The Old Bill tried locking the gates to the station but it was kicking off with some Blues outside the station in the amusement arcade across the road, who Everton thought were the only ones there. We forced our way past the police on to the street and I ran into loads of scallies, knocked one out and kicked and punched others. Then I was grabbed by the police and arrested and kept in until the end of the game and met the guys at the station for the trip home.

We stopped at Crewe to change trains and bumped into Liverpool coming back up from the Midlands. We clashed with them on the stairs and I was one of the first in, as I hated Scousers, so I steamed loads before the police arrived and was arrested again. While I was in custody they phoned my mum to tell her I had been arrested and she replied "What, again?" and the officer said, "Yes, twice in one day."

That day I was wearing my green flying jacket, purple cords and yellow leg warmers as I was going to a funk jazz all-nighter – dress sense or what?

When away fans came into Birmingham, not only might they get a beating but they were quite often relieved of their clobber, as several Chelsea fans in flying jackets wandering around Birmingham one Saturday will confirm.

By 1982, CC, Glenroy and DG had got a flat in Trident House in Birmingham city centre behind Broad Street – a few years before it became known as the Golden Mile because of all the bars springing up. The younger Apex lot went round from time to time and had their fighting skills tested against the three older flatmates, who they thought highly of. As the older lads were also now going out in the city centre, it was a natural progression that the firm grew in size. The firm would hit the pubs as early as possible on match days, especially for the big games, as well as fighting the Villa C Crew, who had a presence in the city centre.

The flat became a focal point. Plenty of parties were held there, with one in particular standing out. Loads of lads turned up, with girlfriends in tow, carrying cans, wine and bottles of spirits, much to the enjoyment and surprise of CC, while Glenroy and DG were out rounding up more guests. The fridge and sinks were filled with booze and more kept arriving. But just as things got going there was a knock at the door. Someone opened it to find the police outside. They ordered all the women out of the flat immediately and told the black guys to move to the left and white guys to the right. Everyone thought the black lads were in trouble, knowing how West Midlands Police usually operated, but instead they were told to leave and all the white lads were arrested. It transpired that Davenport Brewery near Broad Street had been broken into and relieved of its stock which had found its way to the party. One of the lads, ironically a black guy, had put the window through and people got in and helped themselves. DG and Glenroy returned to an empty and locked flat, unaware of what had happened.

November 1982 saw the name Zulus adopted after that famous game at Manchester City [see Chapter 1], and it quickly overtook Apex as the banner for the lads. Under the Zulu umbrella, several small groups had their own nicknames in the 1980s: the Sauce Force, Brew Crew, Suicide Squad, Super Slobs, and the most well-known, the Junior Business Boys, who were the first to use calling cards. The Business Boys were much younger, between fourteen and sixteen years old, and appeared around 1982–3. They totalled about sixty lads and sometimes waited outside the ground for the older lads. They also hung around New Street, watching and waiting for away fans and checking out what they wore. At first the youths, who were from many different areas, were called the Zulu Apprentices, but later this changed to the Junior Business Boys [see Chapter 5].

The Sauce Force were Mods and actually formed at the end of the 1970s. They dressed in typical Mod style but sometimes wore Fred Perry tops – both a Mod and a casual staple – and Farahs. They drove Lambretta motorbikes and hailed from Chelmsley and Castle Bromwich. Around fifteen lads still go to St Andrew's today.

It was to Merseyside, birthplace of the scally/trendy/casual scene, that the Zulus made one of their first forays. Like Liverpool, Everton's fans were known for their penchant for blades and their racist tendencies, so when 700 lads – black and white and newly christened as the Zulus – headed north in December 1982, it was bound to be eventful. The Zulus positioned themselves in the stand behind the goal, which was half away fans and half Evertonians. The locals repeatedly indicated to the Zulus that they were going to get cut up, and flashed blades. Although the Zulus retaliated with abuse, there was a feeling that they were going to get it at some point. CC went to the toilets and bumped into one of the lads from the Sauce Force, who had several cones of chips propped up on a shelf. The pair discussed Everton's ominous threats and what they should do, and formulated a plan.

The lad persuaded CC to take an empty cone into a cubicle and shit in it before handing it back to the lad, who was now closely guarding ten other empty cones, kindly donated by other lads, which were neatly lined up and covered in tissue on the shelf. Back on the terrace all eyes were on Everton as the contents of the cones were chucked in their direction.

It looked like white tissue streaming through the air as several "shit bombs" landed on the bemused Evertonians. Naturally they touched themselves after they had been hit, soon realising to their horror what it was. The Zulus were greatly amused at seeing the Everton end clear amid mass episodes of vomiting. A good result, they agreed.

Thousands of Blues also went to Southampton that December 1982, and CC, Glenroy and DG wanted to be the first ones there. After a Friday night in Boogies, a bar in town that the Zulus practically lived in for a few years, they stayed up and caught the 5.30am train, along with others from Acocks Green and Billesley, arriving just before 10am. Their first job was to check out the shops in the town centre. They discovered a sportswear shop that stocked ski gear and their attention turned to a load of bubble coats, also known as puffa jackets. They relieved the store of around fifty jackets by grabbing what they could and running out. As there were so many of them, the shop workers couldn't do a thing. The jackets were proudly worn by the lads in the ground before they were spotted by the Old Bill and arrested.

Fattie and CC got into a side stand and attempted to get on the pitch. CC managed it and ran straight to the Southampton end, the Milton Road Stand, believing everyone was behind him.

He shouted at the Saints to come on and join him, and as they started to leave their seats and climb over, CC took a quick look behind him to check everyone was there ready to kick it off. He was the only one. None of the others had followed and now it was too late. He ran back to the centre circle but was tripped by several marauding Southampton fans and then kicked around the pitch until Fattie came to the rescue, charging from the Blues end armed with a retractable umbrella, a weapon favoured by many because it was just the right size and shape for whacking people. Lashing out at the Southampton lads, he forced them to retreat to their end. His adventure was later featured on *Match Of The Day*, much to the amusement of everyone.

On a cold Friday in December 1982, the firm made the journey to Swansea on a minibus for a night game. The Vetch Field's wooden gates were no match for the lads, who forced their way in without paying. They had already taken over the city's pubs and were feeling pretty invincible, like superstar hooligans. But after the game they were brought back down to earth when they got a right kicking. Swansea managed to pick people off on the way back to the minibus, isolating them down side roads, and when everyone got back to Brum it became clear that they'd had a good going over.

Each trip around the country brought a sense of the fashions prevalent in different areas. In London, flying jackets were the thing and you could always spot a fellow football lad in amongst the shoppers: the wedge haircuts, Slazenger jumpers and Stan Smith pumps were part of the unofficial uniform. But the further north you went it was obvious they were slower to catch on to the casual vibe. A trip to Sunderland around this time confirmed that they were still in a bygone era, with the terraces filled with fans with long hair and wearing donkey jackets and hobnail boots. By 1983, when the Zulus were properly formed and a force to be reckoned with, it was time to turn their attention to the south, to the London firms that were ruling supreme.

When it comes to the top hooligan firms of the last thirty years, Liverpool may have been the first clobbered-up outfit but

West Ham's Inter City Firm (ICF) have earned themselves a much respected place in the top five, if not the number one slot. For several years, they led the way. Each police force knew what to expect when West Ham were coming, and they were right to anticipate aggro. But the thing that annoys many rivals is that they fail to admit when they have been done by any firm.

When Blues played them in the first game of the season, it had the makings of a massive row. More than 300 Zulus went down on different early morning trains, many tooled up with machetes, hammers, hatchets and other weapons to meet their feared rivals. Those that had already arrived couldn't help but be impressed by the number of lads filing out from the platform. But before anything could happen, the police ushered everyone in one direction, letting them think they were getting an escort to the ground.

Instead, the police pinned them up against a wall outside the station and indicated that they were going to search everyone. With that, the clattering of weapons dropping to the floor could be heard all along the line. Any stragglers not caught up in the original police dragnet now ducked their heads and continued on their way to the ground. It meant there was still a Zulu presence at Upton Park but greatly diminished. Mobile units of officers with dogs were waiting at coach, bus and tube stations and also on main routes to the ground and when they believed there was trouble they pounced and carted lads away to three nearby police stations.

The number of arrests – 236 including sixty juveniles, the Junior Business Boys out in full – was a record for any outbreak of hooliganism in England at that time. One hundred and seventy one were charged with public order offences and the media described it as the most violent start to a season ever. Blues manager Ron Saunders called for hooligans to be birched. Yet little fighting took place. The arrests also provided an unexpected opportunity for the lads to get to know one another better, as so many had travelled and ended up crammed in police cells together.

The Apex

Cud: Loads of us went down on several trains and the older lot had got to London early. The police were waiting, though there weren't any West Ham about. As the lads got off the trains and walked through the station, they were singing and not causing any major trouble, but were arrested pretty much straight away. No one took a huge firm to London in those days and it was the first time we had.

Those that weren't arrested got away and met up with the others and went to the ground. I was on a train with Gnocchi, one of the older lot, and about four others and we were surrounded by West Ham. It was heavy. We knew it could go off and there were no other Blues to help. You might as well stand and show no fear because you have nothing to lose in situations like that, but a couple of the lads with me weren't so sure when I stood up and said, "Come on then!" West Ham looked at me, but instead of clattering us they said, "Leave 'em Brummies, fair play."

That game was a watershed for the younger lot who were out that day. It was probably their first major away game and they got to see what it was like. Because so many were arrested – young and old – and the court hearings were in London, everyone got to know one another more and bonded. The Zulus had been around for about a year and was made up of a hard core of lads, but there were a load more around who had not yet met each other. That day changed all that because of the large numbers.

As the firm grew, the more rows they had, the more united they became and, like an army, everyone had a different role. Confidence would grow or shrink depending on who was stood next to you and while the venues differed, each week the front line would usually consist of the same faces all ready to tear into their opponents. On the day we've always had a good turn out of black guys, better than any other firm.

JJ: People were still learning the score, but when a load of coppers meet you at Euston station on the way to a West Ham match, the working assumption is that you'll get an escort to the ground, at worst. Maybe just get parked in a pub somewhere. But the Met had other ideas in 1983 and bundled 236 of us in vans. It was comical really, but you certainly got to know your comrades better with fifteen to twenty in a cell for a long day. When we finally got out, in twos and threes, I recall a few tasty West Ham heads hanging round the railbar seeing if anyone was in the mood. No one really was. It was a crappy day, but did quite a bit for "bonding".

The next clash came when the two teams met in an FA Cup match at St Andrew's in February 1984. The Blues trounced West Ham 3–0, and the Hammers responded by seeking to force the game's abandonment by massive pitch invasions, prompted when Billy Wright scored Blues' third goal in the 79th minute. Ted Croker, the FA Secretary, was quoted in the papers as saying he had "never witnessed scenes like it". An FA inquiry followed, resulting in both teams facing two-year bans from the Cup if their fans became involved in further disturbances and a warning to all First Division teams that they must consider erecting fences to prevent similar incidents.

Small pockets of trouble started when Blues scored their first goal. West Ham, sitting in the Paddock area, moved towards the Railway End where Blues were celebrating and some rushed to meet them. After a few seconds the police stepped in and began grabbing people and arresting them. But when the third goal went in, West Ham charged on to the pitch, holding up the game for ten minutes. Blues captain Kevan Broadhurst was punched in the face, and when play resumed with only five minutes left, West Ham fans broke through a fifty-strong police cordon and back on to the pitch. The referee then led the players off and told them he was prepared to wait until 9pm if necessary. More than 100 people were arrested before, during and after and thirty were injured, including a police motorcyclist who was struck on the head by a flying 2.5lb chunk of cast iron, which threw him off his bike.

"We had a decent mob in the Railway End that day and they came on to the pitch after we scored, they were right up for it," remembered JJ. "Blues had it with them on the pitch and most of the action was in the Blues' third of the pitch. I remember some people would not come out of the Kop, there were fences around it but still, I thought West Ham had a better show because not enough Blues came out of the Kop to take part. They brought it to us for as long as it took the police to get it under control and they kept bringing lads over from the main stand where some Blues lads were. It was one-to-one fighting and the match was stopped."

According to CC, "Blues were going wild trying to get to West Ham. We wanted them. We'd had enough of them Cockneys bashing everyone all the time. We assumed they were all NF, we had such hatred for them."

Much later, in the late 1980s when England were playing Holland, CC, Cockney Al, Glenroy and a weightlifting Villa fan called Eddie went on a ferry from Dover to watch the match. On the way over, they got chatting to some ICF lads and other Cockneys. They were suited and booted, sipping champagne, looking the part and saying they wouldn't get pulled by the law because of how they looked. But as the journey progressed, they directed some racist comments at Glenroy – "fucking nigger" and "black bastard" and so on – and after a while he decided to do something about it, despite the rest of the lads reminding him there were only four of them. He got up on a chair and said, "Who is the hard bastard then, let's have it." All fell silent until someone piped up, "Come here." They looked towards a group of lads sat to one side and were encouraged to join them. "Take no notice of those shit, wanky Cockneys" they were told. It turned out they were some Wolves lads, all in their mid-forties, who pre-dated even the Subway Army. The four went to sit with them, had a few drinks and chatted to them for the rest of the journey.

On the way home on the same ferry, it became apparent that someone was taking photographs of the groups of lads on board. The ferry was full of different firms and some were playing up and having a bit of banter with each other. One of the Wolves lads went over and decided to have a word with the photographer. In his thick Black Country lilt, he said, "Alwright, you ay with them, and you ay with us," as he pointed to lads in different directions. "Am yow with *The Sun*? Give us your camera." At this, he picked up the startled photographer and started to dangle him over the side of the ferry. The armed guards on board, eager to disperse any football-related trouble, drew their guns and told him to put the guy down. He complied but the photographer left the scene and locked himself away in his cabin for the rest of the journey.

Wally: I missed the one in 1983 when more than 200 Zulus were rounded up and arrested at Euston. I also missed 1984 when they came into the seats at St Andrew's and it went off on the pitch. West Ham claim to have done Blues that day but I was told they didn't have it their own way.

The one major row I have been involved in with the ICF was in 1986 at New Street Station. They got absolutely annihilated. New Street Station has two glass door entrances either side of the escalators and about fifty ICF were hanging around at the bottom of the escalators which take you up into the Pallasades Shopping Centre. I'd just got into town with a good firm from Bordesley Green and a couple of us had gone to the station through one set of doors. As we came through, I saw Cud with a handful of lads come through the other set of doors and bump straight into West Ham.

West Ham clocked the Blues lads, did an about turn, picked up the pace and went after them, but unbeknown to both groups, our Bordesley Green lot were also there. We took the ICF by surprise, as they thought they were heading the charge. We steamed straight into them. I jumped into the middle of them and unleashed a Jiffy of ammonia. A full-on attack took place between east London and east Birmingham, with no Old Bill in sight. A handful of us were in the middle of them, giving plenty, while the others were attacking from all sides. We chased them off the station, bashing them all the way.

By this time we were joined by a lot more Zulus but the original onslaught was even numbers. We reached the island at Smallbrook Queensway and ended up chasing them for miles. They didn't stay together in a firm and we gave up chasing the last ones by Edgbaston Cricket Ground, about two or three miles out of the city centre. I'd like to see what they have to say about that day when they write a book and tell both sides of the story. If they wrote a book called *The Times We've Been Done* it would be a bestseller, because everyone has had enough of the one-sided stuff they come out with. Before any of you West Ham jump the gun and have a pop at me, I don't see how anyone could not put the ICF in their top five over the past thirty years. Personally, I'd put them number one.

When I was around sixteen and Brains was a couple of years younger, we went to Arsenal. In the ground some Arsenal couldn't believe we were Brummies because of the way we were dressed. At the time Blues still had mobs of skinheads, so I can understand their shock. I don't think we watched much of the game, we were stuck at the back of the North Bank listening to the words, "Look at these fuckin' Brummies."

At the time clothes like Fila, Pringle and Farah trousers were the latest trends down south and two Brummies had gone south of Watford and matched the best of them. While I was going to Arsenal, I didn't really get involved with the main firm, although I knew some of them. They didn't then have as good a firm as some of the other London mobs, but that would change later on when they got it together.

As I was playing a big part in the new firm coming together at Blues, my trips to Highbury were coming to an end. The old skinheads firms from Chelmsley Wood and Lea Hall were now more in the background but lads like Ashford and Jayo were still active. They'd be at the Nightrider pub on match days but we'd be at New Street waiting to spring an attack on any ways fans. Blues were not rated at the time but that was about to change.

In 1983, the lads enjoyed some fun at Southampton after managing to get in the Southampton end, amazingly with the blessing of the local constabulary. Their coach dropped them off at the wrong end but the police let them go in anyway and just asked them to behave, which of course they all said they would.

It was the first season the volatile Mark Dennis played for Southampton after being transferred from Blues and when the match kicked off the 50 or so lads started singing and waving at Mark and the 3,000 Blues supporters at the other end happily waved back. Although Southampton didn't have a major firm, their lads clocked Blues and paid them a visit and a few scuffles ensued. The police soon arrived and marched the lads round the pitch back to the away end amid rapturous applause from the rest of the lads and sneering comments like, "Bloody hooligans, should be caged," as they passed the family seating area.

JJ: We took a big firm to Sheffield for an FA Cup match in January 1984. Four coaches left Brum early and arrived before the pubs opened. One lad made a good living out of the coaches, but of course sometimes the mob got watered down a bit with normal fans travelling with us so he could fill up the seats.

We landed in two pubs in Sheffield. The day started early when it became clear that Sheffield Wednesday, who were also playing at home in a Cup game, were not impressed with us landing in their pubs. They gathered a big mob together and brought it on at the top of the main shopping street. We came out of the pubs and ran up the hill. Glasses and bricks were flying in to the Sheffield lot and being returned, in fact so many people were throwing stuff from behind the front line it hit some of our lot who were leading the charge.

I was surprised it came to a bit of halt, as I expected us to go right through them, but they held their line and it became a bit of a stand-off until the law intervened. Most of us moved on to a pub quite near the ground. We must have been a bit slack, as no-one had noticed a mob of Sheffield United group up and come down to the pub armed to the teeth. The first thing I knew of what was to follow was a bicycle flying through the window, followed by a big roar.

The first reaction is to get out of the pub and engage as there's nothing worse than being penned in, but the amount of ammo that kept on flying through – bricks, bottles, road-mending gear – was not easy to avoid. There was no way out round the back, so the only chance was out of the front door, which some tried. There was at lot of brass and memorabilia on the walls – well we were in steel country – like swords, rifles, carriage lamps and so on. It all came off. I remember one lad, a chef by trade, grabbing a wired-up carriage lamp clean off the wall, dashing out the door, bashing some Blade with it and retreating as fast as he went out. It was that kind of day. Some lads found bayonets on the wall and jabbed them through the windows, prompting one of the Sheffield lads to shout, "The fuckers have got guns!" One of our lot cut a tendon in his finger while lobbing something out and it's still crooked to this day. As a fashion note, I know I lost my Burberry scarf in the melee. It also kicked off in the ground. We had a good firm in the seats down the side, which I guess is where we always headed for in those days, hoping that our opponents would have the same idea.

Cud: I thought I'd have a go, so me and Brains went out but the doors were locked behind us. We got chased all the way down the road until we found a hardware store, where we got two shovels. We went back and they were chucking bricks and all sorts at us but we managed to bat them back at them using the shovels. I skimmed my shovel into them and it knocked two of them down and Brains threw his into the window of the hardware shop and then got chased. Someone in the pub had grabbed a sword off the wall of the pub and he came out swinging it. They fought him with some sticks they had, just like a sword fight, while some others managed to find mops and buckets from inside the pub and used them. It was mad and very funny.

———————

As a pledge to their beloved BCFC, Cud became one of a handful of people to start wearing a thin gold chain with the Blues emblem on it in the early 1980s. A girl he knew had ordered a few pendants to be made in Birmingham's Jewellery Quarter for her and striker Noel Blake. One of them fell into Cud's hands and he wore it with pride, but within a year it was no longer an exclusive item as more were made and sold amongst the lads. Many still have them more than two decades later.

Blake, a former Villa player, was a good mate of some of the lads and many thought of him as a "closet Zulu" rather than a player. He would go out drinking with them and indulge in a few escapades at away matches, and was even arrested along with two other closet Zulus, fellow striker Robert Hopkins and goalkeeper Tony Coton, one night outside a club on Broad Street, supposedly down to a Villa fan stirring things up.

Although off the pitch the firm was reaching new heights, on the pitch things were different. Blues managed to score only thirty-nine goals in the 1983/84 season, in front of home crowds hovering around the 14,000 mark, and ended up in Division Two. Ron Saunders strengthened the squad during the summer, and 1984/85 would see the team climb back into the top flight. It also heralded a new era for the Zulus, in a season that would see them achieve complete dominance in their city centre, find a leader for the firm, cause a row at almost every game, and rise to become one of the top five firms in the country.

Chapter Four

The Leader

WHEN SPURS CAME to St Andrew's in 1984, Blues won the game 1–0, but "the Yids", as their hooligans were known, got the off-field victory that day. They exploited the Zulus' lack of organisation and planning to turn them over and achieve the best "result" by any firm at St Andrew's in the past twenty years.

Cud: About sixty of us went behind the goal where Spurs were. The Old Bill kept us apart at first, but as kick-off neared, more and more Spurs kept coming in and filled up the seats around us. Twenty more Blues came in but there were now about 250 Spurs by us. We didn't really know or recognise any of them. Although the boys we had there were top notch, we should have had more, but no-one knew who was around and a lot bottled it, we just weren't organised.

The match started, and after some more Spurs came in they shouted, "Tottenham," and we shouted, "Zulu," and went straight into them. Suddenly all we could smell was ammonia. They were spraying us and it got in people's eyes. It was toe-to-toe stuff until the Old Bill managed to wade in and began getting us out of there. I moved away and jumped on to the pitch to avoid the coppers, pretending I had got some of it on my face, and walked into a casualty area. A few of our lot were in there by now having their eyes treated by the St John Ambulance. I waited but decided I had to get back out, so I left and walked back the way I had come.

I met two of our lads, Trev and Noggin, and we walked past Spurs to go into the Kop, but they gave us shit and took the piss over what had gone on, so we thought, fuck it, and jumped straight back on to the terrace to go behind the goal again. We sat down right in the middle of where we had been moments before, with Spurs a few rows behind us. They goaded us and were singing, making me feel all the more frustrated, so I decided to go further back towards them. I think they were more shocked at what I was doing than I was. The two lads I was with said, "This is mad, let's get out of here." We exchanged some verbals with them and then I realised what I was doing and decided to get out of there. We left sharpish but intact. No-one laid a finger on me or the other two. Was that out of respect? I'll never know.

We got Spurs out of the Railway End later and I clearly remember a half-caste guy in Burberry raincoat, one of their top lads I later found out, come striding past us. He was the last one out. He looked at us and nodded. We knew what that meant; they got the result. They looked good as a firm and were the first ones I noticed wearing Stone Island and Armani.

After the match we chased them silly round the ground and the town until evening came, but not many can claim a result at St Andrew's. Outside, with West Ham it's been fifty-fifty, and we had a good off with Man United once, but that day with Spurs led to us realise we needed organisation. Afterwards, in the Crown, people were arguing with each other about what had gone wrong and what should have happened. People were vexed as they realised that there were a lot of lads out but not in the right places and really more could have been done. We agreed we were going to get turned over by all the big clubs if we didn't have a leader, so the talk turned to who it should be.

A few names were put forward, including mine. I declined at first but then they were on my case to do it. The lads said I was respected and because I knew both the younger lot and the older lot, we had the numbers. There was still a bit of in-fighting going on but people said if we all stuck together and got it together we could be something to be feared. No matter how good one local area might be, they couldn't row with the big firms like Soul Crew, West Ham and Spurs on their own. We needed to operate with one voice or it wouldn't work.

I told them that if I did agree to take the job then what I said went, and since that day, with the help of other right-hand men, like Wally, who have sway, we have done it. Other lads brought their loyal boys and together we got proper results from then on and took on the West Hams and Millwalls.

Before me a guy called Gnocchi was the figurehead in the mid to late 1970s, but the numbers weren't as big as they were after the Apex. He had a load of geezers but I brought the younger lot in and we merged and grew. I was a figurehead. If I didn't go to a match it wasn't like the firm stopped functioning, other capable guys took over. Over the next two or three years we rose to become one of the top five firms in the country and those years sealed our reputation. Ask any firm.

So that day with Spurs was a blessing in disguise really because it made us sort things out. You're either up for it or you're not. Others had tried to lead the way but it never really happened and we weren't organised. Someone just needed to take charge and then I stepped in and sorted it with the others. We were a proper firm. My weekends and evenings were taken up with it all but I worked during the week. For others though, it was their life 100 per cent of the time.

I never lost my bottle when it mattered. I was game and when I was there I called the shots and we got results.

Now a fully fledged, organised and capable firm, with Cud leading the way, the Zulus were poised for domination. They took on every firm they encountered and were victorious on most, if not all, occasions throughout the season. An unofficial "League of Shame" drawn up by police and football chiefs in the mid-1980s put them in fourth place, with West Ham top, Spurs second, then Manchester United, and then Birmingham City.

"The 1984/85 season was when the hooligan scene was peaking and we were having a mad time," said Big C. "We'd been relegated but things began improving and it seemed that every game something happened. It felt like out of twenty-four clubs, twenty had outfits, so it was always going to go off. Maggie Thatcher said she was going to clamp down on it and she took it on and won in her own way, because it was dying off by the late Eighties."

The problem of hooliganism was the subject of heated debate within the Government. A report by the Department of the Environment in 1984 concluded "although soccer spectator violence is not an exclusively British problem, it is a serious problem for this country . . ." and made twenty-two domestic and international recommendations aimed at football authorities, governments, and law enforcement.

The Zulus' mad journey that season began at Oldham on August 25. Upon arriving at the ground Blues let rip at the gates and stormed in. Hundreds forced their way into the visitors' section as police failed to maintain order, with three officers, including a chief inspector, injured during a stone-throwing barrage. Police described the scene as "just like a miners' picket". Blues won 1–0 and fans bombarded cars and houses with stones as they left the ground, resulting in sixteen arrests. One newspaper article reported that a twenty-six-year-old unemployed toolmaker from Lee Bank, Birmingham, was arrested before the game after being found in possession of a cabbage filled with metal spikes.

One Blues lad, The Pogue, didn't find events too amusing. "The police were trying to force us back around the station in an alleyway," said Big C. "They set their dogs loose and one of them managed to get a hold of The Pogue's knackers and refused to let go. The dog just swung between his legs for a while until he was called off by a handler. Another Kings Norton lad, Cooky, was savaged by a dog and his trousers were ripped to pieces. He was taken to hospital and the nurses photographed his injuries."

When the Zulus returned to Birmingham there was more trouble when it kicked off with some youths in the city centre and nine more were arrested.

The next away match was a night game at Fulham and the lads hired a coach with their regular driver, who would usually be drunk and happily chat to those behind him, jokingly taking his hands off the wheel at the same time. It wasn't a mighty clash, more of a funny night out. They arrived late outside the ground and tried to scale a fence to get in, but the police spotted them and took them to the away end. Blues won again 1–0, ensuring the team's third victory in a row. The lads enjoyed a few scuffles on the way back to the coach and someone managed to topple a copper from a horse by grabbing the horse's back leg. They scarpered and made it back to the coach and headed back to Brum.

On the train on the way to London for a game against Crystal Palace a few days later, they stopped at Coventry to see that Chelsea were making their way off the platform. As soon as the train pulled in, the Zulus got off and steamed in to the unsuspecting firm. Chelsea were outnumbered and took a quick beating before the Zulus jumped back on the train and continued on their way.

No-one expected much at Palace and they were right. Blues won 2–0 and on the way back on the train the lads chatted and played cards and were treated to an announcement on the Tannoy system by the Junior Business Boys. "Ladies and gentlemen," it began. "This train has been taken over by the Zulu Warriors." Everyone burst out laughing and discovered that the Juniors had chinned the train guard. Back at New Street, the police were waiting but most managed to escape their clutches.

Leeds in December was a high-risk fixture that the firm was waiting for. Between the Palace game and then, however, Portsmouth were the only visitors to provide any action. They came to St Andrew's in September and sat in the paddock, all kitted out in red Benetton jumpers. It was a night game and

Blues lost 1–0, their first defeat in five games. Blues failed to reached the 6.57 Crew afterwards although Pompey did have a scuffle with some "civvies" and claimed a small result.

It was well known that few clubs took a big firm to Leeds; it just didn't happen. But when the time came to play them at Elland Road, about 250-300 lads caught an early train on the Saturday morning, arriving tense but ready at about 11am. As soon as they stepped off the train they were met by Leeds Service Crew – and the police.

The Zulu chant went up, followed by a charge that prompted numerous passengers to turn and flee. The lads stormed out of the station, chasing Leeds into the town centre as nearby pubs bolted their doors. But the police took swift action, and after calling for reinforcements they managed to round up about three quarters of the Blues firm and took them to the ground well before the three o'clock kick-off. As usual, some escaped and made their own uneventful way to the ground. The Zulus were put in a top tier and the Leeds support behind the goal began zieg heiling in their direction. In response, someone let off a flare in the middle of their crowd. The police rushed up and asked whoever had the fireworks to hand them over. No-one did.

The head of match-day police operations in West Yorkshire was apparently disliked by many visiting fans, who often encountered him at Leeds, Huddersfield or Barnsley. He got the nickname "Rudolph" for his big, strawberry nose. After the game, buses were waiting to take fans to the train station but Rudolph told the lads they would have to pay. When they told him in no uncertain terms to fuck off, he made them all jog the few miles back instead. The younger and fitter lads were OK but the more rounded gentlemen amongst them – Fat Greg, Fat Gary and Fatty Pie – struggled. Most reached the station in time for the next train, although some missed it and a spot of "verbals" went on between the remaining lads and the police while they waited for the train.

Because Cud was seen as the ringleader and was involved in the banter, Rudolph wouldn't let him on the train, no matter how much they tried to persuade him. As the train pulled in the lads got on and, annoyed at Cud not being let on, unscrewed all the light bulbs in their carriages and chucked them at the officers lined up along the platform.

Cud's brother and two others got off to join him, only to then be told, "The motorway is that way," as police pointed out of the station. Cud and the others protested, saying they would be killed if they went out of the station and faced the Leeds hordes dotted around town, but it fell on deaf ears. The train left and the lads travelled back to Birmingham in darkness.

Cud and Co. left the station and asked some of the other lads who had come up in cars if they could get back with them, but there was no room. Then ten Leeds appeared, shouting, "D'ya want it?" One of the lads, Ozzie, did a martial arts kick and knocked one of them out on the floor. When they next saw the police they said they had been attacked but the coppers warned them if they hung around they would be arrested, so they decided to look for a coach back to Brum.

As they walked they heard "Kill the niggers" and 150 Leeds lads came sprinting around a corner. They turned and ran back to the station approach and kept on running, through an area where staff were sorting postal deliveries, past the station entrance where they spotted a meat wagon parked outside, and then through a fence on to a platform. In the chase they had split up and Cud and Ozzie ended up on a train bound for Sheffield, where they bumped into a few more Leeds lads and had a quick tussle before getting on a train to Derby. Cud then rang someone in Brum to come and pick them up. The others ended up in Stratford.

Racism was rife among northern firms, and at an away match with Barnsley, Leeds again turned up. The police were there too, and during an exchange with some Zulus they said, "We don't stand for your sort, your black geezers up here." In return, the Zulus taunted them with their version of a chant sung during the miners' strike: "Zulus, united, will never be defeated."

*　*　*

Big C: There were black guys in the Blackburn and Huddersfield firms but there was always a racist undertone in northern mill towns, though Oldham and Man City were not as bad. It seemed to be a Yorkshire thing. But when it's not present in your own firm you don't see it as much. Leeds for example could be pink, black or blue; they're just Leeds to us and they are going to get it. They're the ones who make the distinction and were always racist, along with Chelsea, Liverpool and Everton.

One time in the 1983/84 season, me and Cud were walking in front of the whole Liverpool firm near the Bullring. There were a few coppers around but all we heard the whole way to New Street was, "Give it the darkie, give it the darkie." They wanted me as well but they wanted Cud more. It made no difference to us, he wouldn't leave me and I wouldn't leave him.

Ron Saunders' summer purchases – and an arrival that October, twenty-one-year-old keeper David Seaman, signed from Peterborough for £100,000 and described by Saunders as "bloody marvellous" – quickly gelled with the other players, and by Boxing Day they were in second place. Equally, the Zulu firm had now grown enormous and could pull 500-plus on match days. Any rivalry between the different areas in the city was all but over and the lads' escapades were forcing other firms to sit up and take notice.

Also, around this time several girls started linking up with the firm. Not afraid to stand and fight by whacking members of rival firms with Burberry umbrellas, Karen, Paula and Donna were as game as the rest of the Zulus. They hung out with the lads at Gino's café and the Bullring shopping centre, and went to home and away matches kitted out in the casual fashion of the day. The same age as the Apex lads, they came from the same areas – Balsall Heath, Northfield, Ladywood – and became part of the firm almost from the beginning in the early 1980s and made their mark.

The trio were joined by Marion around 1984, and then two other girls, Mandy and Donna. The girls became "Burberry queens", wearing the label that was most favoured by Zulus – skirts, hats, waist-length jackets – and carrying the useful, but apparently innocent, Burberry umbrellas. They were clued-up and if the police arrived during or after a scuffle they would link up with lads, pretending they were in couples, successfully dodging any unwanted attention. They would also be out at Boogies with the lads at night after matches and at weekends, drinking with the best of them.

While it wasn't unheard of for firms to have a few girls in their midst – Leeds had a well-known girl called Angie – it was fairly uncommon. Generally, if any were involved in a fight, lads would avoid hitting them if they could. However, Marion in particular was hardcore, knew how to fight, and gave as good as she got. She would tuck her hair up under her hat and get stuck in without hesitation. Once when fighting, she was hit by a lad and when he saw she was female he began apologising.

They stuck with the firm until around the mid-1980s, when they began mingling with Wolves' Subway Army. As they drifted more towards Wolves, something that didn't go down too well with the Zulus, they were seen less and less, although Marion and one of the Donnas were still around and in touch with the lads during the rave era.

As the season entered 1985, it saw the mob engage in some daunting, if occasionally amusing, episodes. For Sheffield United on New Year's Day, a firm got off an early train at Sheffield station and were immediately confronted by a posse of local lads. The police were also present but couldn't stop a flare being launched into a crowd of Sheffield. Instead of dispersing them, the flare flew up one of their lads' trouser leg, much to everyone's amusement.

The police soon took control and marched them to the ground for 1pm, two hours before kick-off. In the ground, about forty lads positioned themselves in seats at the back of one of the side terraces above the pitch. Word had obviously spread about the flare incident amongst Sheffield supporters and they were looking to retaliate. They decided to confront the Zulus and more and more of them came up to where they were sitting, ready for a fight.

The lads were prepared and launched themselves towards them, shouting the by now infamous Zulu chant. They steamed in and Sheffield were sent spilling and tumbling back the way they had come, amid a mass of fists and kicks and resounding cheers from lads in the away end, who were able to witness it all.

Sheffield were pushed back down the stairs and several Zulus jumped the dividing fence and created more havoc. Police appeared and began chasing the Zulus nearly out of the ground, before restoring calm and walked them round to the away end. An escort back to the station after a 4–3 victory for Blues prevented much trouble on the way back.

A month later, about 100 or so lads, dressed in Fila, Benetton jumpers, Farah cords and Trim Trabb trainers, got the train to Manchester Piccadilly and walked to Manchester Victoria for a connecting train to Huddersfield. As they made their way to Victoria they encountered some Leeds Service Crew in a café. With Leeds was Angie, the female hooligan often seen with them, kitted out in the latest gear like the rest. A toe-to-toe battle began inside the small café but the police weren't far away and the Zulus split up around the city centre.

About twelve of them made it to Victoria Station, including Bobby, Big C, Balla, Big John, Ozzie and The Pogue. As they waited for their train, 150 Leeds turned up on their way to Man City, and despite the overwhelming odds, Balla reckoned his dozen could have it with them. A brief stand-off ended when the police told them to back off and the Leeds lot moved on without any trouble, a case of the Boys in Blue saving the day, as they'd have stood little chance.

When they arrived in Huddersfield, one of Huddersfield's lads, a half-caste with a goatee beard dressed in mandatory Fila and Tacchini, immediately gave it the "big 'un". But the lads continued on their way, found a pub and sank of a few before the game – and spotted Rudolph riding past on his horse.

In the ground they stood behind the goal and could see a dozen large blokes standing in the middle of the crowd. They were big, older lumps who hadn't adopted the casual dress. They wore working gear and looked like miners. A few lads decided to go over and confront them, and the "miners" were subsequently bashed all over the place, while the rest of the lads from Huddersfield just watched from the side. Everyone returned to Brum happy in the knowledge they had had a good day out and Blues had won 1–0.

A visit to Oxford in March was to be the team's sixteenth victory in twenty-six matches, but the fun and games started the night before. It was decided to have a night out in Oxford and get togged up in blazers, ties and Farahs, which would also be worn to the game the next day. Twenty lads, dressed in the height of 1985 fashion, met in the Old Crown pub in Birmingham city centre and got in cars for the journey to the Riverside Hotel. The landlady was told they were the BCFC reserve team, a story that was accepted without question, and the lads checked in with four to a room.

Everyone dumped their stuff and headed straight into Oxford to sample the pubs, clubs and local talent. They ended up in a club called Boodles, but proceedings were brought to halt when the door flew open and in came the Junior Business Boys, followed by one of the club's doormen with his shirt in ribbons after he had been slashed outside. They had been refused entry, had rushed the door and the doorman, and there they stood in the doorway. It was clear everyone had to do one, so the lads left and bowled down the street in the early hours of the morning looking for another club.

The police soon appeared and were met with a huge charge towards their van, which was pushed over amid chants and verbal exchanges with the surprised coppers.

They were chased down the road and the lads ran into another nearby nightclub, Downtown Manhattan, where they chinned the doorman and one lad, Convy, grabbed the till.

Another car was tipped over and then a group of local lads appeared with the doormen and tried to kick it off with them. They succeeded in getting into a fight but it didn't last long, with most of the locals being put down rather quickly. It was practically a riot as the lads ranted up and down the street with nobody able to stop them, but after a while they all decided they should split up, call it quits for the night and head back to the hotel.

The next day they knew they couldn't wear the planned outfit of blazers and Farahs for fear of being spotted by the police, so civvies it was. They made the news the next day: "Police are looking for twenty-five men in morning suits in Oxford . . ."

On the way to the ground they walked through a park with football pitches and re-enacted Scottish fans' actions when they played England in the 1970s by hanging off the goal posts before encountering the police and having running battles with them.

About forty Zulus went into the away end and Blues invaded the pitch when they went 3–0 up. Some Oxford came on too, and minor scuffles broke out, but the police soon stopped it and frogmarched the firm around the pitch to the away end. They got a standing ovation and the chant of "Zulu, Zulu, Zulu" rang in their ears.

Almost two weeks later, Blues were playing Blackburn Rovers, and up to 200 lads made their way by train, with more in cars. They congregated in the town centre and the younger lot, who had arrived earlier, staked out a pub Blackburn were drinking in. The Zulus tried to engage them by shouting abuse and taunts, and tried to kick in the pub door, but no-one came out and they gave up, making their way further into town.

They wandered into a shopping precinct and about halfway in spotted a jewellers' shop minus any grills on its windows and door. The rather naïve positioning of a rubbish bin with a concrete base just yards away also didn't go unnoticed by the thieves in the firm. These lads weren't interested in having a row or even going to the matches most of the time, they were mainly there to see what gear they could reap from different areas to sell on at home. They would go to away matches and do their bit, obtaining clothes or jewellery, and rarely left empty-handed. Within seconds the bin was launched into the shop window, followed by a mass of hands feverishly picking over the goods, which were then rammed into coat pockets and bags. Satisfied with their haul, they bid their farewells to 150 or so others who had stood and watched, and hotfooted it back to Brum.

As they left, the police arrived with a Blackburn lad. The Zulus were forced to stand up against a wall while he pointed out those he believed had caused trouble at the pub earlier on. As they assembled along the wall, various weapons and Vicks bottles filled with ammonia were dropped on the floor. The Blackburn lad pointed out about a dozen Zulus, who were mostly black and not actually involved in the pub incident, and they were promptly taken to the station and strip-searched.

The rest were frogmarched to the ground, apart from about eight who managed to slope off down a side road. Inside Ewood Park, the eight – Big John, Big C, Glen, Convy, The Pogue, Balla and two Kings Norton lads – went into Blackburn's end and were immediately spotted and surrounded. The only options were to stand and fight or get out on to the pitch, so they stood and had a toe-to-toe battle for a few seconds before the police waded in and tried to fish them out.

In the melee, one of the lads was jeered by Blackburn for wearing an Aquascutum jacket, which they maintained was just for women. A gap began to emerge around the eight and then the fists and punches came flying in. The lads in the away end on the other side could see what was happening and tried to climb fences to get on the pitch to help. The resulting battle forced the match to be momentarily stopped while the police got them out and marched them round to the away end to the usual ovation. Ron Saunders, however, shouted, "You are all scum," from the dugout, which some thought was high praise indeed coming from someone they considered to be "a twat". Despite losing the match 2–1, the Zulus had a "nice little result" and no major casualties.

On the day of the match at Portsmouth a month later, about 300 lads got the 6.20am train from New Street, arriving in Portsmouth for 9am. A minor internal dispute at a party the night before had resulted in Big C getting a busted hand and black eyes, so he was already injured as well as nursing a hangover. Everyone headed to the Sir Robert Peel pub, and word soon spread around town about the hefty presence. Pompey rang the pub and a meet was arranged at the Guild Hall in the town. A huge roar went up when they knew they were about to go into battle.

They finished their drinks and headed into the town centre to wait for Pompey on the vast concrete steps in front of the Guild Hall. Out came the ghetto blaster and someone put on some reggae. Shoppers were then treated to the sight of 300 black and white lads dressed in Burberry, Tacchini, and Fila, topped off with curly perms, Chris Waddle-style mullets and a smattering of diehard skinheads, dancing on the steps. Those who stopped and clapped were soon in for a shock when a huge roar went up, signalling the arrival of Pompey. A flare was immediately fired and bounced off the steps followed by a volley of bricks, and a rocket put a stop to the music as it landed on the speakers. There was a stand off and the Zulu chant went up but the Old Bill arrived and put a stop to any major fighting. They were the only ones that could claim a result that day.

Although they weren't rated that much as a thug outfit, Charlton were getting things organised and they had one of the biggest ends in the country before they moved stadiums from the Old Valley. Nothing much happened before or during their game with City in April, except for a few Millwall lads taking pictures. This was something that happened from time to time, other firms taking note of what rivals were up to. The lads left the ground before the end of the match, pleased with their team's performance in a 2–1 victory.

They wandered around the Charlton end and some hid behind a corner to wait for any rivals. Some soon appeared, the nod was given and they all scrambled from behind the wall. Scuffles broke out and the unsuspecting Charlton lads were chased down the road. Once again the police appeared and moved everyone on but the lads were happy to head back to Brum unscathed.

Blues' 2–0 home victory over Cardiff at the start of May confirmed promotion to the old Division One. The team's success was described in a local paper thus: "Birmingham City, eternally the team in whom ambition meets frustration, completed more on Saturday than anyone would have forecast a year ago." The match was a celebration rather than a confrontation, despite Cardiff's own violent reputation. "Cardiff had a good firm that day," said Big C. "Blues invaded the pitch but I heard the police say, 'Let 'em on, the next home match is Leeds and no-one is getting on.' How wrong could they be?"

The second last match of the season was against Middlesbrough and fell on a Bank Holiday. Keen to make the most of the weekend, around 100 lads decided to have a night out in Scarborough on the Sunday before the match. The Junior Business Boys had the same idea and were already causing mayhem in the seaside town when the convoy of Zulus arrived.

The two groups caught up with each other on a road near the town centre. The Zulus learned that a Leeds fan had been stabbed and the police were on a mission to find those responsible. They split up and the older lads drove off but not long afterwards several officers, in cars and vans, appeared and pulled over three cars from a convoy, while others sped off. They searched the vehicles and their occupants and found a scabby knife, used for stripping wire, and a metal bar on the floor of the car that The Pogue, Big C and John were in. The officers already had some Zulu calling cards in their possession and told the lads they were going with them to a nearby police station "the easy way or the hard way".

Sixteen lads were nicked in total, including The Pogue, Big C and John for unlawful possession of a weapon, and were chucked in an outside cell and held there for several hours. One of the lads, Morph, had a bit of draw down his boxer shorts, so the lads had a smoke to help pass the time. After a few hours someone asked how much longer they would be detained but all the desk sergeant came back with was a list of their previous convictions and said, "Every one of you cunts has records or are known to the police." In the end, John was the only one charged, as the "weapons" were found in his car. He was later sentenced to six months in jail even though he wasn't anything to do with the stabbing incident.

They were eventually released in the early hours of Monday morning and told, "You've got fifteen minutes to get out of town and if you are seen here again you will be locked up until Monday." With that, lads drove to the outskirts of Scarborough and got some shut-eye in their cars before driving to Middlesbrough.

On the day of the match, they parked near a train station and made their way to the ground, having a few scuffles along the way. The firm numbered more than 200. Middlesbrough were a hard firm to judge. They didn't travel well but you could usually count on something happening when you visited them. Not much went on inside the ground, and after a goalless draw the police segregated the road, forcing opposing fans to walk in opposite directions to prevent any trouble. Around sixty lads, including thirty Junior Business Boys, had other ideas. They kicked down a barrier and ran as quickly as possible down a side street, confident they hadn't been seen. They carried on walking, laughing and joking, along a main road.

They soon became aware of a huge contingent of Middlesbrough lads watching them. More and more seemed to appear: hundreds of menacing-looking lads, waiting to pounce. It was obviously going to go off, and their sixtysomething against 700 or so didn't seem fair. But the Zulus were ready; running was never an option. Even if they had wanted to run, they'd have been chased down.

Boro's so-called Frontline crew would emerge as a serious firm, but in 1985 not all Zulus rated them that much. This encounter with them was to be a real eye-opener for the small bunch of Brummies. They knew they had bitten off more than

78

they could chew and were about to find out just how capable they were, while wishing they had perhaps stayed with the main escort. By now the police had got wise to what was going on and a few officers were within shouting distance on one side of the road, but instead of calling for back-up or trying to prevent it kicking off, they told the Zulus, "Let's see how good you guys are," and stood back, expecting them to get a pasting.

The apprehensive lads formed several lines in the road, ready to take on what was coming. As Boro launched themselves, the shout went up amongst the Zulus to "stand" as the punches, kicks and headbutts came flying in. The fighting was intense and lasted several minutes. The huge swarm of Middlesbrough kept coming at the Zulus who still stood, fighting off everything that came their way. When the police saw that the Zulus were giving as good as they got, they started to panic and called for back-up, which quickly arrived. The officers started to try and break it up by wading in and dragging the Zulus out as best they could, despite their pleas to be left alone for five more minutes. Some Boro had pulled out blades but the police made a beeline for them, with one of their lads, Ali, grabbed straight away.

The fight was over as the police regained control. The majority of the Zulus were escorted down the road back towards their cars, with Boro on the other side of the road. A few verbals were exchanged as the enormity of what had just happened began to sink in. They knew they would eventually get done but they were proud to have held it until the police stepped in. As they walked, the lads got a bit of a spring in their step and someone started singing a reggae song by Tipper Irie. Soon everyone joined in: "It's good to have the feeling you're the best – yes!" It would be sung after other major clashes.

But with the mayhem splitting up many of the group, virtually none were able to get their lifts home and were stranded and skint in Middlesbrough. They decided bunking on the train was the best option and made their way to the station, where they caught a train only to find that loads of Tottenham lads were on it after a match with Newcastle United. The police were quick to act and maintained a presence in the carriage between the two sets of fans, stopping any trouble, before telling the Zulus to get off and change at Darlington. Some cops got off with them and said they would be taken home in police vehicles, being passed on to neighbouring forces, county by county, the further south they headed.

Pretty pleased with this idea, they all got into the vans, but as soon as they reached the A1 the doors opened and they were booted out and told to make their own way back. "Birmingham is that way!" That left hitching as the only option, so they stood at the side of the busy road with their thumbs out hoping to get a ride. It wasn't long before some were picked up, with Wally and a couple of others getting "a right touch" with a lift from a soldier on leave going home to Alum Rock in Birmingham. Others weren't so lucky and didn't make it back for two or three days, ending up in Leeds only to encounter a firm there and receive a bashing, adding to their misery.

Some Juniors had no complaints. Three of them jumped in with a stripper and her manager, with one lucky lad, Big Stig, literally getting a "ride" home in the back thanks to the scantily clad stripper – as described in the next chapter.

Chapter Five

Junior Business Boys

By David George

Dedicated to Little Darren Blunt, Kings Norton; Paddy Burke, Sheldon; Neil Wilf Williams, Chelmsley Wood; Simon Court, Chelmsley Wood; Neil Macatee, Winson Green. RIP chaps, we will never forget you. Much love.

NINETEEN EIGHTY-TWO saw many different styles of music pumped out in the charts, as artists experimented with new sounds. Toni Basil was dressed as a cheerleader and singing about Mickey, Hall and Oates said, "I Can't Go For That (No Can Do)", and Kool and the Gang were asking everybody to "Get Down On It".

A number of older guys from the Chelmsley Wood Trooper, including Pipkin, Jenkins and Bobby, were proper tidy dressers very early, and wore V-neck cashmere sweaters and Adidas Samba before we knew it was a style. A handful of younger lads from the Trooper went to St Andrew's in the early 1980s, but never had enough money to pay into the ground. We used to climb over the massive blue metal fence into the Kop, nearly killing ourselves in the process, just to watch our team, with players such as Kenny Burns, a defensive monster who never shied away from a tackle, Archie Gemmell, who used to skin people on the wing, Tony Evans and the superb Trevor Francis. Those football days were very exciting, and to stand in the Kop End at St Andrew's, watching the game and listening to the home supporters singing, was one of the highlights of being alive for a young Brummie.

Not being a very good thief, I used to try and get hold of bits of clobber, but most of the time I was wearing cheaper versions of the more expensive stuff. Near the end of 1983, style had certainly moved on. The young Trooper dressers were very much into their sportswear and trainers, and didn't mind how bright and outlandish their clothes were. From meeting other like-minded individuals from other areas in Birmingham, we met up with good heads from many other manors and became friends. The Juniors came mainly from Lea Hall, Chelmsley Wood, Kings Norton, Bordesley Green, Stechford, Yardley, Acocks Green, Sheldon, Meadway, Cotteridge, Leamington Spa, Damson Wood, Handsworth, Small Heath and West Bromwich.

Each area in Birmingham had a group of individuals who were addicted to the football culture and the fashion and style that came with it. Clothes were a symbol of a good mob back in the day, and if you were to name the top ten firms, then you would also be naming most of the best dressers in the country. Round south-east Birmingham, Lea Hall were the first to be dripping in Fila BJs and Farahs, as they had a lot of good thieves who were very busy. Eamon had the knack of getting us chased through the Bullring by the local townies, who regularly demanded his clothing, but never succeeded in getting it. The townies didn't really bother me in the early days, as my clothes were not up to par, which was a blessing on the one hand and a nightmare on the other. People who came to Lea Hall or Chelmsley in those days also risked being mugged or taxed for clothing. I saw a number of people pursued from the shopping centre for the crime of wearing a well-known sports label.

As youngsters, we would walk into town after home games, following the older lads in order to see what they were up to, but a lot of the time they were not happy with a bunch of kids bowling behind them. The Juniors got to know one another when crews from other areas popped down to their local pubs and had a drink with them. The Bulls Head, Kings Norton, the Yew Tree, Yardley, the Happy Trooper, Chelmsley Wood, the Broadway, Bordesley Green, the Tavern On the Green, Lea Hall, and the Custard House, Small Heath, were all popular places where the Juniors created a bond of friendship that brought us together as one.

The first titles used at St Andrew's to describe the youngsters were the Zulu Apprentices and the Zulu Juniors, but a number of us changed it to the Junior Business Boys – Pride of the Midlands, as we wanted a different name to the older firm. It derived from the act of "doing the business", as in getting a result, bashing the shit out of a rival firm. A number of girls from Solihull and Leamington Spa associated with us in the mid 1980s. Jane, Vanessa, Jo and Sharon were all quite active on the football scene because they liked our cheek and the feeling of danger when we were out and about.

From travelling to away matches, and sometimes being pursued by rival fans, we learned at an early age that when the shit goes down and you haven't got your friends with you, just a bunch of average fans who look the part but will run and leave you at the first sign of trouble, then it's going to be a very long, nail-biting day. Therefore, as important as Doing the Business was being with the right people, who will cover your arse when it's bang off and up in the air.

Looking at our old pictures, you can see that there were no scary-looking people, just young, working class lads who were willing to stand up and be counted and defend themselves against people who wanted to cut them up or knock them out. In the early 1980s, Birmingham's firms had the largest concentration of ethnic minorities supporting any team, and white fans from most other parts of the country enjoyed trying to wind up the black supporters, by any means necessary.

Manchester is one of those places that reminds me of the mentality of Birmingham fans, because when they want you, then it really is game on. In 1984, 500 Birmingham landed at Manchester's Piccadilly Station and began marching down to the shopping centre looking for hooded leathers, Nani Bonn, Hugo Boss and Best Company sweaters, Benetton cords, Fiorucci dungarees, Adidas Munchen, Nike Internationalist, Docksteps shoes, Allegri jackets and Aquascutum. Burberry cashmere scarves wrapped high around the face was the uniform, and we looked good, trust me. Birmingham's dress sense had evolved so quickly that on their travels up and down the country, other fans in places such as London, used to stop, and pause, step back with their hands held up in front of them, and ask, "You Gooners or Yids?" This on one hand was a compliment, because both of those firms were hot to trot when it came to garments of quality, but it was also an insult; we didn't want anyone thinking that we were from London, as most of our main rivals come from the capital.

Chains were pulled from shoppers' necks as we walked into Manchester. A numbers of lads who travelled with Birmingham were professional thieves and took advantage of any violent situations to make a shit-load of money on the side. Sometimes, when a fight took place in a shopping centre, a group of lads would smash up a jeweller's or a clothes shop in broad daylight, take their ill-gotten gains, and bugger off home on a coach or train, not bothering with the football match at all.

Birmingham marched into the Arndale Centre and immediately a jeweller's window went through. People were leaning into the broken window and pulling trays of gold rings and chains from the display. Some local shoppers were screaming and running away – the sight of 500 fans coming towards the average individual tended to make them very nervous.

A number of Manchester City fans were unlucky enough to be collared by Blues and some took a good slap as we all tried to find exits. A security guard was thrown from an escalator on to his face and then Birmingham met Manchester's heavily armoured riot police, who escorted Blues out of the Arndale and towards Moss Side.

As we neared Moss Side, seven Juniors – me, Elvis, Skully, Eamon, Coaly, Jeff and Ears – who were walking 100 yards behind the escort, crossed over the road and took a diversion to find some action. We reached City's ground before the escort and decided to stuff our faces with crisps and fizzy pop outside the newsagent's across the road. As everybody munched away, we could see a huge firm coming towards us with a number of black guys at the front. We gave them a quick glace and carried on eating, because as far as we were concerned, this was Birmingham's firm. When they reached 100 yards from us, my can of pop was nearly shaken out of my hands by Eamon pulling at my sweater.

"That's not Blues, it's the fucking Guv'nors," he said.

With our average age being fifteen and there being seven of us, we were certainly not equipped to deal with 400 Mancs, mostly in their twenties. We backed slowly off around the corner and walked into another firm, the Young Guv'nors, also known as the Man City Snipers. They were around twenty-strong and one guy in particular was looking for some action.

He bounced into the road, pointing at Skully and asking for a straightener, just him and our man. Skully smiled and walked into the road and the two youngsters clashed on the corner near the newsagent's. Skully put the Manchester lad on his arse and started to get the better of him, but as this was happening, the Guv'nors arrived and the situation was well on top. A number of the Young Guv'nors ran into the road and started to kick Skully on the floor while he was filling in the Manchester lad. I threw a half can of pop at one lad, just missing his head, and we bounced into the road to back Skully. But just as I was right in front of the Young Guv'nors, a policeman on a horse grabbed me by the scruff of the neck and dragged me off up the street.

The Junior Business Boys were now well and truly out-numbered, but they did not run. Instead they punched and kicked anyone who came close as they were backing off, and as luck would have it, Birmingham's firm landed at the ground and saw what was happening.

As the Juniors tried to stay on their feet fighting the Guv'nors, Man City gave it the big one and roared forward. Fats snatched a large stripy umbrella from Elvis and ran straight into them, immediately bending the brolly over one of the Mancs' heads. As I was hopping up the road, being dragged away backwards on tiptoes, I could see that the small-scale scuffle had turned into a full-scale brawl involving at least 200 lads on either side trying to knock each other out. I was dragged through Man City's firm and told to stand where I was, surrounded by Guv'nors trying their best to intimidate me.

The police threw me into a room before the game started and told me that I was being arrested for violent disorder. Having such a baby face, I convinced the officer that I was thirteen and I had lost my dad near the shop outside the ground. Amateur dramatics help at this stage if you can wobble your bottom lip and make out that you're about to cry. The police officer let me go and I walked round to the away end of the ground and paid in.

Right next to our stand, the Young Guv'nors were sitting behind the goal. We got about thirty Juniors together and walked to the fence to have a look at their numbers. A few Mancs clocked us, and as quick as lightning, the whole firm stood up behind the goal. There must have been around 200 in the seats, beckoning us to climb over the fence into their end, but we were game, not insane. We looked at each other and started laughing, "Fuck that, you're having a laugh!"

Even though they were around the same age as us, they were well and truly the biggest junior firm I had ever seen, but they never travelled to Birmingham with it and never tried it on with us in any numbers around our ground. At the time, no other junior firm had the better of us at home, and most would always stay with the much older lads so they wouldn't get beaten up and mugged.

The Junior Business Boys in the early to mid 1980s were on a mission to show their biggest local rivals that when it came to bottle and getting the job done, we were the firm to beat. From my experiences of knuckle against the Villa Youth, we have never been run by them, but I have been sparked out cold on the ramp near McDonalds by the C-Crew's firm.

In 1985, Blues were playing at Villa Park and the Juniors wanted to pay the Villa Youth a visit at their pub, the Crown & Cushion in Witton. A thirty-handed firm of teenagers from Yew Tree, Acocks Green, Bordesley Green, and Chelmsley Wood caught the bus from Birmingham city centre and got off one stop before the pub. As we got off, everybody was pumped up and ready for action, eyebrows dropped, shoulders back, and arms going like window wipers as we all bowled towards the back of the pub's car park.

These Juniors were the ones you want on your shoulder when all hell has broken loose and your friends have been kicked unconscious in the street in front of you. No dummies here, just the proper get-the-job-done firm, was on its way to show Villa what we were all about. As we reached the car park, with everybody talking through gritted teeth and adrenalin flying high, two Juniors walked round to the front of the Crown & Cushion to check on numbers, as sometimes the Youth can pull a huge fuck-off firm of more than 200 chaps. The two reported there were fifty Villa Youth in the pub plus your average supporters, which was just right for us because we didn't mind being outnumbered if it was only the Villa.

We bowled towards the front of the Crown & Cushion and all rushed the door at the same time. Some of their Youth were standing right outside the doors as we took them out. Villa ran back into the pub as we tried to get in through a second lot of doors, but due to a hail of glasses coming at us, we backed off outside and let them come out to us. The double doors flew open and Villa came steaming out of the doors, throwing bar stools, ashtrays and pint glasses which clattered to the ground.

As soon as they had nothing left in their hands, we rushed the door again, smacking as many Youth as we could. The Villa managed to lock the second lot of doors and then started to mouth off at the windows at the front of the pub. We were tempted to cave in all of the windows, but sirens could be heard in the distance and thousands of Villa fans were walking past us heading for the ground. We casually walked off, disappeared into the crowd and began the five-minute walk towards Villa Park with not one adult saying a word to us. Even though the road was full of Villa fans, they were not firm, just your narrow-minded average Villa supporters.

THE JUNIOR BUSINESS Boys were up early, planning to show the older crew that they had more bottle than Unigate milk. Thirty Juniors travelled to London for a match against Chelsea in 1986 and landed at Euston around 11.30am. We bowled up the platform all smiles until we got to the barriers. Euston Station has a very large concourse, where people stand and look for the time and details of their train's departures. On this day, the station was full to bursting with Manchester United's Red Army. Around 500 men, mostly wearing designer gear and leather jackets, were standing in the concourse, obviously waiting for more Mancs to come off one of the trains. As much as we were game in those days, this was beyond anything we could deal with and we turned and walked back down the platform a little way.

"What we gonna do?" was what everybody was asking and we came to the conclusion that we should front this one out and see what happened. We all looked at each other and heartbeats were going like the clappers. We turned towards the barriers and reached for our tickets. As the last Junior came through the barriers, a few Man U clocked us but didn't say a word. We bowled straight through the middle of the Red Army, shoulders back and arms swinging. We were only thirty-handed but the Mancs either moved or were pushed out of the way. We were all at least a foot shorter than everyone on the station, and people were looking at us and mumbling to their friends, "Who are these lot?"

We bowled out of the glass doors and got out of the station without a scratch, which was a fucking miracle, and as soon as we got outside we all let out a huge sigh of relief. Then the glass

A gathering of Zulu Warriors, past and present, in the streets of Birmingham.
The Zulus were one of the first, and certainly the biggest, multi-racial hooligans gangs. © *John Alevroyiannis*

Cud and Wally, Zulu stalwarts who represented two different aspects of the firm. Cud was strictly "in it for the knuckle", while Wally and his crew were more criminally inclined. © Nick Bowman

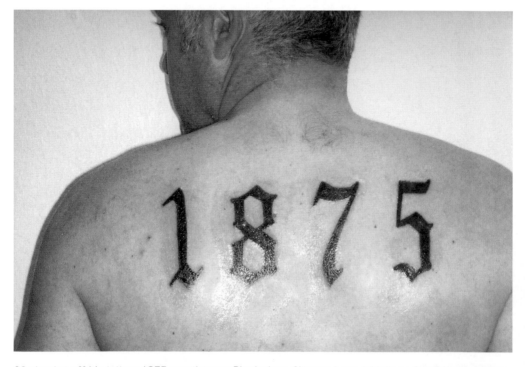

CC showing off his tattoo: 1875 was the year Birmingham City was born, initially as Small Heath Alliance.

A gathering of Junior Business Boys from Solihull, Small Heath and West Brom.
The Juniors were a younger offshoot of the Zulus.

Juniors Business Boys searching for Leeds in Birmingham city centre in 1985. From left to right:
Lawless (Bordesley Green), Coley (Yardley), D (Solihull), unidentified (Kings Norton), Dean (Balsall Heath),
Cotts (Yardley/Yew Tree), unidentified, Paul (Bordesley Green).

The Kings Norton lads gather on a snowy day in the mid-Eighties. The Zulus united many previously antagonistic factions from different areas of the city.

Even the blazer was a casual fashion statement. Some of the lads sport natty threads in a club in Oxford before a mid-Eighties match.

Hanging around outside Bar St Martin in Brum city centre on a match day.

A group of City lads in the back of a van hired for a trip to Cardiff, a moody away fixture.

The most infamous day in St Andrew's history: the riot when Leeds United came to town. Here fans move onto the pitch armed with debris in an attempt to reach the Leeds fans at the other end of the ground.

Carnage as bodies fall and the police, including those on horses, back off from the Zulu onslaught.

Fighting breaks out on the fringes as police battle to keep rival factions apart.

Riot cops in helmets make a mass charge to force the hooligans back onto the terraces.

Police grapple with fans while one tends a fallen colleague. The violence was overshadowed in the media by the Bradford City fire on the same day.

A collapsed wall outside the ground destroyed several vehicles and tragically led to the death of a teenage fan.

doors opened and at least 200 Mancs came bouncing out of the station shouting at us.

"Oi, you fucking Birmingham, come on then, you cunts."

Come on? Come off it! We shot off up the road, pursued by a large contingent of United's firm but they only chased us for 100 yards or so, which was a relief. But then we were set upon by the police in two meat wagons, who stopped us on the main road. Being a bunch of confident, cocky Brummies, a few of us tried to do our best version of Cockney accents, which went down like a lead balloon. One officer laughed and said, "You're from Birmingham, aren't ya? You're playing Chelsea today. If you're thinking of going up to Chelsea with numbers like this, then you'd better think again."

The police drove off and left us standing on the main road about 400 metres from Euston. We were on a mission to go to Chelsea and have it large before the older crew got there, but we decided to change the script because we'd just had a reality check. We got some food from a convenience store and sat about on the high street waiting for the Zulu Warriors to come in at Euston around an hour later.

The Blues firm came bowling out of Euston 400-handed with a huge Zulu Warriors flag. We could have screamed with delight at the time because we certainly could not have gone and had it at Chelsea with thirty. It would have been a death wish. We were just young kids with heart and a lot of bottle, but we also realised that sometimes it is best not to bite off more than you can chew.

LICHFIELD IS A picturesque place on the outskirts of Birmingham; it has an air of old England about it. It also had a firm of Villa Youth that were giving one of our lads, Slick, grief for being a Blues fan in this pretty little town.

Slick told these locals that he would bring the JBBs up to Lichfield to sort them out. They must have thought that we would never go, but in those days we could assemble a sixty-strong firm of Juniors with just one or two phone calls. On this day in 1985, the Juniors met in Birmingham and travelled to Lichfield by train. It was a Bank Holiday and quite warm as we marched through Lichfield looking for the fairground. The big hitters from Small Heath, Yew Tree, Chelmsley Wood, Kings Norton and Bordesley Green were all out. Thirty or so Villa Youth were standing about at the fair but as soon as they saw us, they all seemed to want to go home really quickly.

"ZUULUU!" We ran them straight off the fair and bashed any fool who wanted to dance with us. Disappointed with the feeble local opposition, the Juniors left and caught the train to Sutton Coldfield, another area full of Villa Youth who needed a reality check. On the way, the Juniors were so bored they split into two firms and decided to bang it off with each other. It was supposed to be a friendly scuffle but some people get far too carried away when clenching their fists. Cud let off a fire extinguisher and sprayed white powder all over the carriage, which blinded most of us. A lad from the Yew Tree had just bought a wicked Burberry leather and it was ripped to shit. He wasn't happy and let everybody know, which calmed us all down again before we got off in Sutton, heading for the Falcon Lodge estate.

As we bowled through their manor, there was nobody about, and any people who clocked us didn't want to know at all. The place resembled a ghost town, so we jumped on a bus to Erdington, where we got a quick drink in the Parrot pub. It was well and truly a Villa pub and a group of older Villa lads didn't take kindly to us being in there. We thought nothing of it, as the crew we had out on this day was proper tidy. We smashed a couple of windows and invited the Villa for a dance outside but they declined, so we left and headed off up the main road looking for another venue.

As we reached the traffic lights at Tyburn Road, a car slammed on the brakes and all the doors flew open, with Villa's older crew now running from the motor at us shouting, "Come on then!" We backed off as they threw bricks and all types of crap at us before jumping back into their car to make a getaway. Unfortunately for them, their car stalled at the lights. The Juniors picked up the bricks and crap that had been thrown at them and ran at the car.

"ZUULUU!"

They were going nowhere. Every window was smashed and the Villa were properly dealt with. These grown men were nearly crying in their car as they were punched, stamped and kicked. The traffic was moving all around us at the lights, and people were sounding their horns in the street, as the thirty Blues smashed the Villa to pieces. Once the windows had gone, one Junior used a huge pole to smash into the faces of the Villa lot. Another lad, Bellamy, jumped up and down on top of the car, denting it so much that his feet were sometimes connecting with the heads of the Villa inside.

The police turned up and a number of Juniors were arrested, including Bellamy, who had got a bit carried away on the car, but most sloped off and stood at bus stops going in any direction. It always helps if you carry a pair of clear-lens glasses and a newspaper, and start reading and looking over the top of your paper.

Oxford, the city where knowledge, buggery, and power rules, is not the type of place you would wish to go to if you are working class and real, unless you enjoy speaking to snobby, spoilt, privileged children who would not give you the time of day because the majority are so far up themselves they should be called butt plugs. We arrived a day before the game against United with a decent firm of lads who where only interested in having a drink and a good time with the local ladies.

Oxford has never had a firm of much use, this not being a region in the UK where casuals are prominent. The older chaps were around sixty strong, with a firm of twenty Juniors. The older lads slapped on the double-breasted blazers and hit the town. I never liked the double-breasted blazers with the gold buttons as I thought that they looked tacky, but nevertheless, most of the older lads put on their glad rags. The Juniors marched around the town stealing from stores and generally having a tickle.

When the older Zulus ended up in a club in town, the Juniors tried to get a bit of action and approached the door. One of the six bouncers was being the usual cocky steroid freak and didn't realise that the situation was out of his hands. The bouncers were arrogant and rude and told us to go away. Even though most of us looked around fourteen years old, the majority were in the last year of school, or had left the year before. The bouncers were rushed and one was wet up to fuck with a blade repeatedly run across his face at high speed. He ran back into the club with the whole of his face dripping in blood and people started screaming. The Juniors left to find another place to drink.

On the day of the game, some Blues fans stole students' bikes and rode around town, generally taking the piss. A firm walked round to the away end, broke down a fence and 300 bowled into the game free of charge. If firms were classed as radio stations, Blues were Medium Wave, and Oxford were FM, fucking miles away. I know that their so-called firm is called the Warlords, but the last war they were in must have been with swords. If I was a teacher marking Oxford's firm, I would have to say, "Very poor indeed, see me after class."

Birmingham won the game easily 3–0, and to top it all, managed a pitch invasion into Oxford's end of the ground, fighting the police and anyone who put a book down long enough to protect their teeth. Walking back into town took forever and a number of Yew Tree who were walking ahead of the Blues escort were lucky enough to get a decent scuffle with some local black lads who had hung around town. One of the Oxford lads pulled out a kung fu rice flail and started flinging it around his body in the middle of the main road in front of eight Yew Tree lads. The Yew Tree chaps watch him for a few seconds, as he was quite skilful, but then got bored, so Mark grabbed him by the hair and levelled him, the Oxford lad nearly ending up under a bus. This was the only row all day except with the Old Bill, who are always up for a bit of knuckle wherever you go.

The day before a game at Middlesbrough, twenty Juniors travelled to Scarborough and made sure that everybody in that town would remember them. The lads, from Yew Tree, Lea Hall and Solihull, exchanged words with a group of scooter boys who gladly obliged in fighting them within ten minutes of their arrival. The fight was over as quickly as it started and the Juniors entered an amusement arcade, where some rocked the machines from side to side in order to get a bit of change. When the manager approached, he figured his best option was to kick them all out and shut down for a while. His plan failed; he was knocked out cold.

Throughout the day, the Juniors were fighting anyone in Scarborough, including arcade workers, scooter boys, locals coming out of pubs and some squaddies who chased a number of Brummies up the road with an axe. In the evening, a few Juniors were chased and split up and one lad got his nose broken. Later, not having anywhere to sleep, they sneaked on to a bus parked at a depot for a bit of shut eye, but one lad got carried away with the idea of driving the bus around town, started it up and smashed it into a wall.

The police rounded up the Juniors in the morning and placed them on a bus, which was escorted out of the town by a large contingent of the local constabulary. After a few miles, with the police still following, the Juniors threatened the driver and ordered him to pull up at the next pub. They went in and a couple of lads started fiddling the fruit machine with a strimmer and making some good change, while another lad sneaked up stairs and stole some money left lying around.

I started early on the day of the game and caught a 10.30am Special for Middlesbrough. We were escorted out of the station and straight on to buses to the ground. As I looked out of the window, I got a real vibe of the place. It was very rundown and reminded me of TV documentaries about Eastern Europe, with grey, shabby buildings and the population looking like they had seen better days. I smiled to myself as I was glad to know that after the game I was going home to civilisation, to Birmingham. The everyday people looked rough as hell and I had an uneasy feeling while travelling through this northern hole. Today was going to be eventful, I could feel it.

ZULUS

As we arrived at the game, Blues were mob-handed and sitting together behind the goal. Boro had a proper good firm and we knew that their Frontline had some big local chaps who can throw it down. Near the end of a very dull, 0–0 draw, Birmingham fans started to sing to Middlesbrough, "On the pitch, on the pitch, on the pitch." The police marched in front of the goal to stop Birmingham fans from going across the pitch, but they had no intention of doing it, they just wanted to hot up the spot, or create a scene. The final whistle blew and Middlesbrough fans from all over the ground ran at Birmingham fans behind the goal, only to be stopped by a huge line of police. We stood up in the seats to check on Boro's numbers and they were huge.

As we left the ground, most of the Birmingham fans were forced on to buses to transport them back to the station, but around seventy of us marched around the ground looking for the Frontline. Big, ugly, northern racists were everywhere. Most of them had only been walking upright for a few months and still didn't know how to make fire. Birmingham's numbers were small but if you had seen the seventy that had gone walkabout round the ground you would know that it was the real deal. No slackers here, this was need-to-know time. The firm bowled on to a huge main road and could see in the distance a huge firm walking towards them. This was the Boro Frontline, an electric firm of more than 700 lads now running towards us.

My heartbeat was going like a pillhead's as I tried to get my bearings and began pulling on a piece of fencing with a lad from the Yew Tree. "Make a line, no one run. Fucking STAND!" Blues had a few tools that had been quickly grabbed off the floor and made three solid lines, all standing shoulder to shoulder with each other. If you have seen the start of the Great North Run, then you will have an idea of the size of the firm that was running at Birmingham. The Frontline hit and all hell broke loose. Bodies were hitting the floor on both sides, but Blues held it together. In situations like this, Birmingham are one of the best for standing and trading, putting people on their backsides.

94

Blues stepped forward and bashed a number of Boro who had run too far into Birmingham and were being chinned by the second and third wave of lads. Some Frontline were standing way back and throwing house bricks, but they were hitting their own people on the backs of their heads. A few Birmingham put their years of martial arts training to good use and sent some Boro fans to the floor with axe kicks and roundhouses.

After a few minutes of us showing Middlesbrough that we can come to their manor and go wherever we want with no problems, the police turned up and escorted us to the train station. Their Frontline followed us all the way, shouting racist abuse and showing us all that they were not happy with what had just taken place on their turf. Birmingham had had no choice but to stand, as it would have been insane to run from a firm of this size. I realise that some people will say that this is nonsense, but we don't need to make up stories, as we are known for good reasons to be one of the best in the country.

As we arrived at the station, we were told that the last train back to Birmingham had gone but we could go to York and change trains. At York we were forced into police vans and driven out of the city. The police dumped us on the hard shoulder of the motorway and said, "Birmingham's that way." We thumbed lifts, which seemed to work well for a number of people. Applehead and Jeff were sitting in the back of a car being driven by a burly man who was travelling to Leicester with a blonde woman who was a stripper. Allegedly, this woman was a darling and very horny indeed. She asked the two young Brummies if they fancied a bit of how's your father while in the car. The two lads declined, as the idea of having sex with a stripper in a moving car while her manager was driving didn't seem a good thing to do.

The car stopped at a service station, where they bumped into a few more Brummies who had been successfully thumbing. Jeff explained the stripper situation to Dave – also known as Big Stig – who rubbed his hands with glee, and swapped cars with Applehead for the journey home. It was Dave's lucky day, as the stripper undid his trousers and sat on him in the back of the car. Jeff was laughing like Sid James out of the window as the stripper had her way with Dave.

Around fifteen less fortunate Juniors, including me, were still walking on the hard shoulder when it started to get dark and we decided to find another route. We arrived at a small chip shop in a little town and one of the staff remarked to her colleague that we were the first black faces she had seen in years around there. Realising that black people were not in abundance in the area, we got one of the white lads to go into the local village police station to get a lift to the nearest national rail train station. The officer drove us all to Leeds train station, where we realised that the night was not over by a long shot.

As we jumped out of the police van and walked into Leeds station, we were spotted instantly. The Very Young Team (VYT), Leeds' juniors, bowled into the station. There was an uneasy silence but then things settled. The Leeds lads were OK, and one in particular called Eddie seemed to be proper clued up and on the ball. We sat and chatted with them and some of the Brummies even went with the VYT to a café. I thought better of it, as Leeds are not known for their hospitality, more for putting you in hospital.

While the Blues Juniors and the Very Young Team chatted about the next week's last game of the season against the Yorkshiremen at our ground, you could see the Leeds lot looking at the Brummies' clothing and vice versa, but nobody said a word. Then doors flew open and forty Leeds Service Crew bowled in looking to do some damage. We had nowhere to go except outside or to stand and fight. I was kicked around the floor for a few minutes, but managed to keep my teeth in my mouth. The Service Crew filled us in but this only made the following week's game of the season even more important to us.

The Leeds riot at St Andrew's was just seven days away.

Chapter Six

The Leeds Riot

IT WAS A crucial match for Leeds United. They were chasing promotion, and arrived early at New Street with one of the biggest away firms to ever land at the station. It was by now impossible for a large number of Zulus to wait there on a match day because of the police presence, so they hovered in nearby doorways, watching and waiting. The usual jibes ensued from those who did go near their mob, but the police soon moved them on before starting to escort Leeds away from the station. Many managed to slip the escort and ventured down into Hurst Street, an area now known as the Chinese Quarter, and started drinking in the Australian Bar.

As the morning progressed, the number of Zulus dotted around town in various bars began to swell in preparation for the last game of the season. They soon discovered where Leeds were drinking and some decided to pay them a visit. The Juniors, who made up the largest contingent of Zulus that day, got tooled up and headed off towards Hurst Street proclaiming, "We'll show you older lot how to do it."

They stood outside the bar trying to coax Leeds out, but they were having none of it and stayed firmly put, singing, "We are Leeds." Frustrated, the Juniors started chucking things through the windows in the hope that this might entice Leeds into a scuffle, but in the end it took a canister of gas to shift them before the pub was blitzed.

When the police arrived, a lot of Leeds scattered into other pubs, where they were set upon again. The Juniors carried out a vicious attack on a pub called the Fox, also on Hurst Street, causing thousands of pounds' worth of damage and some bad injuries. Road works went flying in the direction of the pub and the glass front door was smashed as Leeds tried to dodge the missiles while being chased around the street. Again, the police managed to get an escort together and marched Leeds and their casualties to the ground.

As more and more disturbances broke out across the city, the air rang to the noise of police sirens racing to the next incident. The mayhem carried on into the early afternoon and all the way from the city centre to the ground, with cars, vans and coaches set upon and occupants dragged out and beaten.

"Everyone has their own story to tell from this day," said Cud. "There were that many people involved – at least a thousand came out. Leeds plotted up in the Aussie Bar in town before the match and some Blues went down there and gassed it. I knew it was going to go off when the Juniors went off to Hurst Street. There were loads of them and there was trouble in quite a few places. All you could hear were police sirens; it was mayhem, a really crazy day. I went offside for a bit as it was getting on top and a 'naughty forty' of us went to the ground."

Blues, already promoted, needed three points to take the championship, but only if Oxford, their rivals for top spot, lost at home to Barnsley. Leeds had to win to gain promotion and four other clubs had to fail. Blues manager Ron Saunders called for a "showpiece match" at the highest professional level but he didn't witness anything like that once the game kicked off.

Many Leeds fans didn't arrive in the ground until after the 3pm kick-off. They went into the Tilton Road End corner section and were so tightly packed in police had to open the adjoining area. The news that Manchester City were two goals up at Maine Road, thus ending any chance Leeds had of gaining promotion, soon filtered through and a short time later a refreshment stand was dismantled. A few of them jumped over into the seating area in the main stand, which was empty, though other Leeds supporters in the Tilton reproached their own hooligans, singing, "You're the scum of Elland Road," and with that they retreated into the Tilton.

Planks of wood and other potential ammunition were handed down from the back of the terracing through the crowds to the front near the pitch, and when Blues took the lead with a Martin Kuhl goal a minute before half-time, that proved to be the catalyst. Both firms piled on to the pitch. "I scored, got flattened looked up and saw they were coming over the fence and thought, I'd better get out of here," said Kuhl later.

Chaos reigned for thirty minutes. The air filled with missiles as officers tried to restore order and several limped off to safety. Then, more than a dozen officers on horseback charged on to the pitch from the tunnel under the Ansells Clock. A second wave of missiles flew in their direction including rocks, bottles, planks of wood and even a kettle. Leeds manager Eddie Gray and Blues secretary Andrew Waterhouse walked to the Leeds end to appeal for calm so the match could resume, but they were met instantly with another volley of missiles and turned and fled, defeated.

More officers, kitted out in riot gear, appeared and stood on the pitch, waiting for things to settle down, just as loudspeakers informed fans that the match would not be abandoned despite the bedlam. Some Leeds fans then started to remove the missiles and some of the debris, which helped the second half of the match to be played.

During the game, the Blues fans realised that Oxford were on their way to take the championship and, with Manchester City doing well, neither side had much to play for. When the final whistle went, signalling a 1–0 victory for Birmingham, Leeds supporters chucked plastic seats towards the police and began battering down the fencing with the pieces of wood from the dismantled canteen. Meanwhile, Blues invaded the pitch from the opposite end and engaged in running battles with the police.

*   *   *

Cud: We went into the Railway End, into the seats upstairs, and our youth firm were below us. Leeds were chanting and then did the refreshment stand and ran down the aisle attacking the Old Bill with the bits. When Leeds got on to the pitch and charged the police to try and get to us, the Junior Business Boys below us jumped on to the pitch and, as one of them called others on, the younger lot looked up to where we were and said to me, "Are we fuckin' gonna do the business or what?" We came down to the bottom tier and stormed the pitch. There were running battles with the police and our lot got through the police line level with the dugouts to some Leeds, but the Old Bill separated us.

Leeds were well up for it though and if they had done what we had done and got together on the pitch then it would have been a proper tear-up. We were trying to get to them and some of our lot did get to some of them in the side seats.

There were about 1,000 on the pitch just tussling with the Old Bill and we got nearly to the halfway line, but by this time Leeds were just watching in shock. The mayhem went on for over an hour on the pitch – fighting with the Old Bill and generally letting rip. I watched the Juniors going mad and then I went outside to see if I could find Leeds to try and row with them.

———————

The police's main objective was to keep opposing supporters apart and mounted officers charged into the marauding Zulu Warriors, who were by now breaking up the advertising hoardings on the edge of the pitch and using bits as missiles against the police. Whenever the Zulus surged forward, away from the seats and further on to the pitch, they were met with a charge from the officers on horseback and backed off towards the stands.

The line of riot police guarding the Leeds end, while keeping out of range of the missiles, managed to clear the vast majority of Leeds off the pitch and back behind the fence by around

5.30pm, although those still hanging around enjoyed a quick game of footie while others had a go at ripping the nets.

The area behind the goal gradually emptied and most congregated in the left hand side of the Tilton Road stand. Meanwhile, extra officers brought in to help joined the line on the pitch facing Leeds. Some Leeds threw various missiles at the executive boxes for a while before turning their attention elsewhere.

Wally: They are the most famous football vandals in the world, when I hear of Leeds, that's the first thing that comes into my mind. That's what they are famous for – besides donkey jackets. There seems to be a lot of rivalry between the two teams now and most of the games between us are subject to a twelve o'clock kick-off and a very large police operation. This stems from the infamous riot of 1985. I'd only been out of prison about a month by then and went along purely as a spectator. A full-scale battle went on with Blues and the Old Bill.

It was started by the Juniors and loads of young kids from children's homes. The club had decided to give away thousands of tickets to children's homes across the city. A few of the main Juniors were in these homes at the time, so they recruited every young loon in the system. Blues smashed up their own ground and attacked the Old Bill with all kinds of weapons. The advertising boards were used to mount charge after charge. It was absolute mayhem.

I still have an official video of what happened on the pitch. The commentator at one stage says, "Look at the clock, it's 5.40pm and the Blues' fans are still on here attacking the police." He points out that although some Leeds fans to the left of the screen were throwing a few missiles at the police, most were watching events going on at the opposite end of the ground and were more interested in that than anything else. At one stage, you are able to see more Leeds fans come back on the pitch with a ball and start playing football by the goal. They then tried to rip the nets down but couldn't manage it.

But at no time did Leeds try and get to Blues. The only rioting going on was Blues attacking the Old Bill. More than 100 officers were injured on the pitch that day – a record until Millwall played us at their ground in 2002. It wasn't until after six o'clock when the police managed to regain control inside the ground and outside was a similar story, with the Old Bill getting legged everywhere.

A fifteen-year-old Leeds fan lost his life that day although it was not directly connected to any fighting. A wall collapsed in the Leeds end as they surged towards the back when they heard Blues outside St Andrew's, and it crushed him.

This was the same day as the Bradford fire, so the incident didn't get as much publicity. After the game Leeds fans' coaches and vans were attacked. Leeds may have instigated things in the ground when they smashed up the refreshment stand but that was about all they did that day.

Cud: Several Blues ran outside the ground and started throwing bricks into where Leeds were inside. The Old Bill charged into Leeds from the pitch and, as they had nowhere else to go, they were pushed against the wall and it collapsed. We didn't know anything about Bradford, we were too caught up in what was going on to know about anything else.

Newspapers reported that after the game 200 Leeds fans attacked a coach carrying guests returning from an Indian wedding in Preston. Five people were injured, all the windows were smashed, and a terrified driver commented, "I put my foot down. They would have lynched all of us if I had stopped."

More than 100 people appeared in six courtrooms soon after that fateful May 11, and the Government was prompted to appoint Mr Justice Popplewell to carry out an inquiry into both the riot and the terrible fire at Bradford City, which claimed the lives of fifty-six people. Birmingham City made appeals through the media for Zulus to come forward and talk to club officials but, unsurprisingly, no one took them up on their offer. Popplewell, who described the Blues riot as more like the Battle of Agincourt than a football match, heard from fire brigades, police, football clubs and sporting associations during his inquiry. He highlighted the necessity of spectator safety at football grounds and advocated identity cards for fans, although plans to introduce such a scheme were shelved after the Hillsborough disaster in 1989.

In an interview with *The Times* in May 2005, the twentieth anniversary of the Birmingham riot and the Bradford disaster, Popplewell said, "Arising out of the riot at Birmingham's ground ... one of the most important of my recommendations was the introduction of closed-circuit television in a dedicated area of the ground, with experienced police officers in charge. Because they are now able, with their highly sophisticated equipment, immediately to identify and arrest troublemakers, they have managed to reduce the level of violence inside the ground. Sadly, it can still continue outside the grounds and at places, particularly abroad, that are without CCTV."

Wally: The next time we met Leeds was the semi-final of the Coca-Cola Cup in the mid-Nineties. We lost the first leg at St Andrew's 1–0 and had to be at their place for a twelve o'clock kick-off on a Sunday. Between seven and eight coaches, all full of lads, left from the Fox Hollies pub in Acocks Green at 8am.

When we got off the motorway and were coming into Leeds, two police motorcyclists starting escorting the vehicles from the front. As we got nearer to Elland Road, we were getting snarled up in traffic and slowed down. I decided to jump out of the exit at the back of our coach and stand on the road. When I got outside, someone shut the door behind me and then the rest of the lads starting laughing and pointing at me from inside. Then someone else decided to come outside and join me, then another and another, until all of the lads piled out of the coaches except the front one, I later found out. We were all laughing and the coaches continued on their way through the traffic with the police escort, completely unaware that they were guiding empty coaches – apart from one – to the ground.

We made our way to the ground, 400 of Birmingham's finest looking for Leeds. When we got there, we went to the Leeds end, saw them and charged into them straight away. It was a big fight but the police soon arrived on horses to separate us. They took us round the back of the ground and kept us under a bit of a tunnel for a while, where they steamed into us with their truncheons.

In the ground there was the usual racist shit from Leeds, but what really pissed off a lot of us was that they sang, "Where were you in '85?" in reference to the riot at our place. They were trying to take the glory for something that wasn't theirs. They'd started it, I'll agree with that, because they took the canteen apart and got on the pitch, but they did not do anything when they were on there. That day was Birmingham against the Old Bill.

PART TWO

PART TWO

Chapter Seven

Villa

FAR AND away the team Blues dislike the most is Aston Villa. While researching this book, everyone I spoke to expressed the same amount of hatred for the team that shares the second city with Blues. It takes different forms with different people. "When it comes to Villa, I usually don't sleep the night before a derby game," said GG, an old-school Chelmsley Wood hooligan. "It really affects my life. I can remember a couple of carloads of lads going over to the Holte End on a Sunday night before a game – since we've been in the Premiership – and painting the lions by the ground blue and then seeing people having to clean them up in the day." While the rave era did improve some relationships between the two firms, on the whole, from the first major clash outside Villa Park back in 1975 to the infamous Rocky Lane battle in 2002 [see Chapter 17], the hostility has remained and is, needless to say, mutual.

Their history, of course, goes back much further than the 1970s. According to Birmingham City FC's website, the first game between the two clubs was on September 27, 1879, and Blues won by "one disputed goal to nil". However, other record books say it was on November 5, 1887, in the FA Cup second round, which Villa won 4–0. Both teams began competing, along with ten others, in the Football League when it was created in Birmingham in 1888 by a Scotsman frustrated at the lack of organisation and reliability of team fixtures across the country.

Seventy-five years later, the two-legged League Cup final of 1963 pitted Blues against Villa and provided many a "Bluenose" with a sweet moment to savour, the sight of their team lifting the trophy at Villa Park after a 3–1 aggregate win. But both teams were later relegated to the Second Division – Birmingham in 1965 and Villa in 1967 – prompting derbies that attracted huge crowds at each ground.

It took Blues seven seasons to reach the top-flight again, where they stayed until the 1979 season. They may have had a star player in Trevor Francis, but Villa won the League Cup in 1975 and 1977, were First Division champions in 1981, and then won the European Cup in 1982. Birmingham made it back to Division One after the 1979/80 season, were relegated again in 1984, but they were back up a year later, 1985 (when they suffered a shock defeat against lowly Altrincham in the FA Cup).

Over the years the two clubs have inevitably swapped players and managers. Dennis Mortimer, the Villa captain in 1982, was one of fifty-four players who would represent both clubs. Ron Saunders, who led Villa to success in the early 1980s, resigned in February 1982 and became the manager at Blues a week later, taking over from Jim Smith until the 1985/86 season. As a player, Birkenhead-born Saunders scored more than 200 goals as a centre forward and was leading scorer for Portsmouth for six consecutive seasons. As a manager he tasted success at Norwich, had a short stay at Manchester City, then joined Villa and in 1981 led them to the First Division Championship. He resigned in a row over his contract before Villa had lifted the European Cup, and his move to Birmingham was a huge surprise. He went on to complete a hat-trick of West Midlands managerships when he took charge of West Brom in 1986 before leaving football completely the following year, aged fifty-five.

Villa failed to sustain the League domination they enjoyed under his tutelage and they dropped into the Second Division five years after winning their European triumph. Blues managed to slide into the Third Division in 1989, where they stayed until the 1992/93 season, when the Premiership was started. Blues, suffering financial problems, won the Second Division derby at Villa Park in September 1987 but then lost the second clash at St Andrew's.

In the autumn of the following year the teams met three times in forty-four days: a two-legged League Cup tie which Villa won seven-nil on aggregate, and a Simod Cup match, formerly the Football League Full Members Cup, or "Mickey Mouse Cup" to players and fans. Villa won the latter match 6–0. Their games were played before dwindling audiences. Around 20,000 watched the first two clashes but a dismal 8,000 turned up for the Simod Cup.

There were many memorable clashes for Blues lads in the 1970s, when the title "the English Disease" was used to describe hooligan behaviour. These included the first major encounter with Aston Villa in 1975/76. Villa were back in Division One after five years in the lower league and won 2–1. The *Birmingham Post* said it was a "peaceful, entertaining match, a credit to the city". It was actually anything but.

Cockney Al: On September 27, 1975, when I was fifteen, me, Jayo, Junior and Tony Austin, three black lads who were older than me, went to Villa Park see Blues play Aston Villa for the first time. They had come up the previous year, along with Man Utd and Leicester. About sixty of us caught the train from Marston Green, a few miles south east of Birmingham, and at each stop more and more got on – lads from Lea Hall, Stechford, and Bordesley Green. We got off at New Street and walked the two miles or so to the ground; there were no police escorts in those days. We encountered some Villa lads on the way and had a few little battles with them, getting into the spirit of things.

When we got near Queens Road police station the road was a mass of blue and white. We got to the ground and some were still fighting, as we had to queue next to Villa to get in. When the match kicked off, about twenty of us decided to go into the home end and play up. We stood about a third of the way up the terrace in the Holte End, which was one of the biggest ends in the country at that time. There were several thousand Villa and the twenty of us. We just stood in there, not doing anything. We weren't wearing club colours, just a Blues badge under the lapel of our jackets. Eventually they sussed us and fights broke out. There was a mad surge towards us from all sides and the Old Bill ended up dragging us out and put us in the Witton end.

After the game, which we lost 2–1, about 250 lads from each firm congregated in a park right outside the ground. We faced each other, six to ten deep from opposite ends of the park, eyeing one another up. We all knew it was going to go off and we suddenly charged together, but just as we were about to meet in the middle, coppers on horses sliced through the action, knocking people over and preventing a major clash. They reared up on horseback and lads scattered, fell and ran every which way, hiding behind trees, shitting themselves. The horses didn't trample anyone, they just stepped over the bodies cowering on the floor. It was hair-raising stuff and we all scarpered.

That set the scene for all the next meetings. We would bash anyone when it was Villa, I'm ashamed to say. It is pure, pure hatred with them and always will be.

In 1977/78 season, one lad, Tony Gardener, decided to walk across the Holte End wearing a Blues hat, taunting Villa. About fifty Blues were in the Holte, and after Gardener's march the Villa fans threw pies at them and made threatening noises, but did little else.

One cold, snowy Saturday in the early Eighties, Blues didn't have a game but knew that Villa were playing at nearby Coventry, so around sixty lads, including Cud, Balla, Selby, Frankie Monster, the Malcolm brothers and several Juniors, decided to jump on a train and pay them a visit. They arrived in Coventry around 10am thinking they would surprise Villa, and headed into town to find them.

En route they chased a few local lads and relieved them of their designer clobber. But Villa remained elusive, so they settled in a pub until around midday. Word would have spread that the Zulus had landed in Coventry but no one came to seek them out. Getting bored, they decided to head back to the station, and on the way bumped into some other Zulus who had come over after hearing that's where everyone else was. They eagerly reported that they'd seen loads of Villa at New Street getting ready to come over, so they all marched back to the station to greet them.

When they reached a subway, Cud, Selby and Balla told the rest of the firm to wait underneath while they went out the other side to scout for Villa. As the three walked up a slight hill away from the subway, they came face to face with about 200 Villa, some chucking snowballs and play-fighting each other. Villa clocked them and stopped in their tracks. Cud could see their main guy, Black Danny, quickly looking around for the rest of the Zulus.

"What you saying?" asked Cud. "Are we going to have this or what?" With that, he sent Balla back to the subway to alert the rest. He didn't have to go far, as the lads were close by and they came charging up the incline shouting, "Zuuluu," before laying into Villa.

"People were getting KO'd everywhere, with everyone going hell for leather, but we met little resistance," said Cud. "We chased them back into the station and they went flying over the barriers and we were laughing at them running away. The Transport Police were soon around and it was all over but we were still laughing.

"I have to mention one time, though, when Villa chased us. I was walking by Birmingham markets by the Matador pub one evening with CC and another lad, probably going for a drink, when we saw about seventy Villa coming down a spiral staircase nearby. They saw us and we knew it was the old C-Crew. I recognised a lad from my area who started to give it the big one.

"When they got to the bottom, we turned and ran. We went round this corner by the markets and saw some big trolleys loaded with vegetables so we pushed them back round the corner into Villa and took out about ten of them. We were laughing so much it was hard to run but they never got us.

"That lad wasn't seen around our area for about three years after that and his claim to fame is that he chased me. He knows who he is but he's alright and I see him around now."

At around that time, when the Villa C-Crew was operating, they also came out on top against the Apex, the forerunners to the Zulus.

Wally: I will gladly throw my hands up and admit there was a time when Villa had a better firm than Blues. This was in the early Eighties, pre-Zulu days. At the time they were winning the League and the European Cup, so things were going well for them. Although they had the firm at the time, they were not rated by any of the major firms at all, never have been and never will be.

In our days of the Apex we weren't organised at all, we were only a bunch of sixteen and seventeen-year-old kids. Once the Zulus started and we had a decent firm, their days were well and truly over and it's been the same now for more than twenty years. Even in those days, it would be Blues looking for them and it would only be the odd occasion they'd be looking for us. One year, around the start of the 1980s, they came into the Kop End of St Andrew's where the clock used to be and they still haven't stopped talking about it. Only a few of them will admit they were there early and it didn't really go off. Also, in those days they knew the Blues area was the Tilton Road End, right next to the away end. Why go into one end when you know that the main boys are in another?

They had a result one year when they ran Blues from the Hole In The Wall. Other than that I cannot think of much else that they have done. But when we got it together we really took the piss with them big style.

112

A lot of our hatred towards them is because they have always given it the racist shit. In my time in football, the most racism I have experienced has come from them and the Scousers. From the C-Crew right up to the present day with the Villa Hardcore, they are racist through and through.

Cud: I remember one time around 1984 when we chased Villa all over the place. We left the ground early and decided to meet them under the subway by Birmingham's fire station, where we've met a few away fans coming from Villa Park before. About twenty of us spread out and walked down the stairs to wait. As we went down the steps we got a huge waft of draw and discovered about 200 Blues already there, smoking while they waited. We had a spotter on the lookout and he said he could see police on horseback escorting loads of lads.

We waited for the right moment and then the Zulu chant went up and we pounced. The lads scattered in all different directions and we chased them and bashed them all over the place. The police escorted some back into town and chased us too so we split up and re-grouped at New Street to see if we could have it with West Ham who were also around, but they had gone.

We usually had scouts at a pub right across the road from New Street to see when the fans arrived. The Old Bill knew this so we had to keep moving to different pubs so they wouldn't know where we were before games.

When Hofmeister beer was on sale and "Follow the Bear" was their slogan in television adverts, some Blues became aware there was a life-size bear promoting the drink in the Windsor, where Villa were drinking, and they decided to borrow it. A short time later the bear made his way into the bar with some lads following behind shouting the slogan, mimicking the advert. The bear stayed in Boogies for about a week.

There was always action to be had with Villa, whether it was 250 lads buying tickets to sit in the seats at the Witton Lane end, next to the Holte, much to the annoyance of their lads, invading the pitch at one match each time Blues scored (three times), or "taking the piss" in the Holte End.

One victory Villa can claim is the Hole in the Wall row in the mid-1980s.

It was quite late at night and the older Blues lads had been drinking in a pub in the city centre. As Cud walked through town with Brains and Fattie, he saw the younger lot walking up a road and go into the Hole in the Wall, which was a mainly Villa watering hole.

Suddenly, Villa came storming out of the pub tooled up, pushing Blues outside, where it kicked off. They tried to hold it but they had come unstuck and Cud could see it was Villa's main firm. They stood their ground as glasses were sent smashing on to the floor around them but the Old Bill appeared and broke it up. "Villa got the result," said Cud. "We went there without numbers and got done. Yet although I was a major scalp to them, they never really came near me."

Players from both teams were also aware of the hatred that permeated the second city. At a derby in October 1983, which Villa won, Blues' Noel Blake, a Zulu favourite, head-butted Villa midfielder Steve McMahon in the tunnel after the game for an earlier tackle on Kevan Broadhurst. And rumour has it that when Robert Hopkins was playing his last game for Villa before transferring to Blues, he wore a Blues badge over the Villa emblem on his kit. When Villa fans spotted this they started booing him, so when he came to take a corner he just kicked the ball out for a goal kick. Blues midfielder Martin Kuhl, seen as one of the team's hell-raisers along with Hopkins, Blake, Tony Coton and Mick Harford in the mid-1980s, had a pig's trotter thrown at him in 1985 by some Villa fans. So he took a bite out of it.

While the derbies were relished by the two firms, the teams' managers were also aware of what was at stake. "I've been involved in derbies in Manchester and Madrid but I've never sampled anything like those in Birmingham," said former Villa manager Ron Atkinson.

In March 1986, more than seventy people were arrested after running battles after a derby at Villa Park in what was said to be one of the worst days of violence in the season, with fights before, during and after the game, coupled with pitch invasions as Blues won 3–0. When 800 Blues arrived back at New Street on a train from Witton, it went off again between them and other lads getting trains to their various destinations.

The fighting wasn't just at derby matches. When Villa played Luton in August 1985, Blues were at Everton. When they arrived back after losing 4–1, they heard Villa were drinking in the Old Contemptibles pub on Newhall Street, and about fifty set off to find them. They linked up with another thirty or so on the way and chucked bricks, bottles and a road bollard through the pub's windows.

Villa came out but Blues charged them, pushing them back inside where the battle continued for a few more minutes before everyone dispersed, no doubt due to the arrival of the police. There were other, smaller scuffles around closing time but the lads put that down to word spreading about the earlier battle, causing other eager Blues lads to look for some fun.

Wally: Even though Villa had a better firm in the early 1980s, Blues have always run the city centre. From the mid-1980s they couldn't come into town, even when they were playing at home. They used to use the Windsor in the middle of town but eventually, as the Zulus got bigger and better, they just couldn't stand the heat. Before Broad Street and the Arcadian had the major nightclubs in town, the main place was John Bright Street, with clubs like Boogies and Edward's. Villa never ever came near the place; we had the run of it. I only ever saw one Villa lad in that area and that's because he used to work in one of the late night chippies.

If we wanted it off with Villa, we had to go to Villa Park when

Blues had a shit game. I used to go over there a lot, mainly with
my firm from Bordesley Green, and we would slap them silly
week in, week out. They reckon they done us once against
Arsenal. One of our lads, Cockney B, got slashed. Personally I
didn't see it that way, but if that's how they want to call it after
the untold number of times we landed on them, then they can
have it. Think about it. A firm keeps landing at your ground
when they're not even playing you, taking the piss and you only
claim one result. Shame on them!

They always knew when the Bordesley Green boys landed
they were in serious trouble. The biggest liberty we took was one
year they played Millwall. I think it was an FA Cup game. We
hadn't met Millwall before so it was the first time they had been
into Birmingham for many years. We took a firm of about 150 to
Villa Park, not for them but for Millwall. We marched up to the
Witton Arms pub, as we had heard Millwall were getting off at
Witton train station. Villa had a firm of about 200 outside the
pub. They could see us approaching but made no attempt to
front us.

I bowled straight over to them and told them, "We ain't come
for you today, we're here for Millwall."

"Yes Walton, OK," was their response. That's the God's honest
truth and Villa know it. They saw our firm that day. We weren't
there to play games with them. We saw Millwall as they came
out of Aston train station but they had a large police escort and
the Old Bill lined up between us and stopped anything going off.

Another occasion we had it with them was at the fire station
on the edge of town. When I say we, I was with the Zulu Juniors,
but Villa didn't hang around too long. So that was it for them. I
never saw the C-Crew until the rave scene started later on. It was
only because of that scene that they were ever allowed back in
town and certain heads were having it with them. Yes, you've
guessed it, the Bordesley Green firm, but more about that later.

They were unheard of firm-wise until a certain person called
Fowler started showing with a new firm called Villa Hardcore. I
had never heard about him until we played them in a friendly at

St Andrew's when the new stand was opened. Nothing went on before the game, but afterwards, in town, we heard they had a firm in the Square Peg. About thirty of us landed up there but it only went off for a short time before the Old Bill turned up. Saying that, it didn't really go off, all they did was the typical Villa trick of throwing beer glasses. When the Old Bill arrived I just remember someone bouncing up and down in front of me saying, "Come on Walton, I'm Fowler, I'm Fowler."

Me and Brains were on the corner and I said, "Listen, if you want it with me, shut your mouth. The Old Bill are there so let's me and you go round the corner."

"I'm Fowler, I'm Fowler," he kept shouting, and bouncing.

The Old Bill dived on him and nicked him. All he had to do was shut his mouth and come round the corner with me. I asked around after who he was and was told he was putting himself up as Villa's top boy. One of our lads saw him a few weeks later and he said he hadn't got a problem with any Blues, but wanted it off with me.

So now I've got a big-mouthed, racist Villa fan trying to make a name for himself and he thinks he's going to do it off my back. No fucking problem. He's been going to the England games and making a name for himself mainly as a bully, giving it the big one to lads from Second and Third Division teams. Now he wants to go Premier League hooligan. I read in one book that Villa were getting the upper hand these days. Well, let's set the record straight here. Since that first meeting with Fowler, our paths have crossed a few times and only once has he got away lightly. The first time was at Rocky Lane, the same place it went off when we first came up.

Even though it's close to Villa Park, Shanahan's has been used by a lot of Blues lads as a late-night drinking den. Some older Blues lads were in there one Saturday afternoon when Villa were playing at home and Blues were away to Oxford. There were only a handful of them and they'd been out for a few days and nights drinking and on the marching powder. They were lads, but not into the violence any more, and Fowler and about fifteen others turned up, giving them grief. It was the last match of the season so a lot of our lads were in Oxford. I didn't go but I got a phone call to say what was happening in the pub and to get some heads together to go over there.

I got in touch with some of the lads coming back from Oxford and arranged to meet them in town. A minibus turned up, not very full, but we decided to go over there anyway. When we pulled up, the five of our lot in there were just coming out and Fowler and his boys were about to attack them when one of Fowler's lot clocked us and in a little girly voice said, "Stephen there's loads of them." There were no more than ten of us and the other five made it even numbers, but they were on their toes straight away.

I had eyes for only one person, Fowler. His boys went one way and the snidey fucker tried to sneak off on his own. Every hooligan knows the move, when the Old Bill land and you try to walk off on your own and pretend you're not with the others. Well, Fowler tried that one – hands in pocket, head down and off. I kept my eyes on him. I shouted to one of our lot close to him that he was trying to sneak off and he brought him down with a flying rugby tackle. He and the rest of them got smashed to bits. Fowler and another one were kept on the floor and eventually taken away in an ambulance.

We sent people back to the pub later and the report was that the pub was sealed off and loads of Old Bill and forensics were there. We thought he must have been dead, so phone calls were put into the hospital by us pretending to be family. But he was alive, so we had a good night's sleep.

The next time I came across him, I didn't get involved. I'd just got into town on my birthday for a night out and I bumped into a firm of forty Blues from Sheldon. They said Villa were in the Temple Bar and they were going round to have it off with them. About the same number of Villa came running out, the usual thing, throwing glasses. When the Zulu roar went up they were on their toes again. This time Fowler and a couple of others stood but got wasted again. He was left motionless on the floor.

I stood and watched it all and had a good night out. Happy Birthday to me!

Another time was a Sunday afternoon when we heard he had something to do with a football team and used a pub in Erdington after matches. We got a firm together and decided to pay them a visit. I told everyone I only wanted Fowler and if they saw me having it with anyone it would be him and nobody was to join in. We sussed what room they were in and launched our attack. They all jumped over the bar and ran into the next room, where a christening was going on.

I ran behind the bar calling Fowler back but he wouldn't have it. At no stage did any Blues go into the other room. They tried to put it about that we attacked a christening but they know that's a load of bollocks. They ran into the room rather than stand and fight. We left the pub and were going across the car park when Fowler and two others came back out shouting, "Come on you black bastard." I turned around to everyone and said, "Leave this to me."

The three of them had big planks of wood but I flew into them and took the first couple of whacks, then ended up chasing the three of them back into the pub with their own weapon. Off we go chaps, time for Sunday dinner.

I know a few Villa lads who will freely admit that Blues are one of the top firms in the country and, don't get me wrong, they have got some good lads. Over the last few years since the rave scene I've got on well with a few of them and one of my good mates is an ex-C Crew member. I recently bumped into one of their old Villa Youth lads, Mark B. I told him I was helping write a book and he said to me, "Don't make it a one-way thing," which I don't think I have. As I said, in the early Eighties Villa had a better firm than Blues and had a result on occasions. Overall though, it's Blues by a very big margin. He also said that back in the day I was a legend at Villa Park and the Villa Youth firm had a lot of respect for me. Nice one, Mark.

Chapter Eight

The Smoke

Millwall

THE FANS OF Millwall FC have one of the oldest, and worst, hooligan reputations in British football. Notorious long before a 1977 *Panorama* documentary identified some of their gangs – F Troop, Treatment and the Halfway Line – their tough dockland support terrorised many an opponent. Visiting The Den, their forbidding fortress on Cold Blow Lane, was always a perilous experience.

The history between Blues and Millwall dates back to the 1971/72 season, when both teams were going for promotion in the Second Division. Blues were playing at Orient and if they won they would go up at the expense of Millwall. Millwall turned up at Brisbane Road and invaded the pitch in an attempt to get the game abandoned, and there's been animosity between both clubs ever since, although it was to be many years before they met again.

Fizza: Birmingham City versus Leyton Orient, the 26th of April, 1972, was a Second Division promotion decider. On a wet and windy Tuesday night Birmingham fans descended on East London in their thousands. The welcoming party had plenty of time to organise the reception. The football match was between Orient and Birmingham but the violence was between Millwall and Birmingham.

There were plenty of newspaper reports about the flares and pitch invasions by Millwall supporters trying to get the game abandoned, but the real action was outside the ground. I was eleven years old at the time and still at junior school, and the firsthand report I received about that night came seven years later in the New Inn, our local pub in Acocks Green. Paddy Murphy and Pakie Wally were ten years older than us and had many stories of away games, battles won and lost. Orient was a game won but definitely a battle lost. Despite decent numbers and game lads, the Blues fans had found the foreign environment and well organised opposition too much to handle; that, coupled with savage violence and no mercy, had ensured Millwall's reputation, already legendary, was once again confirmed.

That night in East London over thirty years ago was also significant for one other reason and that was the meeting of Millwall and their number one rivals from across the Thames, West Ham United. These were the two most well organised and feared football gangs in the country and they were using a game that neither of them were involved in as an excuse to meet and engage in bloody violence for reputation and kudos only. Birmingham weren't lightweight but it's fair to say neither were we in the same league as the two London firms.

But that was 1972, and within ten years we were challenging the West Ham United gang – the ICF – as the undisputed kings of terrace violence. Out of the Midlands came a firm who learnt the hard way how to organise, how to plan convoys, out-manoeuvre the police, run decoys and inflict savage violence and most importantly command respect. Reputations were made or lost on how well you performed on a week by week basis and camaraderie amongst the lads forged lifelong friendships.

Big C: It was not the done thing for a firm to take a huge load of lads to Millwall. It just didn't happen. They were notorious but when we went there in November 1986 it was one of the biggest-ever away firms of Zulus travelling down to London. Around 1,000 lads made the journey and it was most Zulus' first encounter with them. It was unknown territory, as they were a sort of an enigma, but as the Blues firm was in its prime, Millwall were a target and many couldn't wait to meet them. Everyone knew to go to their place at all was a major event, but to take big numbers was a milestone. I set two alarm clocks to make sure I wouldn't miss it.

Wally: We took one of Birmingham's biggest away firms, with more than 1,000 lads. We took them by surprise, which they admit, but have claimed that we didn't let them know we were coming. You didn't need to be a rocket scientist in those days to know that Blues would turn out at Millwall. They saw the firm we took to Villa Park when they played them there, so surely they were expecting us to turn out at The Den? We didn't travel to London in big numbers, everyone was told to make their own way there and get to Victoria. The meeting place was Shakes. The Old Bill were waiting for us at Euston but not many went by train, so choosing Victoria paid off.

In Shakes there were discussions about what route we were going to take. With a firm of that size, the only way I could see was to go straight in and no messing about on the tubes trying to outwit the Old Bill. If Millwall were out, only one thing was going to happen. So that's what we did. We went straight in. We caught the main line train from Victoria to New Cross. The Old Bill hadn't sussed us at Victoria, everyone was on best behaviour in Shakes and there was no thieving – everyone was there for one thing. I don't think the pub ever sold as much orange juice as they did that day. Even the lads who usually have a drink were on the pop and there wasn't the usual whiff of draw in the air.

When we got to New Cross, the Old Bill were there but not in big numbers and we made our way to The Den. Millwall were nowhere to be seen. The odd few that were there soon scattered.

As we marched to the ground the Old Bill's numbers grew and they managed to contain us for a while under a railway bridge. They started searching people and all you could hear was all kinds of tools hitting the ground. A full arsenal of weapons was left under that bridge.

As the lads came through the arches, a few Millwall appeared and a bit of banter ensued before two others came forward and approached Blues in front of the police. The blokes, who were in their mid to late thirties, acknowledged the Zulus' presence and told them to turn out at Covent Garden after the match. They were recognised by the Old Bill and were told to move on, which they did.

We got to the ground but there were still no Millwall around. We were just getting the ones giving the abuse, calling us cheeky cunts for bringing a firm to Millwall and warning we would get what for afterwards. During the game one of our lot went round collecting newspapers; the next thing you know, the refreshment stand is up in smoke. They managed to put it out before it got serious. It was a pretty uneventful day, and after the game the Old Bill escorted us back. Thirty of us got away and had it off with about thirty Millwall at London Bridge and turned them over. We had just got on a train and they appeared on the platform so we got off and had it with them before getting back on. One of our lot, Barrington, who is a former kickboxer and cage fighter, punched one of their lot so hard his feet lifted off the ground.

———

After a few skirmishes outside the ground, the police escorted Blues back towards the tube, but around ninety lads managed to escape and split up into groups to make their own way to Euston before setting off for Brum. One group reached Euston only to find they had missed the train and plotted up in a bar at the station to wait for the next one. As they headed towards the platform, loads of Millwall suddenly came pouring through the doors. Nobody had gone to Covent Garden and no doubt this had angered them and they were on the warpath. The Zulus were very low on numbers and they knew it. There wasn't much they could do and they admit that if the police hadn't stepped in and formed a cordon, preventing Millwall from getting to them, they would have been slaughtered. That incident is definitely one where police intervention was appreciated.

Big C: Everyone was enjoying a drink in and around John Bright Street before the game at Christmas, 1986, particularly in Boogies, which was a favourite haunt of the Zulus back then, when a firm of Millwall appeared after arriving at New Street Station, just around the corner. Some lads had been involved in the annual seasonal fun and games with the Old Bill during a "Zulu Christmas Party" the week before. They had been drinking in the Kaleidoscope near John Bright Street before encountering some Villa and a dozen Blues started chasing them through the city, ending up near the law courts. Floyd did an amazing flying kick which knocked out one of the Villa lot just before a bus pulled up and a few more Villa lads got off and joined in.

In the melee, Big C had taken a beating and suffered a shattered cheekbone and nose, resulting in a trip to hospital on Christmas Day. This injury meant he was forced to take a bit of a back seat during the proceedings with Millwall a few days later. When Millwall arrived they made their presence known in the middle of John Bright Street, major Blues territory. They announced who they were, which led to a full-on fight breaking out outside Boogies.

A pub full of Zulus set upon them, and unbeknown to Millwall, a load more were en-route after drinking in the nearby Market Hotel. This meant they would be attacked from both sides and were left with nowhere to run. Although Millwall were prepared – one of their lads was seen brandishing a dog chain and whipping anyone who came near him – they couldn't beat the force and sheer numbers of the Zulus.

They got totally bashed and some even suffered the indignity of being stripped naked as they lay sprawled out on the cold concrete.

Wally: That season, the game at St Andrew's was a night match. As with most London teams, they never like to mention when they have been turned over and this was one of those nights. We met in Boogies wine bar in John Bright Street, our stronghold at the time. To be fair to Millwall they are the only team that ever came there during the years we were there. They had done their homework. About 150 turned up and we smashed them to smithereens. We had lads in other nearby bars and Millwall got caught in the middle. They were squealing like pigs as they got smashed everywhere. They had nowhere to run as we slaughtered them. It was only the Old Bill that ended up saving them from more punishment. It was Millwall's firm and their usual rent-a-mob, as some of them were recognised as Spurs lads. After the game they were escorted to New Street but their escort was attacked a few times.

The following season nothing happened home or away. It was a quiet time on the hooligan front as Ecstasy had taken over. We went to their place in the early 1990s, but not in big numbers. Nothing happened before the game and afterwards we made our way to London Bridge station. We had about 100 lads, which dwindled down to about sixty as it looked like nothing was happening. But at about 6pm, a car pulled up outside the boozer and a Millwall lad said something like, "Wait, there's a firm coming." Thirty minutes later there was still no sign so we decided to go looking for them. Me and Eddie M went ahead of everyone else, saw a mob of about 300 Millwall coming towards us, and I ran back to tell the others. Now usually I would be telling everyone to keep it tight and nobody run, but this time I said I didn't fancy our chances but we should give it a go. I remember some of them looking at me knowing it was on top, as they'd not heard me talk like that before.

But there was no time to think, as suddenly a big roar went up from Millwall. We made a feeble attempt to throw some missiles but it was pointless; this mob was coming at us and nothing was stopping them, so it was about-turn and on your toes. They ran us back to London Bridge station. We ran back up the stairs and I made a shout for us to try to get the advantage from the top of the stairs. Millwall came straight at us, as we ran up the stairs they were right behind us. An arm came round me and emptied a tin of CS gas in my mouth. When I got to the top of the stairs the Old Bill were there. I bent over, spewing my guts up, and a copper just patted me on my back and said, "You've got what you came for." So off I go again.

Some of ours got chased and caught in the station restaurant and I could hear the plates smashing. I ran up some stairs, ended up on my own and found a little room to hide in. I could hear footsteps outside and I was gasping for breath from the gas but I had to hold my breath so they didn't hear me. I then heard over the Tannoy system, "Will the people running up the tracks please come off before you get electrocuted." I looked out of the window to see some of our lads running up the track. I wanted to burst out laughing because I knew they were not coming off the line to face that firm. I stayed where I was for a good while, and when I eventually came out a few Millwall were still about. When I got on a train a couple of our lads were on it but we didn't even look at each other, let alone talk, until we got back to Euston.

Everyone had their own story about how they got away that day as it was definitely every man for himself. The lads who ran off down the tracks kept on running and as they passed an old man in a string vest on another platform he made a comment which they'll never forget: "That'll teach you to fuck about down here, won't it?"

The next game at St Andrew's we were out for revenge but there wasn't much of a show from Millwall. When they did turn up their train was late and came into New Street after the game had kicked off. This was the match when they put Blues fans above Millwall in the seats and they got pelted. They even found a home-made bomb that hadn't gone off.

After the game, the Old Bill had to keep Millwall behind for about forty minutes as Blues were attacking the police to get at them. A police horse got stabbed. The Old Bill ended up being the main target for Blues that day but it wasn't the main Zulu lads, it was normal supporters and shirts and a lot of young kids from Small Heath and Bordesley who come out when they know trouble is guaranteed. This fixture is a nightmare for the Old Bill as they not only have to worry about it going off with the fans but over the years Blues and Millwall are by a long way the worst teams for turning on them.

Everyone was expecting a lot more from Millwall that day; every Bluenose wanted their blood. The club had a suspension threat hanging in the balance, and out of misguided loyalty or just to save them getting hit in the pocket by playing games behind closed doors, the club's managing director, Karren Brady, tried to blame Millwall for the trouble. A police inspector appeared on the news, saying it was Blues causing the trouble. They even spotted Blues fans on rooftops with missiles ready while the game was still on. He actually praised the good behaviour of Millwall that day under "extreme provocation". When order was finally restored outside the ground, Millwall were escorted to New Street. The escort came under attack from different firms hiding up back streets all the way there.

The game at their place that season was uneventful. Blues wouldn't sell any tickets unless you travelled by the supporters' coaches. We had a firm of more than seventy lads who went by train, but they were rounded up, put on a bus and taken to some sort of compound in London, where they were held for a while before eventually being taken back to Brum.

The next meeting of any interest was the play-off semi-finals. The first leg was at St Andrew's but there was a no-show from them. The second leg at their ground was when, as most people know, they played up big time. I went by car that day but we took about 400 lads by train. I just missed the firm at Euston and got the next tube after them and headed to Bermondsey. When I got off there were five of us, three black lads and two white.

The London Old Bill started to escort us to the ground, then I heard a Birmingham copper call me by name. I just turned round and laughed. He said, "You won't be laughing in a minute," and told the London Old Bill not to escort us. He was standing there with a big smirk on his face. Now Millwall are playing Blues at the New Den and there are three black geezers walking to the ground. It doesn't take a lot of working out what he was smirking about. But we managed to get to the ground in one piece.

Blues won the game, with Stern John scoring a last-minute winner. Millwall were not happy and we really wound them up. The funniest part was when all the blacks and Asians got together and started giving them the Nazi salute, shouting, "Zieg heil." It was hilarious and Millwall were going ballistic. All the racist chanting they have dished out over the years and now you have got a firm of blacks and Asians giving it them back. We were held outside the ground for ages afterwards so we didn't know how bad Millwall were playing up. They caused mayhem, it was complete carnage. They took their frustration out on the Old Bill that night, and that made my night.

I hope that Brummie Old Bill remembers the old saying, "He who laughs last laughs longest."

Cud: A couple of seasons after the London Bridge battle, Blues were playing Millwall at their place and between 80-100 Blues, including Big Hands, Rockman, Psycho and Daddy C, went down on the train. As soon as they arrived at Euston, the police were waiting. Their feet hardly touched the platform before they were whisked away. The lads told me after that there were around two Old Bill to every one of them. They were taken around a corner, searched, their photos were taken and they had to give their names and addresses before being told to get on some big, green buses with bars over the windows. They were driven to a bomb peck [wasteland] about two miles away and left. The police said there was no way they were going to let them go to watch the match at Millwall, tickets or no tickets. When the match finished they were driven back to Euston and put on a train back to Birmingham.

Spurs

Wally: Tottenham have probably had the best result at St Andrew's in the last twenty years. Most people who were there have told me that when they came on the pitch in 1984 [see Chapter 4] they did turn us over. West Ham have tried to claim they did us in the same season in a Cup match but Blues had it with them on the pitch. Where West Ham do get credit is for the way they did it; one of their lot had a yellow coat on, pretended to be a steward and got the ICF into the seats. That was first-class. It's open to debate about who got the result that day but with Spurs there is no doubt they got the result over us.

In 1987 Spurs played Watford at Villa Park in an FA Cup semi-final. One of our lot used to go to Tottenham and knew a few of their lads, so a meet was arranged for it to go off. Spurs were in a pub called the Craven Arms and Blues were in the Crown, further into the city centre. But what Blues didn't know at the time was that the Old Bill were in an office opposite the Crown, filming everything.

This was to be the main surveillance evidence for Operation Red Card, which resulted in dawn raids and thirty-six Zulus being arrested [see Chapter 12]. There was an undercover Old Bill in the pub with our lot and the signal he gave when he came out was to lift up his hat. Blues done Spurs that day and a couple of Spurs fans got stabbed, but the dirty no-good Yids made statements to the Old Bill. I didn't get pulled in Operation Red Card, I was doing nine months down in Exeter, so doing that little stretch probably saved me from a longer one.

We didn't meet Spurs again until we played them in the FA Cup in the mid-Nineties, when we took a good firm of about 250 down there but the Old Bill got us at Seven Sisters and escorted us to the ground. Both firms also managed to somehow avoid each other at the England–Scotland game in 1999, when by all accounts both teams had the most impressive firms out that day.

On our return to the Premiership in 2002, Spurs brought their best firm to St Andrew's and somehow got out of the away end while the game was on and made their way round to the main stand, where a lot of our lads sit, but the Old Bill intervened before anything happened. Spurs had done their homework that day and knew exactly where to go. The only part of Spurs' account I disagree with is their claim that before the game they were in a pub called the Toad, which is a Zulu pub. Even the biggest Zulu-hating Villa fan will tell you that's a load of bollocks; the Toad has never been one of our pubs. I even had to think where it was.

The same season, Blues took another massive firm to Spurs but yet again the police got our firm at Seven Sisters and escorted them very slowly to the ground. It was nearly half-time before our lot got there. This was a deliberate tactic by the Old Bill. Blues v. Spurs will always pull impressive firms from both sides but the Old Bill seem to be on their toes when we meet each other. I hate to admit this from my Arsenal days but the Yids can put a good firm together and are probably the best to come out of London in the last few years.

David George of the Junior Business Boys recalled the day they bumped into Spurs at New Street Station. Around 400 Blues were on their way to Wolves, Spurs had a match with another Midlands team, and their paths crossed near the stairs inside the station. There was a stand-off before one of the Spurs lads, Carpel, fronted the whole of the Blues firm. He was chased away, along with the rest, but afterwards no one could work out if he was mad or incredibly brave.

October 29, 1986, was a memorable day for a handful of Blues lads. They had a night game at Tottenham and everyone met at Shakes pub in Victoria. Instead of heading to Seven Sisters on the tube, they caught an overland train to another stop near the ground. As the group of 100 walked outside the famous "Shelf" at the ground, they encountered twenty lads and fought toe-to toe for a few minutes before the police brought proceedings to a halt.

Big C, one of the Blues lads, was arrested and chucked in the back of a police van. He could see through the window and although frustrated at being separated from the others he took some solace from the fact that it kicked off again on a corner just yards from where he had been. Cockney Baz, Wally, Betsy and a few others were grappling with the Spurs lot, but he was driven away before he could see any more. As he resigned himself to the company of the Metropolitan Police for the next few hours, the van suddenly stopped and his mates joined him, having also been nicked. There were eight of them in total and off they sped, expecting to be taken to the cop shop, but the officers had other ideas.

They were driven around the ground to the Park Lane Stand, where they stopped again and were abruptly carted upstairs, led into a large gathering of Spurs, and left to fend for themselves. Undeterred, that's where they remained, putting up with cups of coffee and the like being chucked in their direction. One lad's suggestion that he popped to the toilet was immediately dismissed, as splitting up was a definite no-no. Although Spurs knew who they were, they didn't attack them directly during the game. Perhaps they thought the 5–0 drubbing Blues received on the pitch was punishment enough; either way, they would soon find out.

When the game ended and the crowds poured out of their seats, the wary lads followed suit, wondering what could be coming their way. As soon as they were in the corridor going through the exits, Spurs turned their full attention on them and came from everywhere. The small bunch stood together in a tight formation across the corridor near some doors. Fortunately there were no Spurs behind them. Suddenly they were attacked. They tried to remain standing for what seemed like hours. One lad went down but Big C grabbed a hold of him while fending off punches. The fight could be heard by Wally and Floyd and the rest of Blues as they were stood parallel to them outside but couldn't get to them to help. It went on for only about three minutes before the police appeared and opened the doors sending everyone spilling out and providing much needed back-up for Big C and the rest.

When things calmed down and Blues were back up to full strength, they made their way to Seven Sisters. More Spurs came over to them, telling them to meet up at the next corner. Blues agreed and waited but Spurs weren't having any of it and nothing happened. Still, the lads were satisfied with a good day's action and decided to leave for Euston, encountering some Arsenal at Kings Cross where it kicked off again.

The match came just days before an historic clash at The Den, which Spurs were aware of, as one of their lads told Big C. "You've done well here but you've got Millwall next week," he said. Sometime later, one of the Blues' lads, Cockney Al, was talking with some Spurs lads who mentioned the clash and acknowledged that the Zulus did well – always good to get recognition from another firm.

Chapter Nine

The Frozen North

Scousers

WALLY: THERE ISN'T much between us and Everton so they get a shout only to set the record straight regarding a couple of comments they made about us in their book, *Scally*. First of all, they say that since we came up to the Premier League in 2002 our firm has more or less disappeared. They need to ask themselves, why, on police advice was our 2004/5 game at Goodison Park moved to a midday kick-off? I don't think it takes a lot of working out. In the book they make no mention of ever turning up at Birmingham; the author only mentions one occasion when he ended up in the wrong end and had to do one pretty quickly.

One of my first experiences of witnessing football violence was back in the Seventies, when a big mob of Brummies went into the Everton end at St Andrew's singing Everton songs. The Scousers started clapping because they thought they had a good firm turning out, until the singing changed to Birmingham songs. The whole away end had to scatter on to the pitch. They got caught out that day.

In 1985, we played them at their place early in the season. They described it as though we took a massive firm. I suppose we showed them up that day, but there were only fifty of us. I ran a coach for that game and it was made up of Bordesley Green and Kings Norton, with a few different lads amongst us.

We stayed away from the city centre and headed to a council estate not far from the ground. Whatever estate it was, it was a right rough place. We plotted up in a boozer and I remember one of the lads asking the gaffer if there was a shop nearby and he was told to go next door, but came back saying it was boarded up. The gaffer told him to bang on the door and said they would serve him through a hatch. We all went and had a look and couldn't get our breath. This was Smack City a long time before it hit the rest of the country. It was the worst place I have seen in this country.

When we started our march to the ground, a couple of young kids were walking with us. They said they'd never seen a "darkie" before. As we got closer to the ground, without Old Bill, we could see firms of Everton around but they didn't come near us. A few of them tried to steam us near the ground but we had them on their toes. In their book they say there was a big black bloke in a Burberry deerstalker leading our firm. Well, it was a little, five foot six black geezer in a Burberry sun visor at the front, 'cos that was me. There was only one coachload of us, not the massive firm that was described.

The second occasion they mention Blues was when we played them in the FA Cup This time there was a good firm of about 250 that marched to Goodison and we were in an escort. Everton say we didn't try to break the escort, which is true, but did they try to come to us? No, they stood and watched, so I can't see their point. By their own admission they have never taken a firm to Birmingham and twice we have been up there with what they themselves call an impressive firm.

As for Liverpool, it's a similar story in that there is not much rivalry between the two firms, but at least with the red Scousers there has been action and not just words. My first memory of trouble with them was back in the 1970s, when both sets of fans spent the whole game throwing bricks at each other as well as whatever else they could get their hands on. It went on for practically the entire match. As soon as a brick landed on one side it was straight back over the other. A punk rocker Blues fan got hit with a dart more or less in the middle of his forehead and made the front page of most of the national papers.

In their book *The Boys From The Mersey*, they say they ran Blues everywhere after that match. They may well have but this was pre-Zulu days and Blues didn't have much of a mob then. The people like me who later made Birmingham what they are were schoolboys at the time. I'm not trying to take anything away from the Scousers, as it was a mad day and still gets talked about whenever we make trips down Memory Lane.

I remember going to Liverpool in the early 1980s when we were called the Apex. It was a night game and about twenty of us caught the train up there. Surprisingly, there were no Scousers at Lime Street, so the small firm of us caught a bus to Anfield. As soon as the bus pulled off it stopped again and on came a firm of Scousers, who had been watching us all the time, although we hadn't sussed them. We were upstairs and there were only two black lads on the bus, me and Dennis H. The Scousers piled upstairs about twenty-handed and it went off, with them shouting, "Get de darkie, get de darkie."

It was only because we were at the top of the stairs that we were able to hold them off. Luckily for us, the Old Bill got on, as there was no doubt the Scousers were coming for the carve-up and the only blood they wanted was the darkies'. We didn't take that many to the game and the rest who did come were normal supporters on the travel coaches. During the game all the taunts were aimed at the blacks, darkie this and that, it was pure hatred. I have never received as much racist abuse in a football ground as I did that night.

After the game, there was no way I was attempting to make my way to Lime Street. We found out there were empty seats on the coaches. The driver realised he had more than he came with and wouldn't leave until the extra ones got off. I was thinking he was going to have me out straight away, as I was the only black face on there. My chances of getting back through Stanley Park alive were nil, never mind getting to Lime Street. I wasn't moving, no way. There were firms of Scousers hanging around and there was only one thing on their minds: Get de darkie. After what seemed like a lifetime, the driver decided to carry on back to Brum. That was probably the luckiest escape I've had from any football ground.

This was the first time I saw the Arsonist in action, too, the man who tried to burn down the refreshment stall at Millwall a few years later. He's a couple of years younger than me, so he would have been only about fifteen at the time. A lad called Archie fell asleep on the coach and woke up when he smelt burning. He didn't immediately realise his hood was full of newspaper and he was about to go up in flames. Most people won't fall asleep when the Arsonist is around. I've seen a few people flare.

My next trip to Anfield was in the 1985/86 season, when we got relegated, and they did the Double that season. They beat us 5–0, no surprise there. But the night before a load of us spent the night in Southport. It was the usual rabble. The inevitable happened and it went off with the local doormen. They grouped up and came at us with baseball bats, but the weapons were taken and used on them instead. When the Old Bill landed I was still standing there with a bat in my hand – the chase was on.

I had two Old Bill on my case but I gave them the slip and jumped over the back garden of some shops into some bins. I hid amongst them and put a lid on my head and didn't move. I could hear them looking for me but I stayed where I was till about four in the morning. I couldn't get back in the B&B but I found some of our lot who got there late as well, couldn't get digs and had to sleep in the car, so I got in with them. When I did get in B&B in the morning I was gutted when I heard that the Old Bill had fucked off after about ten minutes. At the time, every footstep I heard I thought was OB and I was taking no chances.

We made our way into Liverpool for the match via the A-roads from Southport along the coast, and came in undetected. Around sixty of us parked up and made our way to Lime Street, knowing a bigger firm was on the way by train. This time there was a firm of Scousers at the station but they weren't expecting us to come from behind them.

We chased that firm out of a side door and then another firm of theirs turned up and there were running battles with them. They had us backed up and nearly had us on our toes. I remember Morph come running through, giving a big Zulu chant and that got us all going again. We flew straight into the Scouse firm and had them on their toes but the Old Bill were there and rounded us up and escorted us to Anfield. A few Scousers were coming up taking photos of us. There were no shouts of "Get the darkie" that day. After that, Cud came in on the train with the main firm of about 250, marched all over Liverpool town centre and no one came near them. They'd never seen so many blacks in their lives. I think it was a culture shock to them.

Me and Morph got thrown out of the ground during the game and ended up in Stanley Park, and it wasn't long before half a dozen scallies had sussed us out and started to come after us. I thought back to my last lucky escape and came to the conclusion that this time was carve-up time for sure, but Morph said to them, "Hurry up boys, 'cos our firm's on the way." I hadn't spotted them but when I looked around a massive firm of Zulus were coming through Stanley Park. The Scousers saw the firm, told us we were lucky, and off they went.

The next time we played them was at St Andrew's in the FA Cup and ended in a draw. After the game, the Scousers got some serious hidings in the back streets of Digbeth, getting ambushed everywhere. At this time there were a lot of new faces doing it for the Zulus and not the lads from the 1980s. A lot had dropped out through the rave scene and other things and I was also inactive. I was still going to the games but others were doing it.

We knew they would be out for revenge at the replay. I went on a coach that had all the main heads on board, but we got as far as Stoke and it broke down, so all the main heads were stuck on the M6. We were getting phone calls saying it was going off up there, so a few of us got a taxi number for a Stoke firm and did the rest of the journey by cab. By the time we got there and a replacement coach had picked up the others, we had missed all the action.

Liverpool don't mention it in their book, but Everton say they joined up with them and carried out revenge attacks. But they took their vengeance out on normal supporters who gave as good as they got. Our normal fans class themselves as Zulus just as much as the lads and will stand their ground when they have to. Nothing happened after the game, although we had a massive firm together. The Scousers didn't hang around Stanley Park as usual but they did get up to their old tricks of picking off people going back to their cars.

We met them again in the League Cup final at Cardiff in 2000. They didn't fancy it at all that weekend and we didn't see many of them until the day of the game. The ones you did see wanted no trouble at all. All you got out of them was, "Alright la', we've only come for the footie," and them wanting to shake your hand. Their days of wanting to give it to the darkie were well and truly over and they were under manners all weekend.

Cardiff were not interested in them either. Liverpool are not big enough to get in the way of a Birmingham-Cardiff row. In *The Boys From The Mersey* they say firms only came to Liverpool after Heysel. They may have run Blues in the 1970s but that was pre-Zulu and they have never turned out in Birmingham since the Zulus formed. The way they hid in Cardiff proves the point.

The author also makes a snide comment in his book that we think we're dead hard these days. Would you take the Annie Road boys or the Zulus? In *Top Boys*, people were asked who were their top five firms of all time, and their top five today, and nearly everyone put the Zulus in one of their categories. No-one mentioned the Annie Road crew. I think that says it all.

Manchester

Many see Man City as a similar outfit to Blues. The club underachieves and shares a city with a "bigger" team, but their firm is organised and whether there are 400 or fifty out they're always up for it and will have a good row.

The Frozen North

*   *   *

WALLY: Since that day back in 1982 when the Zulu chant was first heard, we always had a thing about turning out at Man City and always looked forward to going to Maine Road. They don't turn up in Birmingham. I can only remember one time when there was trouble with them in Brum and that was in 1981 in our Apex days. Twenty of them came into the Bullring shopping centre while we were making our way up to New Street Station from Gino's café. We bumped into them on an enclosed bridge that goes over Smallbrook Queensway in the city centre.

One side of the bridge is glass and there is a very long drop to the traffic underneath, so it was a dangerous place to have it off. If you went through one of the windows you wouldn't have much chance of surviving. We had about the same number as them and we steamed into the Mancs, running them back to New Street and a few of them got a good hiding. Some of the birds who used to hang around with us steamed in as well, bashing them with brollies. We chased them back to the barriers and they just jumped over them and ran on to the platforms.

Some of us were still hanging around when, after a while, one of them came back up to the barriers and we started talking to him. He said the others had caught a train back to Manchester but he had bunked the train down and the ticket inspector had just checked their tickets and he didn't have one, so they threw him off. The only way he could get back was to go to the game and try and make his way back with the other Mancs from there. We told him to come with us. He wouldn't have it at first but after a while he agreed and made his way to St Andrew's with me, Carlton R and Tully. One thing about Blues is we don't take liberties if someone is on their own or if there is only a couple of them, we leave things like that to the Scousers.

While I was locked up, Blues had a couple of good rows in Manchester. The next time I encountered them was in 1986, when we had it off in the Arndale shopping centre. About fifty, mainly Bordesley Green and Kings Norton and some townies, had it with the Guv'nors. It was the same result as the Bullring clash. One of our lot let off a flare but it bounced off a wall and hit one of our own lads in the back. We ran the Mancs out of the Arndale; some of them stood and got done and some didn't hang around. The Mancs had made a full retreat but I got hold of one and had him bent over in a headlock. I'm giving him a few shots, shouting to the rest of them, "Come and get your boy." I dragged him along and gave him a few more digs and carried on saying, "Come and get him." They were looking back but not one of them would come and get him. I despatched him with a kick up the arse to run off with the rest of his Manc friends, if that's what you can call them.

We started the walk to Maine Road and a few more had turned up now, so we had a good 150. We were having it off all the way but all the Mancs did was run. We were under escort but we were out of control and gave the Old Bill the runaround. One thing about Manc Old Bill is they never seem to nick you, they just like whacking you with their truncheons instead, which suited me down to the ground.

One of the Juniors, Georgie, got thrown in the meat wagon twice and both times they let him go. A copper on horseback had him by the scruff of the neck at one stage and was giving him a few slaps saying, "Come to Manchester to fight, have ya?" After the game it was the same thing, chasing Mancs all over the place.

After that, any time we played them they didn't show. They must have got sick of us showing them up every time. If one team has had the full brunt of the Zulus then it is Man City. Going to Maine Road was like a pilgrimage because that is where it all started.

It was 1990 before it went off up there again but this time it was with the Old Bill. I had a broken leg at the time so didn't travel up with the firm but we took a good load there. One of the players had got me some tickets but they were in the Man City end. There were quite a few Blues in there but no trouble. Steve Bruce was playing for us then and was getting a lot of stick because he used to play for Manchester United. During the game, for no reason, the Old Bill started getting heavy with the Blues fans in the away end and it went off. Jimmy Sherry got caught on the Sky News camera punching a copper and breaking his nose. Jimmy and Balla ended up getting three years each. This was the last time anything went on with us and City. On their day they can pull a decent firm, but when we played them, because of what it meant to the Zulus, we always made sure we put on a good show.

Sheffield United

Wally: Blues have had some good rows with the Blades over the years but they have never been a problem to us. The first one I had with them was in the late 1980s but it was more funny to me than serious. On the way we were smoking that much weed that by the time we got there I was stoned out of my face.

We bumped into Sheffield's firm at the top of a shopping parade, flew into them and they were quickly on their toes. They kept coming back at us but Blues would have them on their toes again. Anytime anyone came near me I just told them to fuck off and leave me alone. I was absolutely mashed and was enjoying the buzz too much to be bothered with having it off. We had them on their toes a few times but to be fair they kept coming back for more. They also had a few black lads with them that day. Another thing I found funny was that I'm no oil painting but them black geezers in Sheffield are damn ugly.

This was just before the rave scene started so I wasn't really active in the football scene for a few years. When I started going back I missed a mad one that Blues had with Sheffield at their place. Everyone there rated it as a major row and it was up with the best of them. Sheffield have got their own version of events for that day but I wasn't there so I can't comment on that one.

The next season I went up with a firm of 60–70. It was mostly made up of the younger lads that had started to come through. There was a good turnout from the Sheldon lads, they were probably the main ones doing it down the Blues at that time. We all met up in the Mercat pub in the wholesale market, which opens at about 6am. It was supposed to be for the market traders but over the years it's been taken over by people who are still on an E or a charlie mission – the market traders are long gone.

When we were leaving, me and Brains kidnapped a lad from Lea Hall called Spam. He had never been to a match before in his life, now he'd been out all night and got nabbed by us two and taken up north off his face. When we got to Sheffield we met in a pub about ten minutes from the city centre. One of our lot had a number for a Sheffield lad he had met at England games. He tried to arrange a meet but Sheffield wouldn't come to us, saying it was too far and they wanted us to come to the city centre instead. I spoke to the lad on the phone and told him he was talking bollocks. Why do it in the city centre when there is more chance of Old Bill, and then you have got cameras? We were offside and it's down to them to come to us but they wouldn't have any of it, so we stayed where we were.

When we got close to the ground we bumped into a little firm of theirs and had them on their toes. The Old Bill baton-charged us and started whacking us. One copper swiped a kick at me but fell over and ripped his trousers and I stood there for a while laughing at him. He went ballistic but I did my Linford Christie and was off. The Old Bill nicked about 30 Blues fans and guess who one of them was? Yes, Spam. He didn't even get to his first match. Apparently a copper came down the cells fuming looking for a black geezer in a grey coat, I wonder who that was?

When I got into the ground, I didn't last five minutes. I got into an argument with a steward and got thrown out, so I spent the afternoon in the city centre. In their book *Blades Business Crew*, the Sheffield lad says after the game they saw one of Birmingham's main lads sitting on a wall on his mobile and in his Brummie drawl says, "Alright mate," which is true, as it was me. He then says they had us on our toes but tries to make out that there's a firm of us. There were only three of us – me, Morris and one other whose name I can't remember. A couple of them took a few digs at me. There were about forty of them and I recognise the author of their book as one of the ones who was throwing digs at me.

Then one of their lot called me by name, saying they only wanted to talk.

I was just backing off, slagging them for trying to do three of us. The lad that was chatting to me threw his hands in the air and shook his head to acknowledge that they were out of order. He was only a young lad so I don't think he had much pull.

We didn't run from them we just back-pedalled and I slagged them off. I wanted it with them but Morris dragged me away.

One of our lot, Napper, appeared from nowhere and gave one of them a lovely dig. Napper had been at the train station and found some mad tunnel to avoid the Old Bill and came to get us. The BBC don't attack stragglers – don't make me laugh.

Chapter Ten

Cream of the South

Cardiff City

JJ: IT'S ALWAYS odd to read the account of someone else involved in something as chaotic as a football battle. No-one except the copper in the chopper really sees it, and he doesn't see what's going on elsewhere, so any personal account is like choosing "playercam" for a match. A case in point is the day Blues ran into Cardiff at Derby station. We were playing Notts County and on the platform at New Street Station the question was, "Where is everybody?" because we were very thin on the ground for the era, not more than fifty that you could say were regular mob members. Mind you, with Blues you would always count on some pot-bellied loon in a replica shirt or a pikey in a V-neck jumper to come from nowhere and get stuck in with at least as much vigour as the so-called "boys".

The reason for the poor show was a belief that nothing ever happens at Notts County, which was of course true, but given that we were travelling by British Rail on a match day in the early Eighties, that was a rather short-sighted view of the situation, as anything could happen. As for Cardiff describing it in their book *Soul Crew* as being "before the very violent Caribbean contingent" joined the Zulus, this is clearly nonsense. But what they met was a quarter of the regular travelling mob of the time.

According to the Cardiff account, they were on the same train

144

as us, which is quite possibly true. In any event, both sets got off at Derby to change for Lincoln and Nottingham respectively. The Cardiff book described how "150 Pringle and Tacchini-clad Zulus" started it. Well, apart from the inflated number, they could be right. It goes on, "They climbed the stairwell and we moved along the platform then all of a sudden we heard a roar and they came flying down the adjacent staircase punching anyone in sight. We regrouped after the initial shock and proceeded towards them and steamed them off the platform. A few disgruntled Zulus sought refuge, running across the tracks. Although we heavily outnumbered them this was a defining moment in the history of the Soul Crew."

It would be no surprise if Blues had started it but certainly there were so many Cardiff it was always going to be challenging. I was already on the platform for Nottingham before all this kicked off and recall them chasing some of ours down the stairwell towards where I was standing. Looking around, this was getting out of order. There was nothing but railroad behind me and our older heads were in the rail bar across the tracks. So in a rare moment of self-sacrifice, I thought, *Come on then*, turned towards the Cardiff mob and ran into them. I had no desire to become a fallen hero, I just didn't fancy getting run all the way to Doncaster down the tracks, or wherever they led.

They couldn't believe their luck, having someone to try and land digs on, but I think they did more damage to each other as they aimed kicks and blows. It's surprising how painless such an attack is as long as you can stay on your feet. Bar a bit more scar tissue on the forehead, I was relatively unscathed. However, while all this was going on a handy mob of our older lot, including Jimmy S, had come across the tracks armed with all kinds of railway equipment and put up an admirable last stand at the end of the platform. It was like that. Show some resistance and you soon sorted out who really wanted to fight, usually a small percentage of the hundreds you might be facing. Jimmy knocked two clean out before the law intervened. So much for a quiet day.

Once we arrived, we headed for a boozer in Nottingham. One lad went out and before long word came back that he'd been done badly with a bottle by some Forest in town. Going after them, our little mob of fifteen or so, including DD, MM and S, ran into them in a subway. We were quite evenly matched in numbers and weight. They had some big old lads and it went hell for leather for quite a while. I remember DD holding on to some big lump and shouting, "Someone fucking hit him!" and S obliged with a flying kick. Again, I think the law arrived and we dispersed, but it was proper toe-to-toe. Just to round it off, we went into the County end and had a couple of punch ups in there. Like I said, quiet day.

In December 1984, Cardiff and Blues met again and the two firms had a monumental battle before and after the game.

Cud: We got minibuses down to Cardiff and immediately hit the shops, looking for some Burberry and Aquascutum. There were about seventy of us but it was clear pretty early on that no-one from Cardiff was around; they must have been expecting us at the ground. We found a shop with some good stuff and some lads robbed it clean. It was a good haul. We got some blazers, hats, brollies and put them on straight away. Some stuff still had the price tags on.

We then decided to go to Ninian Park and got on a bus. As we got closer, we saw more Blues having a few scuffles but we decided to stay on the bus and get off behind the Cardiff lot, around a corner. It looked like a fashion show, with about thirty black lads and forty white lads in their clobber. When we got off the bus, we sent someone round to distract the Cardiff lot. When they saw him they came running towards him and then ran straight into us. It was toe-to-toe stuff for a while. We stood and some of their lot got put on their arses in the melee. The Old Bill broke it up but it was one of our best rows outside a ground. Broken Burberry brollies were left on the floor.

There was a lot of verbal going on between us and them when the coppers stepped in, particularly between me and one lad. They threatened to arrest us but we went in and watched the match and were chuffed at Blues winning 2–1. After the match, about forty of us managed to ditch the OB and went into town looking for lads up for some more fisticuffs. We saw a couple of dressers around on this long, steep road with a bus station at the bottom of the hill and then we saw about fifteen of the Soul Crew. The Zulu chant went up and some of us went after them.

Me and a couple of others, Sharks and Colton, didn't bother and kept walking. As we walked down the road, I suddenly heard, "Remember me?" I turned round and saw about ninety Cardiff behind us. I recognised the geezer straight away, he was the one I had traded abuse with outside the ground earlier on. As there were only three of us I tried to get them to forget it, but they weren't having it, they wanted to go again. Realising this, I got Sharks to run and get the others who were nearby chasing the previous Cardiff lot. It must have looked like he was bottling it because he just ran off. Meanwhile I tried to keep stalling them by talking them out of it but they suddenly steamed in and Colton and I both turned and ran towards the bus station. As we ran down the hill our lot emerged and began charging towards them. Sharks had managed to find them. The Cardiff lads saw this and as soon as I reached our lot I quickly disappeared in the middle and the fun began. It was toe-to-toe stuff again for a few minutes. All you could hear was the thwack of Burberry brollies breaking after being smacked against different Cardiff lads. We chased them and clattered about five of them in the road.

In their book, the Soul Crew say there were about twenty-five of us wielding blades and we kept coming at them "like robots". Certainly a few were knocked out and kicked but I don't remember any blades there. Then we heard police sirens, so we ran to the top of the road as the others scattered. We told the coppers we had got lost and run into some racist supporters and they escorted us out of the town safely. I have a lot of respect for the Soul Crew. That was a good row and I will repay the compliment they paid us in their book, they are definitely in my all-time top five too.

JJ: I have to say that the trip to Cardiff was awesome before the game.

We rode on a bus round the ground festooned in Burberry, and a big mob of Cardiff saw this single-decker go past with all these black guys in Burberry on and obviously thought, This is it. Although there were no more than thirty, if that, I never felt more confident of a result, as everyone was just absolutely up for it. As Blues ran into this mob, just one lad stood – I think he wrote about it in their book. Fair play to him. Some of the older, fatter ones turned out and made a bit of a show but we totally whacked them until the Old Bill moved in.

Afterwards, I decided to go back on a coach with about forty lads who wanted a drink. We stopped off in Tewkesbury and pulled up outside a pub called the Winking Frog or something similar. I remember a bloke in there wearing a red V-neck jumper who looked pretty tough but also like a lobster. He had big arms like pincers and was rocking back on his chair. I imagine that a coach from somewhere turned up every week and they were more than ready to mix it.

As I recall some locals attacked a couple of Blues lads by a chip shop. A few of us were walking nearby and then more joined in and we started fighting with them. It was mad. There were people coming out of pubs to fight, God knows how many. It was such a funny sight. Two policemen were trying to control everything but weren't doing too well. I caught someone in the doorway of a shop but then a sergeant and his WPC landed on me and took my ankle out. The sergeant was about to put the cuffs on me but then looked up the road and saw others causing more mayhem and went after them instead.

Lobster man was still bopping around at the end, in fact one lad who was a reasonable amateur boxer wanted to tackle him down an alley Queensberry Rules, but it was time for the bus to leave. Amazingly, the sergeant never bothered to look for me on the bus. Which was just as well, as I wasn't running anywhere with the ankle like a balloon.

Newspapers carried reports of the trouble at closing time and reported witnesses seeing "seven different scuffles around a part of the town called the Cross. Reinforcements were brought in from Cheltenham and it took police using dogs some time to restore order. After the arrests, the fans left quickly."

Wally: I have not been involved in any trouble with Cardiff but I have got a lot of time and respect for the Soul Crew. Their book is one of the most honest and straightforward that has been written. I have a good friend in Cardiff called Pablo, one of the main faces around Cardiff. He's not into football but he knows all the Soul Crew and I used to go down there a lot in the early 1990s. When we played them at St Andrew's at that time, they brought a good firm. I went round to their end after the game, which they mention in their book, and told them they were the best firm that had been to St Andrew's for a good few years. Some of them recognised me from my nights out in Cardiff. The Old Bill gave them an escort to New Street so nothing went off that day, and we didn't turn out at their place that season.

The next time we went to Cardiff was in 2000 for the League Cup final against Liverpool. It was expected to go off big time with us and Cardiff but the Old Bill had it sussed. There were bits of trouble but not on a large scale. On the Saturday afternoon, I met my mate Pablo and he took me to a pub in the Docks area to meet some main players from the Soul Crew. I met the Viking and a few others and mutual respect was given from both sides. They said they wanted if off with Blues again, big time. They didn't care if they won or lost, they just wanted the experience of it. It wasn't long after they had given Millwall a serious hiding and they rated us up there with the top firms. But they weren't interested in the Scousers that Cup Final day and neither were we.

A few younger Cardiff came in and said it had just gone off in the town. It wasn't main faces from either firm, as Cardiff were in the pub and I knew our main lads were staying out of the city centre because of the Old Bill. They said to try and get Blues to come to a place called Canton. They couldn't get into the city with big numbers and we wouldn't be able to get out. I agreed with Viking that if either firm could have done it we would have, but the Old Bill had it sewn up. During the night there were little fights going off here and there but most of our firm was drinking in the bars in hotels.

JJ: Wally's account of Cardiff vs Liverpool is interesting as Blues had a massive firm in the city centre at the RSVP bar. We were among the first to arrive, along with Noggin. Cardiff put in an early appearance to let Blues know they were around but not much happened until much later in the day, when the RSVP bar kicked out. The big mob in there split up.

There were a few big rows with Cardiff, including one with A's lot, who really turned them over big time. I think it might have been the younger Cardiff lot and they ran into the heavy mob and got a right roasting. I came out of the pub – annoyingly we'd just bought the only food we were to *nearly* eat all day – as word came that Cardiff were mobbing up outside. It was pretty chaotic, with loads of plod about, but this Taff, not realising we were right by him, just said "Brummie cunts" in that perfect dialect. I managed to cop him with an undercut which shut him up.

Then there was the big bar down the bottom of the main street, which was rocking nicely until a dispute among Blues turned the place into a bit of a riot, prompting the Old Bill to come right in the middle of us all and get pelted.

They retreated out but left this female officer behind. It only became clear she was a woman when someone took her helmet off and this long blonde ponytail popped out. It was a bit surreal. She was taken to the back of the pub out of the way and told to stay put. The Old Bill came back in for her eventually and gassed the place. They were vexed and were whacking loads of people.

There was a funny moment up the road when we came face to face with a few older Cardiff heads and oddly enough a Millwall geezer clutching a handful of bottles. They turn up everywhere. It was clear to both sides that the cameras would make this a pointless confrontation, I think they even mentioned jobs and children. So it was quite a polite discussion in the end, although Mr Den was a bit more grizzly. Their recommendation was to get down to Canton where they were all holed up, but any further mobility was rendered pretty much null after the upset in the big pub with the riot squad, as the groups just got smaller and smaller.

One lad, TD, got a nasty gash in the head from a screwdriver or some such, as he and a few others ran into some Cardiff very late into the night. It was a long day with not a Scouse in sight until the next morning, when at least one got banged outside the ground by another out-of-town legend, Mr C.

When we played Cardiff at St Andrew's right at the end of the season in the late Nineties, much was expected but little happened. But then, a while after the game, a couple of lads ran back to the Garrison pub, where quite a few Blues were drinking, to say Cardiff had landed by coach across the park. It didn't make sense, but sure enough, a rogue coachload had come off the bus to have a go at some Blues lads wandering down the road. As it turned out, the Garrison was full of right old heads and so we flew across the park in a pincer movement and, after head-butting a few bricks, gave them a right old bashing. They were getting whacked as they tried to get back on the coach, really running for their lives. One big fat lump took a brick on

151

the back of the head and splayed out right on the pavement. It looked bad until he got up and waddled towards the bus. The coach got trashed and they spent the evening at Stechford nick; I passed them in the car on the way home.

Wally: We were back in Cardiff in 2002 for the play-offs final against Norwich. With the help of one of the Cardiff lads, we became the only ones to invade the pitch at the Millennium Stadium. Outside the ground, I was approached by a Cardiff lad who had some Nationwide access-all-areas passes that he was struggling to sell. I phoned my pal Pablo to check this tout out and he said he was a good lad and not a stroke-puller, so give it a try. I took one of the passes, went into the ground, walked round, came out of one entrance and went back into another turnstile to make sure it was sound. I went back out and told all of our lot it was sound, so we sold our tickets for £80 and gave the tout, Pugsy, £30 each for the remaining passes. You could go anywhere with them, so we did just that.

One of our lads stood next to Atomic Kitten on the pitch when they were singing before the game. Norwich scored first and then we equalized, that's when we first ran on to the pitch. The stewards let a lot of us on because we had the passes and they didn't have a clue what was happening. The rest just followed. When Darren Carter got the winning penalty we were back on again. They got everyone off for the second time but me and a couple of others fronted it and stayed on. When the players were parading the trophy I walked around with them, holding it aloft. The players were looking at me thinking, *Who the fuck is he?* The lads in the crowd were in stitches.

The Zulu Army chant started going up and soon the whole end was singing it, 35,000 Blues fans singing "Zulu Army" and there I am on the pitch with the players, holding up the trophy because we've just reached the Premier League. The buzz was tremendous. I loved every minute of it.

Portsmouth 6.57 Crew

After an encounter in Portsmouth in April 1985, which the police managed to curtail, the two firms didn't meet again until a convoy of Zulus headed south in October 1986 for a League game. The day was full of surprising and amusing events and provided fond memories, especially for those who indulged in a bit of toe-to-toe action against Pompey – with the Old Bill helping.

Wally: Pompey's 6.57 Crew are another firm with a good name who many people rate. I just missed the game in 1985 when Blues took a good firm down there. Everyone was talking about it when I got out of prison and I couldn't wait to visit. Blues got promoted that season, so I had to wait a couple of years before we played them.

The previous time, everyone had gone by train but this time we decided to go by car. It was before the M40 motorway had opened so it was A-roads all the way. I don't remember where we met but it was the same ritual for any big away game when we went by car. We'd exchange tapes so we had music for the journey. Some cars would have ragga sound systems like Saxon from London, or the Birmingham Sound Now Generation, and other cars would be blasting out soul music. We would also make sure we had enough Rizla and fags for the journey – the amount of weed we'd smoke was mad. We'd be that stoned sometimes it was a wonder we could fight.

The A-road to Pompey in those days was horrible. I suppose the best thing you could do was get stoned and nod your head to the ragga beats. There were about 100 lads in the convoy and during the journey someone decided to start ripping up newspapers and throw the bits out of the window. They landed on the windscreens of the cars behind and then the whole convoy started doing it. At the time we thought it was funny but if there had been an accident we would have been in trouble. That was sheer madness, but you don't think of it at the time.

About halfway into the journey there was a crash, but it didn't involve any of our cars. A woman in front of us had crashed into a wagon in front of her. The car I was in was the first one to get stuck behind it all and with it being an A-road there was nowhere to overtake, so all the traffic was held up. The woman was in a bad way and couldn't be moved out of her car. We could hear her moaning and her car was pretty dented. People had stopped to help but we were all thinking the same thing when I shouted, "We've got a match to get to." With it being in the middle of nowhere it was going to takes ages before the emergency services would arrive. We were already running late and just wanted to get there and a quick decision had to be made, so we bounced the car out of the way. Four or five us got around it and started bouncing it on to the hard shoulder. No-one tried to stop us and when we had moved it I guided our convoy past before jumping back in the car and off we went again.

When we arrived, we parked up on a housing estate and went straight to the game, as it had already kicked off. We all went in the seats on the side on the upper level. The away stand was behind the goal. There weren't any Pompey lads in these seats, so nothing happened. At the end of the game, the Old Bill were escorting us out when I noticed a fence at the back of the stand that divided it in half. I climbed the fence and jumped into the other end. Then one by one everyone else came over. The Old Bill were concentrating on the front so they had no idea that almost sixty of us had slipped out behind them. We came out of the ground, mixing in with the ordinary Pompey fans, but we must have stood out as there were no blacks in Pompey.

We eventually bumped into their firm on some wasteland and a full-on battle took place. We were outnumbered but turned them over. Two plain clothes police officers who used to give Pompey's lads grief were watching. When the uniformed Old Bill appeared and went to go for the Pompey lads, the plain clothes guys shouted and gestured to them, "No, this lot are the troublemakers, they've just turned Pompey over!" The Old Bill couldn't get their breath; they'd never known them to get done at home like that.

After the Old Bill rounded us up, twenty-five of us got out of the main escort but two uniformed coppers caught up with us and walked us back towards our cars. We had to go through a housing estate and ran part of the way to try to shake them off, but although they were quite old, we couldn't lose them. As we entered the estate I noticed all the flats were named after areas in the West Midlands.

On the way a few Pompey popped up and threw bricks at us, but we soon met up with a firm of them outside their main pub. Then something happened which most would find hard to believe. One of the coppers got hit with a brick and said, "Right, I've had enough of this." He took off his helmet, got out his truncheon and shouted, "Come on then!" We all looked at each other in amazement but no second invitation was needed, so we steamed into Pompey, with two Old Bill having it with us. We couldn't believe it but we just got on with it. Again we did Pompey over and then the two coppers said, "That's enough," and we stopped.

We made our way to our cars and waited for the others to land in the main escort, sitting on some grass thinking about what just happened. The copper said to us he had been waiting to see them get turned over for years. In their book *Rolling With The 6.57 Crew*, Pompey admit we did them that day and added that we were the only firm to go down there and take the piss. We had our day that day but I still rate Pompey as a top firm. Respect due, Pompey.

After that, I felt we were untouchable to pull that off against a top firm. A few weeks later I tried it again with a similar number at West Brom, but this time the result was disastrous [see Chapter 11].

———————

After a match at Portsmouth in the early 1990s, a dozen Zulus, including Cud, Psycho, Shirley and a lad from a Birmingham boxing family, walked back to their cars to head home. The first of the three cars, containing Cud, was about to drive off when one of the lads tapped on the window and said: "They're here." The Zulus had parked somewhere offside but about seventy Pompey had found them. Everyone got out and prepared for what lay ahead, while a Pompey lad in an Aquascutum jacket punched his fist into his palm and said, "It's all over for you Zulus."

Cud shouted to everyone to make a line and responded by saying, "We are the Zulus and we don't run from no one." He then flew into them. The fighting was so ferocious that people living in houses nearby ran out to try to stop it. Because black faces were a rarity in Portsmouth, the Zulus also took a lot of racist abuse. Several Pompey lads ended up on the floor and one had several teeth knocked out after being punched with a knuckleduster.

When the police arrived they broke it up and forced the Zulus up against a wall before chucking a few in the back of their vans. The toothless Pompey lad was asked to point out who was responsible for his injuries, but he played the game and winked at the lad who had done it, before taking a look at the firm and assuring the officers he wasn't there. "Pompey thought they could get a result against us," said Cud, "but they didn't know that even though there were only a few of us it was our top lads."

Chapter Eleven

Middle England

West Bromwich Albion

WALLY: ALTHOUGH WE are local rivals, there isn't much history between us and the Albion. They have had it off with Villa quite a lot but in general they are not in our league. They did turn us over one year and it was a massive blow to us. One of their lads, Cola, has written about this in Cass Pennant's book, *Top Boys,* but he twisted the truth.

The first incident he mentions is when they came and smashed up the Crown.

I don't know if this lad ever went to school but he seriously needs to learn how to count. He reckons they were doing OK until another 300 Blues turned up. This is a load of bollocks. When they smashed the windows in the pub there was no-one in there. No more than 100 of us came down from John Bright Street as they were doing it and we steamed straight into them. One of their lot got done with a hammer. It was no contest, they were never in it.

But the second time at their ground, they did do us. It was a few weeks after we had played up at Pompey with a small firm of twenty-five. That morning we met in the Nightrider on Stephenson Street, which was our old pub from the early Eighties. We met there because you could get the number 79 bus straight to West Brom from right outside. Most people just wanted to go on the piss that day but me and a few others got impatient and got on the bus. We didn't even fill the top deck. There were no more than thirty of us. They done us fair and square that day, no complaints. But unless them Yam Yams have got triple vision, they are thicker than I thought they were.

On the way over there, we were talking about what we did at Pompey and thought Albion would be a pushover. We'd done it at Pompey so why not to the Yam Yams? We met up in the Lewisham pub on West Bromwich High Street. One of our lads, Stuart, used to follow Albion so we decided he should go scouting to see where they were and to sort out the row. We didn't think sending one man on his own, who they knew, would be a problem but he came back up the road in tatters. Albion had done one lad on his own and slashed his coat to bits. Not far behind Stuart we could see a firm of Albion coming. They had 150 and the thirty of us made our way towards them and they came straight into us. They spanked us silly.

One of our lot got stabbed and was left on the floor. I tried to get to him but an Albion lad came towards me with a small can in his hand and said, "Yam want this Brummie?" I was thinking, what the fuck is he gonna do with that? Then he sprayed me. That was my first encounter with CS gas and the first time it had been used against any of us. A few of us tried to stand but it was no good. In the end I was dragged out of there by two of our lot, with my Burberry Mac dragging behind me. I was in the middle of two lads, each with an arm around my shoulders. I got a kick up the arse with "yam Brummie bastard" ringing in my ears. That's all they kept saying as they kicked us back up the High Street.

A copper on a motorbike got kicked off in the melee, while me and T ended up in Sandwell General. They had never treated CS gas before and everything they used was water-based, which made it worse, but I managed to make the game for the second half. I notice that Cola makes no mention of what happened after the match. We ran them ragged, but to be fair the damage had already been done. We found out who stabbed T, a black lad called Joey who lived up by the ground. He'd got nicked that day, but for something else, and was being held in custody over the weekend.

On the Monday, Stuart and I waited for him to come out just up the road from the West Bromwich court. We spotted him go into a phone box. Payback time. The following Friday evening we took a couple of vans over to West Brom and paid them a surprise visit. So yes, we did get done by Albion. No excuses but, Mr Cola, you need to go and get educated because 150 doesn't go into thirty.

Wolverhampton Wanderers

Wolverhampton's Subway Army was rated by the Zulus in the early Eighties under the leadership of a guy called Dodger Q. He was respected as their main man long before their current "leader", Gilly Shaw, for whom the Zulus appear to have little respect. The Subway were up there as one of the best firms in the Midlands at that time, along with the C-Crew, before Blues dominated. Their lads would regularly come into Brum, and not just on match days, looking for a fight with Blues. But from 1984/85, when their team joined Blues in Division Two, they seemed to drop off the radar as they fell further down the divisions, until the two firms rarely met at all.

Wally: Before the days of Gilly, Wolves used to have a decent firm. I have a lot of respect for the old Subway boys, unlike that shower they have got down there now. They were very similar to our young Apex firm, as it was made up of young black and white lads just getting into the casual scene. They were as game as fuck and led by a black lad called Dodger Q. But their main mouthpiece now, Gilly, reminds me of Fowler from Villa. I'm sure they were separated at birth. He once proclaimed himself to be the country's baddest hooligan. I know a few Wolves lads

159

from the rave scene and everyone who has a nickname gets it for a reason, and I have it on good authority that he is known as Bullshitter Gilly. Not Fat Gilly or Bald Gilly but Bullshitter Gilly. That sums him up a treat.

But we've had a good few run-ins with the Subway lot. Even if we weren't playing each other they used to land over in Brum in the weekdays and have it off with us. They used to have what we called a "bag man" who carried a bag full of knives, bats and machetes. They weren't shy pulling them out either. Mostly it would be them coming to Brum, although we did surprise them once when we were on our way to Shrewsbury for a pre-season friendly.

In August 1982, we played Walsall in another pre-season game at their place. Before the game, we had a running battle with the Subway lot in the town centre and it also went off with the local Walsall lads. I ended up getting glassed on the ear by one of them using an old style pint glass with the handle. I had to have half a dozen stitches. It was a mad row and went on for ages, back and forth in the middle of the road.

The next time we met was when we drew Walsall in the FA Cup in January 1983. Yet again the Subway lot turned out. When the main row had finished, I ended up with a handful of us breaking away from the main escort. We bumped into a handful of the Subway down a back street and it was off again – and the little bag man was with them. We were jumping in gardens, getting bricks and bottles to throw at them. When we saw the Old Bill everyone dropped their weapons. Theirs went in the bag and the bag man was off. The OB had both firms up against the wall and there was still a bit of verbal going on. I was face to face with one of them and he spat right in my face. It was one of those dirty horrible ones and I was fucking livid and the Old Bill had to jump in again. We eventually got to the game, which ended in a draw, and the replay was set for St Andrew's the following week.

Every time we met Wolves and it went off they were always tooled up, so I didn't intend to get caught short again. You fight fire with fire. I am not going to bullshit and say I didn't know what I was doing. If it went off, someone was copping it, end of story. On the day of the match, I made my way up town and went off to get a Stanley knife. At the time, it was the weapon of choice for hooligans as it was small and easy to conceal. Nothing happened before the game but afterwards a few of us made our way down Garrison Lane, where we bumped into a firm of Walsall. We were all young ten-stone kids but these were great big lumps, fifteen-stone grown men in their thirties.

It turned out they were the main men from a rough estate in Walsall called Beechdale. We couldn't move them so out came Stan. Three of them copped it, one from the top to the bottom of his face, one from ear to ear and one down the side of his face. One of us copped one on the hand by mistake.

The Old Bill had my door off the same night. Me and Balla got nicked and remanded in custody. At the next home game, the OB were at the match with a couple of the Walsall lads, who pointed people out. Dennis, H and Lloyd M got nicked. One of the Walsall lot was a geezer called Migza Heyes. He was supposed to be the main man of the town and had done quite a lot of bird. He put Dennis up as being the one that did him. Four of us were charged, me and Dennis for wounding and affray and Balla and Lloyd for just affray. I spent nine months on remand in Brockhill Youth Prison.

During that time, football violence was on the up and a few other people were to pass through the institution's portals. A Juventus fan came in for stabbing a Villa fan and another lad, Peter Andreas, an Arsenal fan, was up for doing a Man United fan at an FA Cup semi-final at Villa Park. I later read he was the one who got Arsenal top boy Denton the job of minder for the Pet Shop Boys. Peter was the boyfriend of one of them; he later died of Aids. Some of the Subway lot came in but not for football-related stuff, they'd had it off with some biker gang in their town. One of the Subway lot got stabbed and died, but because of who they were, the Old Bill still charged them with affray.

Dodge Q, the main man, was there and guess who else? Yes,

the guy who spat in my face. Of course we had it off a couple of times, once when we was playing football. The screws let you off because they put it down to the heat of the moment.

Another time I was coming back to the wing with my meal on a metal tray, we passed each other and a few things were said. Something made me look back and he was coming at me with a plastic water jug. I turned around, whacked him full on with the tray and it went off again. The screws are pretty lively in the nick so it was over in seconds. I spent a lot of time on remand down the block. I had a few offs with the screws and one time they gave me a good hiding.

A couple of years after I got out, I saw one of them in a sports shop in town when I was with some mates. I pointed him out to JK, who then went up to the counter with a pair of boxing mitts and asked the woman if he could try them out. He hadn't said anything to the rest of us but he just walked up to the screw, knocked him spark out and legged it. I saw the screw again a few years later in Winson Green Prison in Birmingham on another sentence and he didn't recognise me, not when he was standing up.

In October 1983 I pleaded guilty to wounding and affray and got four years. Dennis got not guilty on affray and got two years. Balla and Lloyd went guilty and got two apiece. When we went to the Green, some of Migza's firm were in there. The young offenders were on C Wing and threats were coming across. If they wanted it, no problems, but nothing ever happened.

I was moved to Swinfen Hall, which was a long-term prison for young offenders where you had to be doing a minimum of four years. It was there I met Curtis Warren, who was two cells down from me. He became something of an underworld legend in years to come. I thought he was alright and got on with him. During that time I heard from the lads that the Zulu firm was getting bigger and bigger and making a good name for itself all over the country.

I pretty much kept my head down, although one spot of grief I did get was when someone sent me photos of Blues doing the

Old Bill on the last game of the season against Southampton. They had gone mad when they came out of the ground. It didn't do my parole any good getting sent photos of police vans being turned over and Old Bill getting run everywhere by Zulus.

The stories I was hearing were music to my ears. The firm that I had helped start was now getting rated as one of the best out there. I got knocked back on my first parole, then got moved to Stafford nick when I turned twenty-one, in January 1985. I eventually got parole but they wanted me to go into a hostel to see how I got on. I told them to ram it. I'd been in for more than two years so what did they need to know that they didn't already? I had about five months left and I knew I wouldn't conform to the rules of some poxy hostel and I'd end up back in, so I might as well stay and finish off. April 15, 1985, was my parole date and on that morning I felt gutted, thinking I could have been out, but around 11am my door opened and the screw said, "Pack your stuff, you're off home."

I thought he was joking at first but then I realised he was serious. I couldn't believe it, the Home Office had buckled and let me out. It was the same day as the famous Hagler v. Hearns fight and this was my fight with the Home Office and I had won. I was twenty-one and had just finished a four-year stretch for football violence. Had it broke me? Was I finished with football violence? Was I fuck. The best was yet to come.

In September 1983, Wolves and Birmingham City met at Molyneux. Wolves dispatched a couple of scouts early to New Street to look out for any Blues lads in town. When they spotted some they put it on them, taunting them to bring a firm over to Wolverhampton for a meet. The lads recounted this to other Zulus who had congregated in a city centre pub, and Cud and Bobby decided to make their way to New Street to have a little chat.

They located the visitors and fronted them up. In response,

one of the Wolves lads pulled out a knife and lashed out, missing Cud's throat by centimetres. They then turned on their heels, ran down a platform and jumped on a train heading for Wolverhampton, shouting, "We'll be back in half an hour." Cud and Bobby headed straight for the Nightrider pub, where some 200 Zulus were drinking. Word spread about the encounter, and on the advice of Noggin, one of the original members of the firm, some lads were immediately sent to Woolworths in the nearby Pallasades Shopping Centre to get what weapons they could. They came back having cleaned the shelves out of choppers, hammers and Stanley knives, which were then dished out to whoever wanted them, mainly the Juniors, as the older lads relied on their fists.

The 200 lads then descended on New Street, ready to head over to Wolverhampton, but police were on hand and stopped about half of them getting through and on to a train. It was certain a big firm of the Subway Army would be waiting for them and the remaining 100 or so carried on even though a lot of good lads hadn't made it. They arrived and, as promised, there was a huge firm in attendance, far outnumbering the visitors. The lads at New Street had obviously got back in time to round up a tasty crew.

As the Zulus walked out of the station, there was a head-on collision with Wolves. Any police there found it hopeless trying to contain the throng of Tacchini and Fila-clad lads hell-bent on having it off. Kicks and punches came raining in from both sides in the station car park but there were more Wolves casualties on the floor than Zulus. The Zulu chant went up and Wolves were chased back up the car park, round the corner on to a nearby dual carriageway and further down the road.

In the exchanges near the road, one Zulu, called Tully, ran towards Wolves and used a hammer on an unsuspecting rival, only to be seen by the police. Officers went after him but he darted back into the crowd. Despite attempts by the lads to try and hide him in the mayhem, he was apprehended. When the police regained some sort of order, the distinctive sound of weapons falling to the floor could be heard as the officers began breaking things up.

As predicted, Wolves brought a fairly big firm to St Andrew's for the next match, in February, and about 150 lads congregated in and around the Toreador pub, near Birmingham Market. Cud made his way there and spoke to his cousin, who was in the Subway Army, to arrange a meet for later. As they casually chatted outside the pub, a couple of the Wolves lot, also standing outside on the look-out, turned to Cud and asked, "Is that your lot?" Cud turned to see about forty of the younger Zulus, dressed in the latest sports gear, making their way down the stairs at the side of a ramp which led to the Pallasades and New Street Station.

When the lads got nearer and inquired what the sketch was, Cud assured them everything was sweet, which they accepted until Cud's cousin took it upon himself to fling a bottle in their direction. A shout of "Give it to 'em" came from Cud, which was all that was needed to kick things off. Wolves barricaded themselves in the pub and tried to flee via a back door as, one by one, the windows were put through and the front door wrecked, with Cud watching the shenanigans from under a table out of the way.

Wally: When the old Subway Army firm split up [partly as the result of an undercover police operation called GROWTH – Get Rid Of Wolverhampton's Troublesome Hooligans], the "Dingles", as we call them, were quiet for a few years. We call them the Dingles because no matter what they wear, they always look scruffy and most of them work in scrapyards and factories. Another name for them is Yam Yams because of the way they talk. People take the piss out of the Brummie accent but them Yam Yams are something else. The thought of coming home to a Wolverhampton bird after she's just done an eight-hour shift in the local factory, greeting you with that famous Wolvo saying "Yam o right?" is enough to put you off women for life.

This new Dingle firm is another one of those who think just

because they brought a Stone Island coat and a Burberry hat and go to England games, that makes them a top firm. It takes a lot more than that. A couple of years ago, a few Wolves lads got sent down for attacking shirts at matches. Their targets were not your designer-wearing thugs but normal supporters who wear club colours. The police mounted an operation and rounded them up. It wasn't just a one-off incident, it had been going on for a while. They're also well known for picking off people on their own and dishing out severe beatings. I'm not saying it was their main lads that were doing these things, but they can't deny it was going on. If that was going on down the Blues we wouldn't stand for it and whoever was responsible would get back what they had dished out. Attacking fans in shirts is not on at all.

Not a lot happened with Wolves over quite a while until it went off in Moseley in 2000, when they turned up with the so-called England Hit Squad that was supposed to come and teach Blues a lesson for attacking Villa at an England game in Scotland. Blues have never been involved with the England scene. With our large black contingent, the few lads that did go were always met with taunts like, "Where's your niggers?" It was OK for them to give Blues fans grief, but once we have a firm that do Villa at an England game, we are out of order.

I've got a friend who is also friendly with [leading Villa hooligan] Fowler and lives on the same estate as him. He's a Blues fan but he's not into the hooligan thing. He and Fowler were going to the international between England and Scotland together. My friend phoned me at about 8am to say he was with Fowler and they had a spare ticket for me if I could have a word with the Blues lads that were up there, as they'd heard that Blues were hunting Villa. I told him there was nothing I could do. Fowler had put himself up as my enemy and I wasn't about to save his arse now.

Our mutual friend thought that because it was an England game everyone would stick together. Not Blues, I had to tell him. I advised him that the best thing he could do was go elsewhere. I couldn't phone the lads and say give Fowler a squeeze today, how could I when he tried to build a rep off my back? Fowler and his boys were soon dispatched from the pub they were using. They were outnumbered as Blues had a good firm up there that day.

JJ: Blues and Wolves have been fighting each other since the Seventies. Everyone had heard of the Subway Army, who would lay in wait for visiting fans coming off the soccer special to navigate the labyrinth of underpasses en route to the ground. My first significant hand-to-hand combat with Wolves was an odd one. Watford had played Plymouth at Villa Park in the FA Cup semi and we had a nothing game. I went into New Street, proudly wearing my Ellesse grey and red coat bought from their store in Florence.

In those days, stealing each other's clothes was an accepted pastime, so the coat was an obvious prize. Heading back to north Birmingham alone, I nipped down to the platform but was very aware of some yam yam child – not more than fourteen – getting very excited about the coat. I ignored him and carried on down. I was sitting on the bench waiting for the train – for some reason they thought I was a Watford supporter – and an ugly little group of a dozen or more youths surrounded me.

"Who do youm support?"

"Blues."

"Yer a Cockney, ayn't yer?"

"No."

"Give us yer coat or wim tek it off yer." Or words to that effect.

Not much answer to that but a weary glance and a last calculation of odds. It reminded me of Gimli the Dwarf in *Lord of the Rings*: "Chances of success: nil. Probability of death: certain. What are we waiting for?" So I jumped up and punched the first one to make a break through the group, but their dirty little paws were all over me as some tried to pull the coat off my shoulders and others aimed boots and punches to the head. What was amusing about this scene at 6pm on a Saturday night at a crowded New Street is absolutely no-one took any notice. Either because they became bored, embarrassed, frustrated or late for their train, they gave up the struggle and took off without my coat.

There were many fights with Wolves, including one that someone ought to remember not so many years ago when Blues landed on their boozer right in the town and turned them over big time before the game. I think it was all on camera. They really weren't up to much for a long time, but word came through of "stirrings in the dark lands to the north" and Blues started to take a bit of notice, having more or less given up on the local rivals in the late Eighties to fry bigger fish. A sequence of battles began when we were promoted back to the old Second Division from the Third and this was about the time they were earning a name for themselves. They landed offside in a pub near Digbeth before one match and called it on, but already had a healthy police escort to keep them company.

I recall with some amusement that one of our lot was talking to them on the phone and a notable legend (AA) grabbed it and demanded their presence immediately around the corner to do battle. They jumped around a bit but nothing happened. After the match they came out on the Coventry Road, up for it, and it was one of the last times there was a ding-dong right there outside the bus station, despite the police cordon. One of the reasons for that was the police photographers standing atop the station, who snapped everything. A recent convert from West Brom was arrested that day and spent more time banned from Blues than he had watching them. We played at their place and slipped the Old Bill after the game and caused mayhem in the surrounding streets.

There was trouble at England matches. In Bulgaria, the English were split between two resorts. Wolves ran amok in one and Blues took the lead in the other, 100 miles away. Wolves made a lot of enemies across the country by gassing pubs and breaking glasses in people's faces. They even gassed the hotel lobby where a group of Blues were waiting for their coach home. Blues' friendship with Man City very much began in the other resort, while Villa's offer of friendship was rejected, but without resorting to bullying.

But all this was just a build-up to hostilities that were to follow. I think one of the reasons it got so involved was because of the connection and communication between Blues lads in the Wolves areas – Staffordshire and Shropshire, for example – which made it easy for meets to be arranged at very short notice. For a while it became a sport. Coming back from Everton in the Cup, we landed on Wolverhampton, then they would put in an appearance in Brum, coming from somewhere else. A train ride north wasn't complete without a phone call to Wolves. But what this added up to was a lot of nothing for quite a while, and so, when they announced that they'd be coming to Brum before their Walsall game, it was a bored group that waited for them in the pub at the bottom of the Rotunda.

Sure enough, no show, and everyone went to the game. Of course the call came in again after the game and by this time no-one was interested. But the rumours became stronger and about twenty-five moved up from Digbeth. Two of us decided to have a wander into the station and see if these phone calls were valid. Fortunately there used to be two ways to New Street from the bar where we'd been, divided by a wall. So while we walked one way, towards the station, we saw the mob approaching from it, heading toward the bar. It was hard to say numbers, as usual, but it was more than eighty. We thought, oh bollocks, because we knew how few were in the pub and we were, at best, in no man's land. So all we could do was stand and watch them march up to the pub and attack them from behind, if nothing else.

Whoever was near the door popped out and blasted the first couple. It was unbelievable; the whole Wolves mob just ran for it. I said to my amigo, "Come on, we're in here." Blues ran out of the pub, chasing Wolves back to the station, meaning the gap that had closed behind us was now back in "friendly" territory and we could lunge into the melee that had now drawn its line more or less on the corner where the road turns into the station. It was full hand-to-hand combat, fists flying in everywhere. We were fortunate that the front line was rather narrow, stuck between a row of bus stops and the wall mentioned earlier. And they never tried a pincer move to attack the rear, which would have made it hard. So we just got stuck into them.

Gilly was right in the middle of it. I think he took a couple of digs. More of our lot arrived and it all got a bit fragmented, with some of us going forward and some going back. Plod was trying its best to sort things out. One of our lot, a real headbanger called N, would always go deeper and further than anyone right-minded. Put it down to too much time spent living in a Falkands ditch and cutting Argentinean throats at night for a living. Anyway, he ended up sparked out on the floor in occupied territory and to their credit they did let him up rather than jump all over him. Our tails were up so high that two of us decided to go deep into enemy territory, taking them on right in the station road, which proved a bit rash as we were soon encircled. It was a right old battle. Blues held it despite the numbers. One Wolves lad and four from Blues got arrested, which was a bit ironic considering they started it all.

This was part of a cycle of clashes between us and them at the time. We played them one Friday night, I guess the match was televised. Anyway, the turnout was appalling, fewer than twenty, and we went over in a single minibus. We got dropped off somewhere and they knew where we were, as one of our lot was on the phone to them. I think they thought it was some kind of trap when he told them how few of us there were. Nothing happened before but they were ringing up all through the game, so we said, "Well, here we are."

It's a big open space as you come out of the ground, so we were mindful that it could kick off from any angle and kept it tight. As soon as the first lot had a go, we just weighed into them and they scattered. We were chasing some down a little street, but mindful that it was a short cut to a trap. As ever, the Blues shirts and beer monsters were getting stuck in at the first sight of aggro; I think one got nicked for his trouble. We didn't run into their main mob until we were out by the road to the station and they weren't keen to have a go at us with the law there, so all in all it was an amusing little night out.

Leicester City

JJ: Leicester could always be lively, even back in the late Seventies and early Eighties. We took a massive mob there in 1980, there must have been 10,000 of us on the good old-fashioned soccer special.

I don't recall them being much of a casual firm. It was funny how things changed; you could walk through Birmingham and no-one except a few "in the know" from either Zulus or C-Crew would have a clue what a Tacchini was. Most thought the "T" was Talbot Motors down at Coventry. Benetton was for posh girls. Burberry and Aquascutum was what old men wore. The first bloke I saw wearing a Burberry golf jacket was a Chelsea lad, who was a mate of one of the Blues, drinking in a city pub. I thought, *That's odd, where's all the sports gear?* Within six months everyone had one.

I went on a ski holiday to Italy in 1985 with a largely "non-firm" assortment of friends of various footballing persuasions. It was supposed to be just a break, a winter alternative to sun and sangria. As chance would have it, we ran into about ten Millwall who had the same idea and one from Charlton. At night they all wore paisley or some fancy patterned shirt, buttoned to the neck. Again, I thought, *Odd.* Six months later it was standard dress in Brum. So much for a break from football; it was the only time I've seen it kick-off in a ski resort between two groups. Mind you, it was billed as the Benidorm of the Alps.

There was a bunch of Bristol Rovers lads, with the obligatory Bristol City lad to take all the jokes, who were needling the Millwall lot all week. It came to a head on the last morning when the Bristol spokesman went up to the Millwall group and

171

told them, "Millwall are fuck-all and always have been fuck-all." You can imagine this feedback was not taken well, and the whole pub went up. As our seven included Spurs, Villa, Albion and Blues, we remained resolutely neutral. I've always wondered what happened on the flight home, as they were all headed for Gatwick.

Finding your own pub round the corner from the main mob was a favorite ploy of the older heads. And so it was in Leicester when I ended up with the "All-Stars" of the era: A, Y, and Coxy. It was a heavy mob. Fifteen of us ended up by the ground and Leicester were out in force. We'd somehow come down a street with one mob at one end and another at the other end, being minded by a couple of coppers at best. It looked a bit iffy and they were ranged right across the road. I think we were along the Burnmoor Street side of the ground and there must have been more than sixty on each side.

They soon worked out who we were and started coming for it. But again, how many fighters have they got? It looked impossible odds, but once our heavyweights started bashing a few they backed off. We were going into one lot on one side, then into the other lot, just preserving our zone in the middle. It was again one of those situations when numbers mean nothing; no-one wants to get hurt and they all just want someone else to do the fighting. Sure, if you get overrun then they'll all come in, flailing fists and boots and kicking each other. But as long as the line holds, with all of the group looking out for each other, you can defy crazy odds.

Wally: We have had some good ones with Leicester over the years. You're always guaranteed to have it with them at their place and they have a got a tidy little firm, although they would have to admit that they're not quite up there with the big boys. One thing I like about them is that they always seem to do Villa.

I got on OK with the Leicester lads on the rave scene and used to do a night up there at the Starlight club every Friday. One of our most memorable ones with Leicester is one that didn't go to plan and I have to throw my hands up, as I was the one who fucked it up. Fat Errol still slags me off for it to this day.

It was a night game at their ground. A couple of our lads used to work the markets there and they knew some of their lads and where their main boozers were. We had a good firm of about 150 and we left Boogies wine bar in vans and cars. The Bordesley Green bread vans [see page 179] were out for this one. When we got to Leicester it was dark and we parked up near their main boozer and everyone hid in bus stops and shop doorways out of the way. We left about twenty lads on show in the middle of the road and then someone went to their pub to let them know we had arrived. Their firm came marching down to front our lot in the road.

I came out too early though and everyone followed, but Leicester hadn't got close enough and had it on their toes. If I hadn't come out so soon they would have faced a wicked ambush and would have got it big time. I don't know if they realise how lucky they were that day. It was a great escape for them and they can thank me for it. After the game we were put on buses and escorted out of there.

For some reason, I don't know what sparked it off, but we started to act like Leeds United and the bus I was on was vandalised and got smashed to bits. The only things that weren't vandalised were the wheels. There were two Old Bill on the bus but we still smashed it up. It was driven straight to a police station and about seventy of us were locked up overnight.

We have had a good few rows with them over the years since then but not anything big and always at their ground. They never really brought a firm to St Andrew's until 2003, when about 150 of them came by taxi, which was a good move by them. They turned up about 11am and later said they were told to go to Digbeth. I wish everyone would stop believing everything they see on the Internet; these cyber thugs are unreal. None of our lads would call a meet in Digbeth and then not show. One of our lot was in the area at the time and saw their firm. He made a few calls and got together what he could quickly. About a dozen of them had it with Leicester but couldn't hold them off. The Leicester lad in the book *Top Boys* admits after the game the Old Bill saved them, as we had a massive firm out. I agree with him that Leicester will always have a firm. I've got a lot of respect for them but they are not up there with the big boys.

PART THREE

Chapter Twelve

Operation Red Card

WHEN WALLY EMERGED from prison in 1985, there were plenty of faces in the firm he didn't recognise. The fact that there were a much larger number of black and Asian lads in the firm also surprised him. When he first started going down to the Blues there were only a handful – Jayo from the older firm, Glenroy on the Trooper Mob, Cud and his brother and a couple of others – and he could remember only one Asian guy before he went into prison.

When he started the Apex there were a good few from the town like Lanks, Sharky and Tony M. Then, when the original Zulus started, there were about thirty black lads, but now there were hundreds from all over Birmingham, from the likes of Handsworth, Winson Green and Lozells. One of the Handsworth lot went on to become a major player in the Birmingham Burger Bar Boys gang. There was also a new, younger firm that he became aware of, the Junior Business Boys. Most areas of Brum had firms that were involved with the Zulus, except for north Birmingham, which is Villa territory. The main pub the Zulus frequented then was the Crown at the back of the New Street Station.

The next few years would also see a distinct, though entirely amicable, "divide" in the Zulus. Those who were purely "in it for the knuckle", like Cud, did their thing. By day they were eminently respectable, law-abiding citizens; at the weekend they turned into hardcore soccer thugs. Others, led by Wally, took a different path, and branched into criminal activity as an adjunct to their football exploits.

For Wally's first weekend out as a free man, Blues had Charlton at home. Wally didn't go to the game, but he went to the pub beforehand with Fat Errol and a few others from Bordesley Green. When he walked into the Crown, with all the lads discussing what had gone on at Pompey the week before, a huge cheer went up from the lads that knew him. A few years later, Wally found out from Morph that some people were asking who he was when he walked in that day, to which he replied, "If you don't know who that is, you ain't a Zulu." That's something Wally will always remember. "Nice one for that, Morph."

There were a couple of games left before the season ended, Middlesbrough away and Leeds at home, and Blues were eventually promoted to Division One. Although Wally didn't get involved in any shenanigans at either match, his hunger for the violence was still with him.

Wally: People who don't understand what the football violence was all about will find it hard to believe how someone could serve a four-year sentence, come out and get involved again a couple of months later. All I can give is a straightforward answer: I wanted it. It was in me and didn't go away. I was looking forward to the 1985/86 season in Division One, though when it started a few people had dropped out, as there had been a few nickings for the rioting against Leeds. The Bordesley Green firm, however, got bigger, with two notable additions in Paul and Floyd Gibbs.

During the new season the Zulus split into two firms. It wasn't planned and it wasn't over fallouts. Cud led the main firm, which had the larger numbers and was made up of lads who mainly held full-time jobs, and I led the more criminal-minded lot, which was mostly made up of Bordesley Green, a few from Lea Hall, Kings Norton, and other heads from town. It was pure rabble. The hardcore of it was Bordesley Green.

Paul and Floyd had use of a couple of VW vans belonging to their dad, who used them for delivering Jamaican bread and buns. They certainly came in handy for away matches. The two vans and a few cars meant we always had a good fifty or so of Birmingham's finest. Villa hated the sight of those vans, as they knew what firm would be in them. During the week we would meet up in the Broadway pub and plan what was happening for each game. Some places we would only go for the earner, as we would already know the places that were easy for robbing because they had previously been visited by our shoplifting firms. Bordesley Green and Lea Hall had a good few lads who were out doing the lifting.

A few of the Lea Hall lads went out to Rotterdam robbing when Villa went for the European Cup final in 1982. The Scousers were out there too. The Villa lads at that time were all factory rats. We used to call one of their main heads Red Robbo, which was the nickname of the trade union bloke who used to head the strikes at British Leyland in the 1970s.

When we turned up in another city, although having it off with the other firm was the main priority, also high on the agenda would be thieving. First would be the meeting place and it wouldn't be long before someone would be upstairs in the boozer looking for the safe and the cash, and the store room would always get a visit for the fags and spirits. The town centre would be getting a look at for jewellers or any store rooms that could be had for fags. Many times certain people have turned back to Brum because they've had an earner. We had the firms doing the fruit machines and fag machines and if they weren't fiddling them or breaking into them they would just go missing. Some of the main firm didn't like our antics, as it would lead to visits from the local plod if some gaffer in the pub realised last night's takings had gone or they were looking for the firm that had done the jewellers.

Many times the Old Bill have been in pubs, threatening to lock everyone up because something has gone down. I can understand the lads of the main firm getting the hump about this, as they had been at work all week and had only come out for one thing. So the threat of being locked up for something they're not into wouldn't be too appealing. We didn't have nine-to-five jobs so football was a good cover for us to have an earner. This had been going on for years but now there were a lot more at it. That's how the firm was split into two. Cud just used to call us lot the rabble. We would cause pure destruction.

It worked in our favour having two firms, as sometimes one of the firms would turn up just in time to help the other one out. Our firm would mostly turn up early doors or from the night before. The sight of another big firm landing after the first lot took people by surprise just as they were about to have it their own way.

Every Christmas Eve from the early 1980s until about 1987 some of the lads would have a Zulu Christmas Party in the town centre around John Bright Street. It was the main area in the town for going out and Blues ruled the roost – Villa never made it there, the lads made sure of that. They'd be drinking at the Rumrunner, Boogies, Edwards No. 7 and 8, the Paramount, Rococco at the Tower Ballroom in Edgbaston, Millionaires, Kaleidoscope and the Crown pub. They'd venture up to the top of Broad Street and go to a couple of clubs, Faces and Maximillion's, which later became Baker's, and the Rep Bar, which was part of the Repertory Theatre, on Sundays. After the pubs there were often a few smash-and-grabs.

Wally: One night we went to Faces, at the top of Broad Street by Five Ways Island, and did a clothes shop near there. We'd also go to the Jewellery Quarter; no need to go abroad with the jewellery stores in town. They got done whenever, not just when the football was on. People would mob up and head to the shops. There were no cameras, so you could grab stuff then do a runner.

Watches of Switzerland, which was right in the city centre, got done once. There used to be a Rumbelows opposite it and someone picked up a washing machine and threw it through a window and the Rolexes were gone. We liked our clothes and I remember two lads spending the night in Rackham's department store. They nicked loads of clothes and broke out early in the morning. But we'd also buy gear from Nicholls, Austin Reed and perhaps Rackham's. Nicholls was good for Tacchini and Fila.

I remember watching Wimbledon to see what Borg and McEnroe were wearing. Borg usually favoured Fila and McEnroe Tacchini. I liked to wear Pringle and Gabicci jumpers, Farahs, and some of us wore jeans that were split on the side, as well as Fiorucci jeans. We wore safari jackets, leather box jackets and of course Burberry macs and waist-length Burberry jackets. Aquascutum was about but not as popular with us and we never favoured the wedge haircut which was about in the early 1980s. As times changed we got into the designer gear like Armani. For footwear it was Diadora or Adidas trainers with some into Trimm Trabbs and Munchen. I had some Stan Smith strapovers – Kois – in two or three different colours, red, blue and white, and I loved the crocodile shoes and kickers. Lillywhite in London was the main place to get trainers.

We were always checking each other and other firms out as we passed through New Street. But dressing like a Scouser was frowned upon by a few of our lot; we dressed more like the London firms. I think we were one of the best dressed firms in the country at one point.

It all started about 1979/80. I was just leaving school, our numbers were growing and we took it seriously until we were a full firm of dressers by about 1985. Of course, the firm would go to clubs and soul parties out of town. Someone would hire coaches and convoys of cars would head up to Manchester and Rock City in Nottingham from the Rotunda by Bar St Martin.

Manchester wasn't a dangerous place to go out in like it is now. This was well before "Gunchester" and some great nights were had. Shelley's in Stoke was another popular night out, as was a club in Doncaster on Bank Holidays. There were all-dayers on once a month and we'd follow them.

Most of us were into Chicago house music very early on, around 1986, well before it dominated the rave scene, listening to DJs like Marshall Jefferson and Farley Jackmaster Funk, and the lads went where it was played – Powerhouse all-dayers in Brum and of course, Boogies.

Eddie Fewtrell, a well-known Birmingham figure, owned Boogies as well as other clubs and bars, including Barbarellas, which was a big punk venue in the 1970s. Boogies had three floors – the Kipper Club on the bottom, mainly soul on the middle floor and mainstream music on top. The Kipper Club was listed by *The Face* magazine as one of the top fifty clubs between 1980-88, along with the Rumrunner and the Powerhouse jazz all-dayers.

Wally: We'd be in Boogies on a Saturday night, go for late-night drinks in a shebeen somewhere and then on Sundays get a coach to an all-dayer. As this was before the rave days it was just brandy and weed for us. When we'd hear Afrika Bambaataa's "Zulu Nation" we'd go mad on the dance floor. A lot of Zulus would go to the all-dayers, including lads from Handsworth and Winson Green, and cause mayhem. Someone would go in and open the fire exits so others could get in without paying, the tills or the bar would usually be robbed and the doormen terrorised.

One night at Shelley's it was really mad. The place got destroyed, although it wasn't just the football lads doing it. At one point the MC said, "You Birmingham lot, we do not want you on the scene." He ended up getting bottled off the stage. The Handsworth lot brought the ghetto mentality with them, I guess. Some things that went on were out of order – girls getting their jewellery taxed – but that is what happened. The police came to Shelley's that night and escorted our coach out of Stoke. Before we left, some of the girls got on and pointed a few lads out who had taken their gold and a few were nicked. That kind of killed the all-dayer scene, as no one wanted to put anything on because it had got too dangerous.

One night, a few of the lads, including Norman, were out celebrating a birthday and went to a club called Pagoda Park, down the road from Boogies. They hadn't ventured to London with the rest of the firm to watch Blues play Millwall, although they were expected to land in the city centre afterwards. But when they got to the club, the security had other ideas and knocked them back on the door, a decision that didn't go down too well and caused a scuffle with a doorman, who produced a cosh and whacked one of the lads with it for no apparent reason.

As back-up arrived, the lads scarpered and went back to John Bright Street, where they could see the rest of the firm had returned from Millwall, drunk but ready for more. They met up with Cud and 200 or so lads in Boogies and told them what had happened. Cud stood up and shouted, "Right, who's coming?" The whole pub stood up. The lads then marched out of the pub, walked under a subway, ripped up trees to use as ammunition along the way and arrived at the club.

They confronted the doorman who had used his cosh and Cud and Norman smacked him. That was it for the rest of the security team. They ran inside the club and locked themselves in a room at the back. The Zulus then proceeded to wreak havoc inside the club. Lads could be seen hanging off chandeliers, breaking tables and throwing chairs about, gradually trashing it before leaving and heading back to Boogies, where they carried on drinking. Pagoda Park was closed "until further notice" for refurbishment.

A party at a school off the Stratford Road in Sparkhill around 1984 was a success until someone robbed the caretaker's office. It came about through a friend of a friend of a friend who knew the caretaker and more than 400 people turned up and got drunk.

ZULUS

The place was crammed with Zulus, girls and lads from town, and it went on till the early hours. It would have become a regular occurrence if the office hadn't been relieved of the majority of its contents. The caretaker was not impressed and the perpetrator was sought and efforts made to get the items back. Although the party was cranked up again, quite a few drifted off and carried on elsewhere. But the offender was later tracked down and told in no uncertain times he'd made a mistake.

Another incident where trouble broke out was after Birmingham City's annual supporters' dance. The evening ended up in a brawl and the police were called to the Locarno Ballroom on Hurst Street around midnight after chairs and curtains were wrecked and four people were arrested.

During one of the lads' Christmas outings, two police officers were attacked. As some stood outside the Kaleidoscope bar drinking, one of the lads got a bit mouthy with a couple of bobbies, who told him to shut up or they'd nick him. Wally taunted them, saying they wouldn't nick anyone, to which the police replied, "You reckon?" And with that, two other lads steamed into the unsuspecting officers and bashed them silly all the way round to Nicholls, the designer clothes store round the corner. They were grabbed by the scruffs of their necks and punched and dragged along the road, but must have managed to radio for help, because when they turned the corner the lads saw that the cavalry had arrived and loads of officers gave chase.

Eventually Eddie Fewtrell was made aware of the trouble and made inquiries as to who was the cause. When he was told it was mainly Wally and another Bordesley lad called Errol, he made it clear he wanted them as doormen and they accepted. They were there every night of the week and there was fun to be had all the time. One evening they had a tear-up with twenty postmen taking a break from work at what was then the Royal Mail building a few streets away.

Everyone in the Zulus has many memories of those times, but then Boogies was burned down and Eddie sold up to a brewery for about £10 million around 1987. It reopened, but not as

Wally (in dungarees) at the head of a crew as it marches through an unidentified town shopping centre, a typical Saturday afternoon scene during the 1980s. The Zulus were one firm that always made people stop and stare.

Wally in Burberry Mac strolling past Victoria Station in London with a couple of the lads.

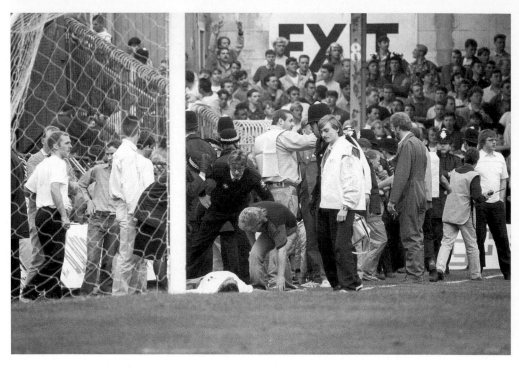

Mayhem in the away end at Blackpool in September 1989 led to bodies
on the pitch and the police losing control.

Operation Red Card was a lengthy undercover investigation of the Zulus
and led to dawn raids and a slew of arrests and convictions.

A Union Jack and the Birmingham Coat of arms displayed before Wembley in 1991. The Coat of Arms flag was "liberated" from the Town Hall before the match. The Lord Mayor appealed for its return but it is now a duvet cover for one of the Zulus.

Something to celebrate, for once: in the fountain at Trafalgar Square after winning the Leyland DAF Trophy against Tranmere Rovers in 1991

A sequence of pictures, shown repeatedly on British television, taken at an end-of-season game at Crystal Palace in 1989. Blues ran on the pitch and attacked Palace fans, with many of them again in bizarre fancy dress.

The Blues hordes at the Millennium Stadium, Cardiff, in 2002, to see their team clinch promotion to the Premier League with a play-off win against Norwich.

Birmingham City and Zulus flags at a pre-season friendly tournament against Deportivo La Coruna in Spain

The good, the bad, and the ageing: Outside the Old Wharf pub for a team photo-shoot © *John Alevroyiannis*

Author Caroline Gall with Cud (left) and Wally outside St Andrew's. © *Nick Bowman*

Boogies; those days were gone. It was now called Old Orleans. A new era was also about to start at St Andrew's in the form of a police operation to bring down the Zulus.

The 1985/86 season was Blues' last in the top division for sixteen years. "We were gone but not forgotten, as we had established ourselves as one of the top firms in the country," said Wally. This was something West Midlands Police were very aware of, and after apparently tolerating their presence for a few years, they eventually decided to set up an operation to target the firm in an attempt to break it up. It was originally named Operation Rorke's Drift after the place where some 4,000 Zulus, angry at the British invading KwaZulu, fought 150 soldiers at an African supply station in 1879. But this was thought to be racially sensitive, so Operation Red Card was launched instead in January 1987.

It is hard to know exactly when the police decided to concentrate their efforts on the Zulus, but after the Leeds riot in 1985, which indirectly resulted in the death of a teenager, and other incidents perceived by police as overstepping the mark, perhaps it was inevitable. The police believed there was a hardcore element in the firm of both black and white, employed and unemployed, who dressed in designer clothes and operated around New Street and the city centre, looting stores and running riot in bars on match days.

A fifteen-man investigation team was set up at Steelhouse Lane police station to compile a dossier of information about the core of the gang and uncover the crimes they committed. Undercover officers infiltrated the firm, its size no doubt making that easier, and travelled with fans to away games, including Leeds and Torquay. Video cameras were used to film trouble-makers. The undercover officers adopted false identities and were not allowed to return to their various police stations for fear of blowing their cover, instead passing information to colleagues by telephone.

Surveillance got under way, unbeknown to the Zulus, in January 1987 and about the same time an off-duty copper came into Boogies for a drink one Saturday night. Needless to say, the bar was full of lads, this time drinking in celebration of Blues' 1–0 victory against Ipswich in an FA Cup match. As everyone knew each other in the bar, a large, well-built stranger walking in and proceeding to drink alone was immediately noticed and aroused suspicion.

Some of the lads engaged in a bit of conversation with him and discovered he'd had a bit to drink, as he told them to shut up with their Zulu nonsense because they didn't realise who he was and they couldn't touch him, or words to that effect. Cud wasn't far away having a drink and when he was at the bar the copper banged into him. He gave him a shove back and turned around. Thinking this stranger was about to punch him, Cud got in first and the guy went down on the floor. Cud left him to it and went back upstairs, oblivious to the fact that several other lads set upon him moments later.

From upstairs, Cud saw the guy was now covered in blood but was sure he had not caused that much damage from one punch. But it emerged one of the lads had stuck a glass in his face, cutting it open. Someone must have called the police, because a short time later about thirty officers appeared and ordered the bar to be closed as they started bagging up bits of broken glass as evidence. Within a few weeks Cud heard the police were after him for the incident because someone had made an anonymous call informing them what happened and saying it was down to him. He handed himself in to sort things out a few weeks later and was charged with wounding. A few months later, he was convicted and received an eighteen-month suspended sentence and a £300 fine. The lad who glassed the copper was tracked down by a bar owner, who told him to hand himself in. He was later sentenced to three-and-a-half years in jail. Cud decided to keep away from matches for the rest of the season and kept a low profile in town, hardly venturing into the city centre bars for fear of the wrath of the police.

Later on in the year, Watford had an FA Cup semi-final match against Spurs at Villa Park. One of the Zulus, CC, used to go to

Tottenham and knew a few of their lads, so a meet was arranged for a fight. Spurs were in a pub called the Craven Arms and Blues were in the Crown further in the city centre. What the Zulus didn't know at the time was that the Old Bill were in an office opposite the Crown, filming. There was an undercover officer in the pub with the Zulus and when he knew it was about to go off, as people headed outside the pub to meet Spurs, he signalled to them by lifting up his cap. When Spurs came down from their pub the two firms clashed near the Crown. In the resulting fight, Blues battered the Yids. A couple of the Londoners got stabbed and afterwards made statements to the police. On the surveillance video, which was shown in court, one officer audibly shouts, "Someone's been stabbed." But when the cameraman tried to film the event, he got the camera tangled up in the window blinds and missed it.

In the first week of October, 1987, 180 police officers raided nearly forty homes in Birmingham and Staffordshire where they believed hardcore Zulu members lived. Men aged from their late teens to forty years old were escorted out of their houses with coats over their heads, past waiting photographers and journalists who had accompanied police, and taken to six different police stations. When the first wave of arrests were made, frantic calls were made by lads who had heard what was going on, warning others to destroy any scrapbooks they may have compiled over the years. Several lads hurriedly went out into their gardens and set about burning treasured memories and mementoes.

At a press conference at police headquarters, the various weapons officers had seized were put on display in a potentially damning exhibition. They confiscated two photo albums, sharpened billiard cues, a machete, knives, coshes and clubs. West Midlands Police Assistant Chief Constable Paul Leopold said, "They are just people who like hitting people. It is an operation that needed to be done for the sake of public tranquillity and for the good of people. We have certainly dealt them a good blow."

The next day the papers reported that a Customs officer and a systems analyst were among thirty-six people who appeared before Birmingham magistrates accused of violence connected with football matches and a gang called the Zulu Warriors. "The gang has been involved in organised shoplifting, public disorder and stabbings and they leave calling cards at the scenes of their crimes: 'You've just been zapped by a Zulu.'" The media also reported that the officers "dressed in the skinhead uniform of jeans and Doc Martens and mixed with known members in pubs and clubs...to record their violent tactics on the terraces and in shopping centres." The Chelmsley Wood lads were the last die-hard skinheads in the firm, but even they had moved on by 1987.

Twenty-one were remanded in custody and fifteen remanded on bail on condition that they stay at least one mile from any Football League ground in England and Wales on match days, from two hours before kick-off until two hours after the final whistle. They were also banned from Birmingham city centre between 11am and 8pm on Saturdays and ordered to report to police stations on Saturday afternoons. The thirty-six accused faced charges including conspiracy to cause an affray, conspiracy to cause violent and disorderly behaviour and conspiracy to assault the police.

Sefton, the Customs officer who was arrested in Solihull, was charged with conspiracy to commit violence and disorderly behaviour at Plymouth. Desmond Hanson, from Small Heath, who was charged with conspiracy to assault police officers and cause violent and disorderly behaviour, was due to get married on the Saturday after his arrest and his bail conditions were relaxed so he still could. Some were charged with extra offences: one with four offences of wounding and Lee Evans with opening doors on moving trains and endangering passengers. T and Floyd Gibbs were remanded over conspiracy charges, with Floyd also charged with threatening behaviour.

After the resulting trials nearly a year later, eleven people were jailed with terms ranging from twenty-one to six months. Two received suspended sentences and thirteen were fined between £75 and £300. Martin Felton, described as "the gang's historian, keeping a diary of the gang's violence during their two-year reign of terror" was sentenced to six months.

In court, the judge said the lads came from good, caring family homes "yet their barbarism was astonishing and depressing". Several MPs said the sentences were inadequate and had let down the police, who had spent two years infiltrating the gang. The club introduced a membership scheme a short time later, which meant anyone who wanted to travel to an away match had to have a card with their picture on it to get tickets. This caused many to stop going down, plus there was a new distraction starting up, the rave scene.

By sheer fluke, however, several prominent lads escaped the dragnet. Cud was away on holiday when the raids were carried out, while Wally was in prison in Exeter serving a nine-month term. There is little doubt that short stretch saved him from doing a longer one.

The first Cud knew about what had gone on was when he bought a newspaper while on holiday. He knew that the police were after the Zulus but wasn't aware of the lengthy surveillance operation they had been conducting. He had already taken a back seat after the incident with the undercover officer in Boogies earlier in the year. After the raids, he heard from the lads that the police were very much aware of him and wanted to know more about him. Feeling paranoid, he stopped going and kept a low profile, although with the club in dire financial straits after falling into the Third Division in 1989 there wasn't much joy to be had as a Blues fan. Gate numbers dropped to between 6,000 and 7,000 in the late 1980s and everything was in turmoil at the club with no fans, no money and a failing board. The future looked bleak.

The operation stopped a lot people going to the ground. Average home league attendance had already started to slide year-on-year during the mid-1980s, and an FA Cup defeat to non-league Altrincham in January 1986 did nothing to win over supporters. Ron Saunders departed not long afterwards, prompting a succession of managers: John Bond for almost three seasons,

ZULUS

Garry Pendrey, Dave Mackay, who passed the mantle to Lou Macari for only a matter of months, before Terry Cooper took over and led the club back up the divisions.

Chapter Thirteen

Rave On

OPERATION RED CARD stopped a large number of lads from following Birmingham City, but at the same time there was a new mass movement that engulfed a large contingent of the Zulus: the rave scene. With the authorities getting the upper hand over the hooligan and talk of a national membership scheme for supporters – which was brought in at Blues around 1989/90 but didn't last long – lads began looking for fun elsewhere, and the dance floor, or nearest field, provided the perfect platform.

While not everyone in the Zulus was interested in pill popping and getting wrecked for days on end, especially when it became apparent that the new movement prompted liaisons amongst lads from rival firms, others turned to organising and promoting nights, dabbling with Ecstasy and the like and generally having a great time as the scene swept the country.

Cud: I stopped going down the Blues for a good few seasons after Red Card, as did loads of others. I took a bit of a back seat after the incident with the copper in Boogies and then the raids went on in October and that kept me away even more. I heard from the lads that the police had been asking about me and I knew they were out to get me and it made me a bit paranoid. I sometimes went to one-off games but really I stopped going all the time I wanted to keep a low profile.

Not much was going on down the ground then. Blues slipped into the old Third Division and everything was in turmoil at the club, no fans, no money, rubbish board, the club just went to pot. I just worked the doors in town and when the rave scene started to kick in I wasn't into that. I was going out to the Midland Hotel, the Exchange and Pagoda Park in town. I knew Wally and that were mixing with Villa for business at that time through the rave scene but I wasn't going to do that.

I remember once when Villa put it on a few of our lot at a do in the Hummingbird [a city nightclub used for many raves] one night and we got a call, as Wally couldn't do anything about it. Me and Psycho went there and saw Garry Little, one of their main faces at the time, and spoke to him. Villa shit themselves and that was it, in the end they were buying us drinks. Although we weren't rowing with other firms we still used to bash Villa, they were easy prey. They wouldn't come to town that much and if they did they got done. They needed major numbers and if they did row with us they would fear the comeback.

The rave phenomenon headed north from London with many memorable nights springing up across the region from 1988 onwards. The scene was an excellent way for the lads to let loose and put on their own events. Ecstasy and acid are certainly not aggro-inducing drugs and the thought of kicking off with someone, or some firm, while off your face was the last thing on anyone's mind.

Amnesia House nights in Coventry and Birmingham proved to be a big success as well as the "Lifestyle" party in a field in Coventry on October 29, 1989. The movement was unstoppable, attracting all kinds of people as well as lads from Blues, Villa, Wolves and West Brom who all wanted a slice of the action. The monthly events at Sky Blue Connection in Coventry were allowed by police and were probably the first legal club raves in the UK. DJs Doc Scott and Man Parris provided the sounds but after six memorable events the police shut it down, prompting the birth of the first all-night rave venue in 1991 at The Eclipse in Coventry.

"The Sky Blue Connection nights became well known and visited by a fair few black Cockney lads who were up to no good some of the time," said Wally. "They were taxing some people but one time they did one of our lot, Stacey, and we thought, that's enough, so we took our revenge. It was decided between us and Villa that we had to kind of join forces to stop the Cockneys. They were soon told in no uncertain terms that they had made a mistake."

Spectrum at the Institute in Birmingham was another success, as was Shelley's in Stoke-on-Trent, put on by the Amnesia lads, Neville and Bambam, proving that the Midlands was a mecca for raves in the early days. And at the turn of the decade it was the turn of some of the Zulus to have a go. Villa had got their event off the ground with RAW at the Handsworth Leisure Centre in 1990, and Wally put on the first Starlight at the Small Heath Leisure Centre in March of the same year, with DJs Mickey Finn, Keith Suckling, Lee Fisher and Neil Macey. Legendary acts such as Moby and The Prodigy performed for the masses as the scene was by now in full flow. Pandemonium also joined the ranks as one of the greats with their all-nighters at Telford Ice Rink in 1991 and a rave at Birmingham's Rag Market in 1991 was another mad one. It was a fast-paced and hectic era but full of good times.

Connections were made between Blues and Villa through the buying and selling of drugs and organising nights, and although things were still a bit edgy, it pacified relations. If there was a big do on in Brum, everyone wanted to go to it regardless of who had organised it. The talk on the terraces, for those who still went, turned to raves, not rows.

Some Blues lads that were still going to some matches can recall coming back from a game in Reading and stopping off for a drink in Oxford. Some guy in the pub approached them to see if they were interested in going to a rave nearby. It sounded good so off they went and ended up having a wicked time.

"There was guy I knew, Keith Baker, who was a manager for a rock group called Magnum who fronted things for me when I did Starlight," said Wally. "When we wanted to put on a night at Villa Leisure Centre or other venues, his record label was called Time and it was respectable, so less questions were asked by the authorities, which made it easier to get a licence. When we put on a do at Bigley Hall in Staffordshire, it was the biggest indoor event at the time, with a capacity of 7,000.

"The police soon got wise though. They monitored ticket sales and just a day or so before, you'd get a huge bill for policing the event, which would be a huge chunk, if not nearly all, of the ticket sales. But what could you do? You couldn't pull the plug, the party had to happen so you had to pay up. Ultimately they knew the footie lot were running the scene and they wanted to bring us down."

But those events were the big ones. In Birmingham city centre in the late 1980s, Tressines was the place to be, even though it was only on a Monday night, with nights put on by Simon Raine, who later went on to to set up Gatecrasher. Bar and club promoters didn't have much faith in the fledgling scene back then and would only allow nights to be put on early in the week. Tressines was the first established club night in the city, swiftly followed by Reflections in Coventry on a Tuesday.

Coast to Coast, run by the Robinson brothers, was soon in full swing in the early 1990s, as was Quest in Wolverhampton, run by Carl and Jez and former British judo champ Kenneth Brown. They also set up a clothes shop in Wolves called Diffusion, which was a good place to sell tickets, but The Depot in Brum – run by the organisers of the swanky all-dayers Chuff Chuff – was the main place to get tickets, buy tapes or even just be seen hanging around.

Outside the Midlands, Manchester had a certain pull for some, although lads distributing flyers for events in Brum were not welcome. "They saw it as you taking trade away from them," said Wally. "It was a complete no-no; if you tried you'd get a beating, one hundred per cent. We'd go to Konspiracy, Thunderdome and obviously the Hacienda in Manchester, and the

Hippodrome in Altrincham, and they'd all come down to us for the crack sometimes. Eastern Bloc Records was good for a few ticket sales but Liverpool was better, even though they were left behind by the scene. But nowhere could beat The Depot. They sold all the tickets for all the raves. It was the best in the country, no doubt about it."

Needless to say, a fashion movement accompanied the scene. Labels such as Mash from London, Naf Naf and Gio Goi from Manchester were much sought after, as well as the obligatory Wallaby shoes. But by the mid-1990s, efforts were being made by the Government to clamp down on rave, and in 1994 they passed the Criminal Justice and Public Order Act, which helped kill off an already dying scene.

After finishing nineteenth in Division Two for two consecutive seasons, Birmingham City finally dropped to the Third in 1989. To "celebrate" plumbing new depths, and with the club in perilous financial difficulties, fancy dress was the order of the day for normal supporters and hooligans alike travelling to Selhurst Park for the last game of the season. It was mainly the crazy element within the shirts who turned up dressed up, but there was a Nazi, Maggie Thatcher, a priest, various animals and blokes wearing stockings, suspenders and make-up, plus a couple of gay Vikings in pink hats with horns. A coachload of nuns also put in an appearance along with a two-man horse that was later seen jogging across the pitch in the subsequent melee.

The average home league attendance that season just about reached 6,000, but a hardy bunch of supporters made the trek to south London to mark their team's demise and the start of a new chapter in the football wilderness. A couple of minibuses were hired from a trusted firm to take some lads down. Aziz Coaches in Highgate was used on several occasions because the bigger firms had got wise to the trouble their passengers usually caused and after a while refused to take them. One time, with a full quota of passengers all smoking weed on board, the Indian driver asked, "Can we open the window please because I am feeling quite stoned?"

On the way to Selhurst Park, they stopped for a drink in Aylesbury, where they ran into some Mansfield Town lads who were happy to oblige in some fisticuffs before the Blues lot went on their way again. To enhance the day ahead, some lads took some speed while others decided acid was the way to go, so for quite a few the day was a haze.

Not everyone had tickets, and when the game was about to start several lads inside pushed open the club's wooden gates, allowing others to get in without paying. The fence at Selhurst Park had replaced a higher barrier in the wake of the Hillsborough Disaster just four weeks earlier, and when Crystal Palace scored, twelve minutes after kick-off, Blues fans charged forward to get to the home supporters. Some supporters packed at the front were getting crushed and police let them on to the pitch, wary of another tragedy occurring. They were on there for fifteen minutes and indulged in running battles with Palace until the police managed to restore order using seven officers on horseback charging across the pitch to disperse the pockets of trouble.

Wally had made it round to Palace's end and as he walked out on to the pitch it took several seconds for him to register that everyone was shouting, "Behind you!" He looked round and saw a large number of Palace coming on to the pitch, prompting him to run as fast as he could to the other end. The referee took both teams off for thirty minutes and the mounted police attempted to usher fans back to the terraces. An extra 100 police were brought in to help the 150 already on duty at the ground and Blues manager Dave Mackay pleaded with Blues fans to behave, while Palace manager Steve Coppell used the public address system to appeal for calm. But Hitler, Maggie Thatcher and a bunch of nuns whacked the crap out of anyone they came across, while a priest blessed casualties.

Cud: We encountered some West Ham before the game and it went off with them outside the ground. It was after the

Hillsborough Disaster and some Blues fans pretended they were getting crushed at the front of the fences. The Old Bill were taking no risks so they let them on the pitch, but as soon as they got on there they went straight to where Palace were and it went off. It wasn't our top lads and nothing was planned.

Blues have always had a mad following, even normal supporters are pretty crazy, and they all just went for it. If you are on the pitch I suppose you have to do something. I was watching it all from the stand but you couldn't tell who was who because of the costumes. It was pretty violent and a load got chinned. One lad, John G, who was dressed up as a priest, was going round blessing people who were on the ground.

JJ: It was the first match I'd been to in the best part of two-and-a-half years, and I'd proudly had the campaign sticker "Blue Nose Day" on my desk for some time. I met up with the old guard in Victoria, and you could sense it was going to be a funny one. A few of the old heads were dressed up – one as a priest in sunglasses. For some reason we improvised by grabbling a load of stockings and putting those over our heads to enter the stadium. That went down well, as we were mixed in with the Palace crowd.

I think I know who managed to cause the first disruption, but in truth it was an accident waiting to happen. The police stormed in and started bashing people. There is a famous shot in *The Sun* of the Hitler guy getting truncheoned. A WPc also gave me a right dig in the back.

Seeing that more fun was to be had on the pitch, I jumped down and walked along the gangway between the Blues and Palace fans. It was badly segregated. In fact, the Blues lot took me for a Palace fan and I took a few kicks in the head, as they were standing on a higher tier. As I protested my Brummie-ness, a south Londoner took exception and took a shot as well, before an old Blues face recognized me and bashed him. Realising the pitch would prove more fruitful, I got on and joined the fun.

197

Blues took it to the Palace lot in the side, I remember a Redditch head doing a right windmill job at their front row. It was crazy, all these cartoon characters and casuals rucking all over the place, a complete breakdown.

The "fun" continued on the way home with some lads taking over Toddington Services on the M1 in Bedfordshire. Diners fled as furniture and crockery was hurled about before police arrested forty-three lads on the coach and found the vehicle packed with drink, from beer to champagne.

This was just one of several incidents of mayhem across the country on the final League Saturday of the season, which saw nearly 300 arrests after games:

- Forty Leeds fans were arrested at a pub in Cheshire on their way home from a match at Shrewsbury after brawling with Macclesfield Town fans who had played at Wembley earlier on in the day
- Two hundred supporters went mad in Weston-super-Mare after Bristol City and Sheffield United played each other
- Fifty-seven Chelsea fans were arrested after trouble at Portsmouth
- Eleven Plymouth supporters were detained by police on their way to Bournemouth
- In Tewkesbury, thirty Bristol Rovers lads gatecrashed a wedding, overturned tables and beat up guests.

Incredibly, for Blues the following season would begin with an even bigger bang, on a raucous, no-holds-barred trip to Britain's most popular seaside resort.

Chapter Fourteen

Pleasure Beach

IT WAS A red-hot day in September 1989 when Blues took over the seaside resort of Blackpool and caused twenty-eight hours of havoc. The team was now in the Third Division for the first time in its history and playing the likes of Rotherham, Wigan Athletic and Shrewsbury Town. This, combined with the rave scene, which was in full swing, and the aftermath of Operation Red Card, led to depressingly low gates, and the worrying financial situation at the club contributed to a bleak period for Blues fans. But when Blues played Blackpool in a League match, those lads still going decided to make a weekend of it.

Many arrived on Friday evening, and trouble started when several lads robbed a cashier at the Slots of Fun arcade in the town at 10.30pm. A car was later turned on its roof and twenty people were arrested overnight. It was clear it was going to be a testing weekend for the Blackpool constabulary.

On the Saturday morning, the mob was out early and the pub of choice was the Dutton Arms on the Promenade. Around 300 lads filled the large bar, with some spilling outside to enjoy the sunshine. The drinks were flowing and more lads were arriving as the morning progressed, with some visiting other pubs before joining the masses at the Duttons. Brummie accents seemed to be everywhere.

Inside the pub, someone relieved a games machine of its contents and someone else got into a debate with the bar staff over their bill, which prompted the end of any drinks being served, much to the annoyance of all. The staff disappeared through a door next to a large glass panel which ran along the length of the bar and within minutes several volleys of glasses and bottles went flying through the air towards the bar. This may have caused some to think a fight had started, and for thirty seconds more and more drinks were chucked, with the broken glass covering the floor, while others helped themselves to refreshments.

The pub's doormen were long gone and when the police arrived, on horseback and with dogs, there wasn't much they could do except try to protect themselves when the bottles came in their direction. Mayhem prevailed and the number of Zulus on the rampage was too much for them to control. With everyone spilling outside, the main Promenade was blocked and traffic brought to a standstill for twenty minutes.

Once the marauding lads finally left the premises, shouting and singing in the sun, the police tried escorting them up a road off the Prom, but as they walked more groups appeared from along the side streets while others slipped away. The town was full of Zulus.

Cud drove up on the Saturday, and one of the first things he saw was loads of bare-chested Blues fans hanging around the Duttons in the hot sun with coppers on one side of the road. The next thing he saw was the air fill with bottles. "It was like the Vikings had taken the town," he said. "There were a lot of lads out but also a lot of normal fans, just piss-heads, who were joining in, getting excited and causing mayhem." Several jewellery shops were damaged as lads snatched items from their displays, while others chased off stall-holders, and again the police were powerless to stop it.

By around 2pm, the majority had been herded to Bloomfield Road but tension built inside and outside the ground, as 200 Blues didn't have tickets. The game was delayed as lads inside tried to smash open a wooden gate to let ticketless fans in.

The Blues end was full to the brim and there were more of

them inside the ground than home supporters. Attempts were made by officials to mend the wooden fence and riot squad officers were brought into the area. Shortly after 3pm, the match kicked off, but within minutes some Blues fans had climbed over the fence separating them from the main area of fans into Spion Kop, while others tried for the second time to smash open the wooden gate.

At around 4pm riot police fought back and let their dogs loose in the crowd, resulting in one Blues lad being bitten twice before the dogs were kicked back. Clashes between the visitors and the police became more heated with proper battles going on, but they were unable to calm things down. Police tried to push them back, leading to a full-scale confrontation. Injured Blues fans were being passed over the fence into the Spion Kop. Some Blues fans had also got into Blackpool's end and the police did not know what to do amid the chants of, "Zulus here, Zulus there, Zulus every fuckin' where" for about twenty minutes.

Lads were scaling the fences and going mad and a rather naïve inspector was attacked when he decided he could deal with the situation single-handedly. He was heard to say, "I'll sort this out," before wading in towards the brawling masses. He was brought down within seconds and disappeared from view as a sea of lads closed over him and pulled him further into the fighting. Twenty riot squad officers battled their way in to save him from the Zulus' clutches. He stood up looking dishevelled and dazed, minus his helmet and the pips on his shoulder. "There was nothing I could do," he later told the press, "I just covered my face and head and hoped to be saved." This was the first time the lads had seen riot police on the terraces, and it was believed to be a first anywhere in England.

Blues scored in the ninth minute thanks to Simon Sturridge, then lost their lead because of a mix-up between goalkeeper Martin Thomas and Vince Overson, who headed the ball into his own net. The game was nicely poised at half time after end-to-end football. Blackpool scored again with a penalty eight minutes into the second half, then hit the winner through Ricardo

Gabbiadini. Blues lost 3–2, not that many were really aware of the score or what had taken place on the pitch, such had been the warfare on the terraces.

They finally left the ground around 6pm after an hour of abusing the police and some more coin throwing. Around 700 Zulus, escorted by police, walked down the road, ultimately ending up near Blackpool Pleasure Beach. Shops had been closed and as they passed a McDonalds restaurant they spotted an employee standing outside, watching the crowds, and singled him out as a target. A few lads ripped off his name badge and pulled his hat down over his face. Some holidaymakers stopped to take pictures of the mob of lads parading down the road but were mistaken for "snides" and had their cameras taken.

They then headed towards the Pleasure Beach but found guards had closed it for the first time in its 100-year working history when they saw the huge mob approaching. Forty did manage to get inside but were rounded up and ejected. Police and staff then watched 400 lads lay siege to "Britain's top tourist attraction", with families trapped inside, no doubt wondering what the hell was going on.

The sea-front donkeys also attracted the attention of the rampaging fans and around 100 lads – largely the piss-head contingent – started chasing them down the beach, much to the surprise of more tourists. A photographer for a Birmingham newspaper was attacked as he took shots of Blues singing; five lads apparently turned on him and kicked him to the ground, while up to 1,000 stood behind them, chanting, "Let's have him." He managed to flee but was too frightened to stay in Blackpool and get medical attention, instead driving all the way to Walsall Hospital.

The lads eventually dispersed, drifting off to various pubs to continue drinking. CC and a handful of pals found a working men's club miles from the mayhem and spent all night in there before going for a curry. Other groups went from pub to pub in the town, causing disturbances throughout the evening. More than 200 were arrested as shops were looted on York Street after people spilled out of pubs at closing time, smashed windows and helped themselves. A café window was also put through during the night and several lads were about to charge in, but when the lady owner told them all to "piss off" they did, much to her surprise.

A twenty-one-year-old soccer referee from Erdington was among four Blues fans accused of looting a jewellery shop. They appeared in court the following month and the four pleaded guilty to stealing jewellery from the Gold Mine on Waterloo Road. Magistrates sat all day to hear more than thirty cases for offences including breach of the peace and obstructing officers. Sentences dished out included bans from attending matches for a year and fines totalling more than £8,000.

After their curry, CC and friends had walked across a bridge towards the town centre. Below was a car park where a coach had just arrived; its occupants were getting off and walking towards the stairs of the bridge. For some reason convinced they were cricket fans, one of the Blues started waving at them. But as they emerged from the staircase on to the bridge, CC realised they were big guys and probably not mild-mannered cricketers.

They were pretty much face-to-face in the middle of the bridge when CC asked who they were. "We are Leeds and we take no shite," said one huge guy at the front. With that, CC rammed a can of Coke from the curry house into the guy's face. Unfortunately he didn't budge. He only got angry and the Brummies got the crap beaten out of them. Two of them ran away, leaving three against ten, and one of the trio was hit by a Ford Capri as the brawling spread on to a nearby road.

Meanwhile, Cud was with a few others at a nearby chip shop when he saw some lads from Acocks Green – possibly the pair who scarpered – who said they had been done over by Leeds in a car park. Cud and Co. had been intending to head back to Brum, but now debated whether there was enough of them to seek out the Leeds crew. They got in their cars, and as they drove out of Blackpool they saw the fight still raging and parked up.

Cud ran in and managed to throw one or two big lads down

the steps towards the car park below, but as he was a little the worse for wear he lost his footing and went tumbling down, past another Leeds lad who helped him on his way to the bottom with a kick. At one stage, Psycho, living up to his nickname, held another Leeds lad over the bridge by his legs and threatened to drop him, but was stopped by the others. More Leeds got off the coach and joined in, but Cud's arrival had saved CC and others on the bridge. They believed they would have been killed if help hadn't arrived when it did.

Fighting continued in the car park and Psycho ran towards the coach and chucked a pool ball at the windscreen. The driver had the vehicle's full beam right on him but his throw went straight through the windscreen, making a perfect hole. Cud grabbed him and they legged it up the stairs and away. The coach also pulled away and before long police sirens could be heard in the distance. CC was nursing a broken nose after being whacked by Cud's brother by mistake, and the lad in the hit and run was salvaged, badly bruised and shaken. The two lads that had run off came back and apologised, which was accepted as they weren't full-on fighters and therefore couldn't be expected to stand and row.

As the police got nearer they knew they had to hide. They ran to find some kind of shelter and found another car park nearby where they scrambled underneath the parked cars and waited while the police walked around the area. After the officers left – some two hours later – they went back to their cars, slept on the seats and drove home once daylight had broken. "It was the maddest day for consistent fighting, 10.30am until 1am for me," remembered Cud. "I have had worse battles but we just took over a town for a whole day. Like the Vikings but without the raping."

Blackpool wasn't the only resort to have the dubious pleasure of the Zulus' patronage. After a memorable stag night in Bournemouth for one of the lads in the late Eighties, it became a bit of a ritual for the firm to go "on tour" there. Each summer they'd go back, with one excursion in 1992 standing out. Between sixty and seventy lads went down on coaches and in cars, including Cud, Mickey F, the Kray Twins, Psycho and some Bordesley Green lads. They had arranged to meet up with a couple of lads who used to live in Birmingham, Froggie and Jimmy G. As the firm walked into town, they were passing a fence when they heard someone say, "There are too many niggers around here." They immediately tried to get round the fence and when they did they saw Jimmy G laughing to himself. He had spotted them on their way and lay in wait.

They hit the bars and ended up in a club. As the rave era was in full swing, some of the Bordesley Green lads decided to liven things up by dropping speed in everyone's drinks. Half of the firm out that night weren't involved in the dance scene and couldn't work out why they felt so good and had so much energy. Everyone was getting into it – dancing, sweating, taking their tops off and generally taking over the place. They were highly amused when they found out why.

In the late 1990s, they left their mark on the resort during another stag do for a lad known as Mad Dog. About thirty of them let rip in a club after a doorman gave Norman, one of the Acocks Green lads, some grief on the door. Once inside they hijacked a bar area, helping themselves to drinks, which obviously attracted the attention of security. One lad, nicknamed Big Hands, told the doormen to "fuck off or cop it" and they were left alone.

Word spread that the Zulus had landed and when they came outside at the end of the night people were pointing them out. They saw the club's doormen again and it went off in the street. Psycho put two on their arses and Big Hands was wrestling a bodybuilder. The lads came to his assistance by chucking bottles at the bodybuilder, the Zulu chant went up and the lads managed to push the doormen back into the club before splitting up into the night. One group went one way and the others scattered in different directions to avoid the police. One lad who jumped in a taxi was amused to hear a warning to cab drivers on the in-car radio: "The Zulus have been spotted walking up a road by a park." Over breakfast in their hotel the next morning they caught up with each other, licking their wounds after another crazy night out on tour.

With Cud and Wally not featuring as regularly at St Andrew's during the early 1990s, other areas and lads moved to the forefront. The two were still known as part of the top tier in the firm but they only came out for the biggies. The dance scene had split the firm between those who went raving and those who didn't and went drinking instead. But the drinkers were still enjoying crazy nights out and a visit to a club in Doncaster around the end of the 1989/90 season saw their coachload of lads impersonate the Birmingham team.

Through playing football for local teams, Cud's brothers knew a guy who owned a club in Doncaster. They spoke to him about an end-of-season party and made out the Blues team were looking for a place to celebrate. Needless to say, the owner was keen to entertain them and said he would sort out a VIP area, champagne and personal doormen. So a coach was booked to take a load of Zulus, all suited and booted, to Doncaster a few weeks later.

They decided who would be which player on the way, and when they arrived they telephoned the owner, who greeted them and escorted them through a side entrance into the VIP area. The drinking began and he told them to enjoy themselves and that he would shortly be making an announcement to the other clubbers about their presence. The lads were a little bit hesitant about this but went along with it.

"Ladies and gentlemen we have some special visitors here this evening . . ."

The music stopped, the lights went up, and the Birmingham contingent was led down some stairs while other party-goers clapped in appreciation. They were having their photos taken, signing footballs and autographs and generally lapping it up until one of the revellers from the crowd came over and started talking to them. He shook their hands saying he was a Blues fan and he worked in Doncaster, but he didn't recognise any of them as players. Sensing they'd been rumbled, they told him to shut up before ushering him upstairs and giving him as much free champagne as he wanted. He got smashed and never said a word.

"To this day we have never heard anything more about that little night out," said Cud. "We had a great time and got really drunk. A few were practically unconscious from the champagne."

Cud didn't start going to the football again regularly until the mid-1990s, and was aware how much more clued up the police had become. The Hoolivan – a vehicle packed with high-tech communications equipment and connected to CCTV cameras around grounds to provide an on-site central police command – had been a regular fixture at matches since the late 1980s. CCTV for the police and, of course, mobile phones for the hooligans, had made a big difference to both. Fights were now nearly always arranged beforehand; the days of just turning up and bumping into other lads were almost gone. The cat-and-mouse of who was in what pub, or not knowing who you would run into around a corner, was fading. When lads went into town they'd ring others to report back on who was around and where the police were.

If the police were around, they'd advise against going in, whereas years before that lads would just turn up and see what happened. Although the fighting was just as vicious, more often than not it had to take place somewhere "offside", and on many occasions Blues sent in a decoy firm so the Old Bill would concentrate on them while the real fight could go off elsewhere.

The 1990s also saw the introduction of stewards employed by the clubs to control fans inside grounds rather than the police, while improved technology saw police using hand-held video cameras to gather evidence. The National Football Intelligence Unit was fully operational by 1990, and by 1992 more than 6,000 names and photographs of individuals were held on computer files. West Midlands Police was also one of the first forces to set up a 24-hour "hooligan hotline", inviting people to report incidents and identify offenders.

Just as each decade had ushered in a new era on the terraces, the 1990s were no different. They signalled a negative for the lads, the end of the glory days. The Seventies had been all about mass disorder and a medley of often bizarre clothing styles. In the Eighties, fashion and organisation became crucial. Crowd perimeter fences were removed in the early part of 1990 after the Taylor Report was published, and standing areas were faded out at leading clubs.

Meanwhile, Birmingham City FC was itself in a period of change. The club was relegated to the Third Division in 1989 for the first time in its 114-year history. Players came and went, attendances reached alarming levels and the club faced serious financial troubles. In April 1989, chairman Ken Wheldon sold up, while Dave Mackay took over as manager from Garry Pendrey, a former defender at the club.

Manchester-based clothing entrepreneurs Samesh, Ramesh and Bimal Kumar bought the club for £1.6 million, and gave assurances they were willing to part with a "fair amount of cash" to help turn it around. In January 1991, Lou Macari took over as manager until the end of season, before suddenly leaving to go to Stoke after an alleged fall out with Samesh. The club's finances weren't improving and it was reported to be losing £5,000 a week throughout 1991. In November the following year, Samesh Kumar's business went bankrupt with debts of £6 million, the brothers' eighty-four percent share in the club went up for sale and the club was placed in the hands of the Receiver.

The following March, millionaire publisher David Sullivan bought the club for around £1.5 million. Sullivan, a graduate of the London School of Economics, had launched the *Sunday Sport* newspaper in collaboration with former soft-porn magazine rivals the Gold brothers in 1986. Inspired by the success of *Penthouse* magazine in the US, he first made money by selling pictures of naked women by mail-order before spotting a gap in the UK porn market in the 1970s.

Seeing there was more money to be made in sex shops rather than magazines, he set up a vast retail chain outside of London in 1978. Within four years the company had more than 125 branches – selling magazines, films, sex toys and lingerie – making it the world's largest sex-shop chain. In 1982 he tried to import a consignment of sex dolls into Britain but they were impounded by Customs and Excise. He took them to court and five years later was credited with forcing Britain to lift its stringent import prohibitions, dating from 1876, on certain material deemed indecent or obscene, because it constituted an arbitrary barrier to free trade under the terms of the Treaty of Rome.

Sullivan and the Gold brothers, who own the Ann Summers chain and Knickerbox, had previously owned twenty-eight percent of West Ham United, but after being unable to join the board, sold their shares. Sullivan, whose personal wealth has been estimated at £575 million, wanted to purchase a club, despite the potential for financial instability, and ended up buying Birmingham City. In an interview with the *Independent*, he said, "The one thing money allows you to do is indulge your fantasies, and the more you've got the more you can indulge. The club was virtually bankrupt. There were bailiffs arriving every day, saying pay up or we're taking away the goalposts, the Xerox machine in the office, whatever. I had to stand at the door with a chequebook."

Karren Brady was only twenty-two when she left her role as an account handler at advertising giant Saatchi and Saatchi to join Sullivan's Sport Newspapers. She advanced to director level within twelve months and when Sullivan and the Gold brothers bought Blues they asked her to head up their latest venture. The "first woman in football" is credited with turning the club's fortunes around. In her first year, City recorded a financial trading profit and in 1996 the club made an overall profit for the first time in recent history. The Stock Market beckoned and a year later the club floated at a value of £25 million, making her the youngest managing director of a PLC in the UK, aged twenty-seven.

"When I started I was something of a novelty," she said in an interview. "We had a turnover of about £1m. We were haemorrhaging money. We had an almost all-standing ground and a team that lacked ambition on and off the pitch. We self-generated the income to rebuild St Andrew's into the stadium it is today, 30,000 seats and sixty-four executive boxes." She has also been listed as one of the 100 most powerful women in the world by *Cosmopolitan* magazine.

The arrival of financial stability was followed by the avoidance of relegation, although not until the final game of the season, but the club began to drag itself out of the doldrums, home attendance started to go up and things started to get back on track.

Chapter Fifteen

Fisticuffs

TERRY COOPER TOOK over as Birmingham City manager for the 1991/92 season and led them to promotion, taking them from Division Three straight to Division One after the League was restructured following the birth of the Premiership. Under Cooper's reign, leaflets were issued through the *Evening Mail* newspaper, supported by the club, appealing for fans to maintain good behaviour at matches. "Keep the peace," fans were told, "Do not lose your temper regardless of circumstances," and similar requests. When Barry Fry took over from Cooper, Blues were still in Division One but they made little impact and dropped to the Second Division after the 1993/94 season. The Spion Kop and Tilton Road ends were demolished in April of that year to make way for a £10 million development.

But despite the dark times that prevailed in the late 1980s and early 1990s, there was one success for the club in the form of the Leyland DAF Cup at Wembley in 1991. About 1,000 Blues lads went to see a thrilling 3–2 victory over Tranmere Rovers and stayed overnight in London. The star of the show was undoubtedly John Gayle, who scored two astonishing goals for Blues. Bobby Charlton, no less, told a TV programme that they were the two best goals he had seen scored at Wembley. The first was a thunderous thirty-yard strike and the second an overhead volley from an Ian Clarkson free kick. Thousands turned out in Victoria Square for a civic reception for the team.

Straight after the Wembley game, Aston Villa manager Ron Atkinson, Blues boss Lou Macari and leading directors the Kumars all went into the boardroom to discuss Gayle signing for Villa for £900,000. Sheffield United manager Dave Bassett made it known that he also wanted the player. With offers ringing in his head, Gayle went on holiday to Weymouth with his family to think about it, damaged his achilles tendon while running and was out injured for the next eighteen months. He later told Macari that he couldn't "cross the border" to Villa after doing "something great" for Blues at Wembley. He left the club in 1993 and went on loan to Walsall, before spells at Coventry, Burnley and Stoke.

Cud: We went to a Croydon pub the night before the game and some lads robbed the machines, which paid for their drinks. We were staying at a hotel in Swiss Cottage and the boxer Marvin Hagler was also staying there. He had a few beers with us in the bar but wouldn't let us take any photos. But we saw him again in the hotel the next day and officially christened him a Zulu – the hardest one. He laughed and went along with it.

The game was incredible. We were two up, then it was two-all, then we won three-two. We went on the piss in the Irish area; everyone made their own way and it became a massive piss-up. A thousand Blues were there and in Trafalgar Square we were all in the fountains and having running battles with police. It was like a New Year's party. At midnight, everyone sang "Keep Right on to the End of the Road", the song that has been sung at Blues matches since the 1950s. It was a great scene, the best ever.

But the following season the club was nearly put up for sale after a game against Stoke City at St Andrew's. With Blues 1–0 up, the referee allowed a challenge by Stoke's Wayne Biggins on goalkeeper Alan Miller which led to them equalizing, then disallowed a goal by Blues' Alan O'Neil seconds later. "Blues got on to the pitch from all sides and started beckoning Stoke to come on too, but they didn't, so lads started climbing the fences to get to them but were punched when they got to the top and just couldn't get over," said Cud. "Stoke never came on."

The players were taken off by referee Roger Wiseman, who had earlier been hit by a supporter, and came back out to play the remaining few seconds without any fans inside the ground. Then-chairman Samesh Kumar was reported as saying "it flashed through my mind to sell the club" in the heat of the riot, but he decided to carry on to "make it clear that there is no way the hooligans are going to beat us". He blamed the referee for the violence that erupted on the pitch and the club was charged with misconduct for his comments, fined £50,000 and ordered to play two matches behind closed doors – though the sentence was suspended.

Manager Terry Cooper was also fuming and likened the tackle on Miller to "something out of a rugby match". But, he said, he despaired over the actions of Blues supporters and when he saw a six-year-old boy crying in the tunnel he told him, "Don't ever come here again, stay home and watch your cartoons." One supporter even squared up to Cooper near the dugouts and told him to shut up and sort the team out or he would "belt him".

Wally: I've always thought of Stoke as an overrated firm, don't think much of the so-called Naughty Forty and I'm dubious about some of the things they reckon they've got up to at Villa Park over the years. My mind was made up when I read their version of the riot at St Andrew's in February 1992. They reckon twenty Stoke came on to the pitch from the main stand. Bullshit. Not one Stoke came on to the pitch. I can only presume that as this happened in 1992 and the rave scene was going strong that the author was on a bad trip.

Admittedly they did a good job in making sure that Blues didn't get into their end, but beat us back? I don't think so. They were on top of the fence and we had to climb up six feet and the level of the terrace from their side gave them the advantage. They were safe throwing punches from behind the fence. All they had to do was jump over and join the fun but they didn't.

There was one year in the mid Eighties when Stoke had their chance to have it with us once and for all, but when it came to it they had it on their toes. Everything had been arranged with a lad from Stoke called Acko. He used to have it with their firm but he was a Blues fan and came to our games as well. He was good friends with one of our lot, Leroy, who was from Bordesley Green, and was seeing a girl up in Stoke at the time. Stoke knew we were coming and that Acko would be bringing us straight to them. When it came to it and we turned up in their town, they came out of their first pub, threw their bottles and were off. Another firm came from another pub behind us and it was the same thing; they tried to ambush us but failed, and once they ran out of glasses and bottles they were off too.

After this, some of the Stoke lads gave Acko grief because they had been shown up big time by a small firm of us on their own manor. All Acko did was bring us to them, which is what they wanted, but they just couldn't take the heat that day. A few of the local black lads in the town came and congratulated us, as they used to get a lot of grief off the Stoke lot and they were glad we taught them a lesson.

———————

Although Blues may have felt they had Stoke's number, it was a different story when they travelled to deepest South Wales to play Swansea, and a salutary lesson that lads from rough towns in the lower divisions can spring a shock on even the biggest hooligan mobs.

JJ: It was a Third Division game in the early 1990s. Looking back, it was pretty daft the way Blues dismissed the trip, as any journey to Wales was likely to be lively. I was going through a "great outdoors" phase and stuck the tent in the car to sample the "land that time forgot" of the Gower Peninsula wilderness after the match. I took the missus as well, as she had become something of an adopted Blues fan. The same formula had worked at Barnsley, followed by a sojourn into the Peak District.

Unfortunately, it looked like a dodgy decision when I ran into Glenroy, who explained he'd been fighting all the way up the road to the ground. Even in the ground they were going crazy. The police watched as some loon ran on the pitch to give us the big "Come on!" This *was* the land that time forgot. It was like a nightmare version of the 1970s, only we didn't have 1,000 blokes in flares and platform shoes with us, just a motley bunch of whoever could be bothered to make the drive. After the match was also crazy; they were just picking people off. I remember telling the missus to keep walking while it all kicked off around us. It was a wake-up call.

The Gower Peninsula was as spectacular as they had said, by the way.

A trip up to Sheffield in the mid-Nineties saw a small number of Blues engage in a heated battle outside a pub, with the Zulus once again ready to take on a much larger group of rivals. The police escorted the majority of Blues fans in one direction but about twenty, including Cud, sloped off and ended up walking through a housing estate. They came out by a pub where Sheffield United were drinking and were soon spotted. Though low on numbers, they weren't going to run.

Moments later, Sheffield poured out of the pub with pool cues, chairs and other weapons. The shout to "stand" went up and the Zulus charged into them, pushing them back into the pub doorway as best they could. Sheffield were throwing things and Blues retaliated with whatever they could get their hands on, even chucking a few wing mirrors plucked from nearby cars.

Suddenly they heard "Get the midget!" aimed at one of the Zulus. He was fighting with one of Sheffield's lads and because of his small stature managed to throw an uppercut into his opponent's testicles, causing him to slump to the floor. But when around 100 more Sheffield arrived behind Blues, they decided to split up and get out of there. "Sheffield have beaten up girls before now, but they were bugged that day because they couldn't finish us off," remarked Cud.

The last game of the 1993/94 season, against Tranmere Rovers, was crucial. With relegation looming, loads of lads went to the seaside town of Southport the night before. It was another riotous affair, with around 100 hooligans rampaging through the town centre and a three-hour street brawl with police, resulting in forty-seven arrests.

JJ: Most of the lads went to Southport and had a right tear-up, but for some reason a mixed bag headed for the old favourite, Blackpool. I ended up away from my regular group and with the Kings Norton and Warwick lot, less than a dozen of us. One of our number ran into a Stoke lad he knew and had a chat with him. He proudly explained they had fifty in town for a stag do but, of course, was not seeking any trouble with us. The words rat and odour came to mind.

We went to a club later that night. There'd been some kind of needle inside with bouncers or locals, so everyone decided to go out together, which proved to be very fortunate. We'd barely got out of the door when the roar went up, "C'mon you Brummies," and more than forty Stoke who had been waiting for us ran across the road. There wasn't much time to assess the situation and I think they were shocked that, rather than doing a runner, we flew into them, banging their front line. We had three arrested in the first skirmish, so we were already down twenty-five per cent in a minute. Police reports in court later said the smaller contingent were more aggressive than the larger group.

Stoke dispersed, circled round the block, and came from the

top of the road, bobbing up and down as mobs have a habit of doing. It didn't look too good to be honest, and I barely knew the guys I was with at that time. What was odd was the way Stoke attacked, almost in a flying V formation, with one lad at the front who really wanted it, two behind him, four behind them, eight behind them, and so on. As it turned out, we had some serious firepower and well-organised lads. The leader of this group had us stand behind a metal rail and wait for them to come at us again before launching in. These were bloody good tactics from a cool head. Anyway, we kept backing them off until the law finally took a bit of control.

It was funny at the end as we were by then down to about six, as another got arrested and another chased as he got caught on the wrong side of the melee. Frankly it would have been no contest if they'd had the bottle to do it properly in the first place, but all this noise, bobbing up and down and the flying wedge meant they must have been pretty embarrassed when they realized how so few had given them such grief.

Blues were relegated to Division Two the next day, despite their 2–1 win, while West Bromwich Albion avoided the drop thanks to a 1–0 victory over Portsmouth. Yet Barry Fry was cheered by fans who got on the Prenton Park pitch after the match, and they also sang in tribute to their team. It was the club's third win in four away matches but their dreadful run between November and March was the problem – two wins from twenty-two games. They were relegated on the number of goals scored.

In January 1994, after City had lost to non-league Kidderminster Harriers at St Andrew's, Wally vented his anger at the players from behind the dug-out in K Paddock as they made their way off the pitch into the tunnel. One player, Ted McMinn, also obviously vexed at his team's 2–1 defeat, ripped off his shirt and shouted, "C'mon then," as he jumped up and down, egging Wally on before disappearing down the tunnel.

The next game Wally went to, a few weeks later, was against Sunderland and he and the lads sat in the same area as before. Before kick-off some of the lads went to get some food and came back with pies. As the players came out on to the pitch to warm up, one of the lads positioned himself by the tunnel and shouted, "Oi, Ted!" as McMinn walked out.

When he looked up, a pie flew through the air and hit him straight in the face. The lad made a quick exit, then paid into the Railway End and stood chatting to a steward who was watching the commotion unfold. The police came round, quizzing various people, including the lad, but the steward, without any prompting, said it couldn't have been him because he had been talking to him moments earlier.

A few weeks later, the lads had to laugh when they read in the newspapers, "Ted McMinn: I fear for my life." It emerged the player had been getting abuse from other fans, and this, coupled with the pie incident, caused him to feel threatened and concerned about his safety at the club. He believed he was being targeted and went on loan to Burnley the following month, before becoming a permanent fixture there in March 1994.

The 1994/95 season was better for Blues, who gained promotion to Division One after beating Huddersfield in the last game of the season, and won the Auto Windscreens Shield against Carlisle United at Wembley. Although the final was the club's fifth competitive fixture in twelve days, a sell-out crowd of more than 76,000 watched them win late on in sudden-death extra-time, thanks to a header from Paul Tait. The Mexican waves surging round the stadium had a huge effect on two Blues lads, CC and Joey, who had necked a couple of Ecstasy pills before kick-off. They were positively rushing throughout the game and enjoying every minute of it.

The successful Birmingham boxer Robert McCracken was a big Blues fan. He wore the club badge on his shorts and is included in the "Famous Fans" section of the club's website, along with Mike Skinner of The Streets, UB40 band members and comedian Jasper Carrott. His family were very much part of the Blues scene in Kings Heath, where the Cross Guns pub was something of a City HQ in the late 1980s.

The Zulus had a Sunday league team, which is still going although many main lads have since retired, and Robert was on the team. He even played about a week before a title fight, much to the amazement of the lads. He lost the fight. As the team's ground was in Perry Bar, which is Villa territory, trouble wasn't far away when they went for drinks after games. But they did well, winning the title and the odd cup when they were in the South Birmingham League, with the help of Cud, Brains and Wally, to name but a few. Ex-Blues players Paul Tait and Liam Daish were even seen on the touchline from time to time.

When they beat a local rival from Lyndon 9–1, they were very surprised to see a former lad from the firm in the opposition. Martin used to be well up for a bit of fighting in the 1990s but he disappeared from the scene. He wasn't seen again until Wally saw him arresting one of his mates in the Lea Village area of Birmingham – he had swapped sides and become a copper for West Midlands Police. Needless to say, he got a lot of grief for that and had to leave the force at one stage because the windows at his home had been put through.

When Robert McCracken was boxing, he pulled a big Blues following and if the opponent also had a following the consequences were inevitable. When he fought Peter Till to win the British title at Watford Town Hall in February 1994, it was chaos. Around 800 lads went to watch and fought with the venue's security amid tear gas. In the middle of it all, some local man stood up and said to one lad, Jamie Q, "Do you know who I am?" Jamie said he didn't care and, bang, put the guy down. A few days later was the funeral of East End gangster Charlie Kray, and Jamie saw that the man he had punched was one of the pallbearers.

That night added to the build-up for McCracken's next fight, the British light-middleweight title at Birmingham's National Exhibition Centre against Steve Foster aka "The Viking", from Salford, Manchester, in September 1994. Foster also had a big and rowdy following, and the contest was portrayed in some quarters as the Zulus v. the Vikings, although Nigel Benn was the main event defending his WBC super-middleweight title against Paraguayan Juan Carlos Gimenez.

On the day of the fight, a few Zulus had been down at Oxford United to see Blues draw 1–1. By the time they arrived at the NEC, the atmosphere was already edgy. There were three rows with a heavy mob from Salford that night – with one shown on television across the world – and there was a well known face in among them, a lad called Paul Massey, said to run the gangs in that part of the UK.

The first row started around seven o'clock by one of the booth bars behind the seating. The Salford lot, not their main group, were apparently singing "Manchester" or having a go at Robert, so Blues chased them into the main bar. They were jumping over plastic chairs to get away and ran out of the fire exit.

That was it for a while, but more continued to arrive and they were sore about the first humiliation. The singing restarted and it went off again. The second fight was bigger and this time the Zulus backed Salford into the arena itself. To them, it was an amusing sight as they were running over the seats in the arena to get away while some pro boxer was still going at it in the ring. The floor was soon covered with booze and wheelie bins were thrown around. One bin came from behind JJ, took him clean off his feet and sent him skidding headlong astride the bin into the Salford lot. The bars were closed shortly after this, or at least everyone decided to take their seats to watch the main event – which was supposed to be the Nigel Benn fight. Significantly, no police had yet arrived inside the arena – the only security was the stewards.

Rows of plastic chairs had been laid out on the floor of the hall around the ring, with the Salford crowd and the Zulus on either side, facing each other, and the bar area at the back. Salford/Manchester were now baying for retribution, and had massed up a bit more. The Zulus were mostly in permanent seating, with the temporary rows of seats, fastened together with metal callipers, separating them from their rivals.

The third fight was not long in coming, and it was brutal. One Zulu started having a row with a Salford lad down in the temporary seating and quickly it became a free-for-all. The fight spread in the main floor and then mobs from either side poured down like ants to join the fray, while plastic chairs flew through the air. Though Salford were outnumbered – there were only about twenty of them at the hottest point of the fight – they were clearly game as anything, and the fighting went back and forth across the floor. The Benn fight was stopped momentarily and Robert McCracken's brother, Adam, appealed for an end to the fighting over a microphone. He even asked one Zulu by name to put down a chair.

Wally was in one of the upper tiers watching events unfold. He could see Salford were backing Blues up and even starting to get the upper hand, so he decided to join in. The fact that it was all being broadcast on television did deter some from getting involved, but not many. The main danger came not from the flying chairs, which were relatively light, but from the fasteners, which soon came loose and were near-lethal. One Birmingham lad sustained a terrible eye injury in the carnage.

JJ: It was like Agincourt. All these metal bars flying through the air, taking people out. One lad lost an eye and the First Aid looked like a field hospital in Vietnam. You just wouldn't get injuries like that normally. Added to this was the fact that there was no policing, so the fight took its course. Everyone has a lot of respect for the Salford lot, they put up a hell of a battle, but in the end we made it three-nil, largely with the weight of numbers that swarmed over them. I had calls from friends in Australia who saw it on television. I don't think anyone could believe what they saw.

McCracken beat Steve Foster to gain the British light-middle-weight title, but the fighting outside the boxing ring captured the headlines instead and, unfortunately for him, did his career no favours. ITV said afterwards they would not show another of his contests, while promoter Frank Warren said McCracken would not feature on a bill of his again, adding that he feared other promoters would also be reluctant to use him. He didn't box again for a while and then lost his next two matches, one being a shot at the world title, although he only lost on points.

The NEC launched an inquiry and police admitted they were "not prepared for the scale or intensity of the crowd violence". To add to the mayhem, there were calls for Jeremy Hanley, the Tory Party chairman at the time, to resign after he described the violence as just "exuberance" on breakfast television the following morning. He later regretted making the remark but refused to stand down amid accusations he "heaped embarrassment" on the Conservatives' law and order campaign.

Fifty police were eventually deployed but only an hour after the fighting had stopped. Only one man was arrested on the night, and that for an unconnected offence, and eight people were injured, but police managed to make further arrests in both Birmingham and Manchester after the event, an action which actually helped towards forming links between the two areas.

The trials were in Birmingham and when the accused made their various appearances they and their friends would meet up for drinks before and after, with the Zulus invited up to Salford for a few beers. Some pleaded guilty to the violence and received prison sentences of between three and six months. Four Zulus and two Salford lads pleaded not guilty and were cleared.

In 1996, Barry Fry departed St Andrew's after a chaotic reign and former playing hero Trevor Francis took the helm, boosting hopes that the club would at last achieve the success of which it was capable. In the mid-1990s around fifty lads travelled to Barnsley by train, arrived about midday and settled in a boozer near the station where they met others who had driven up, bringing numbers up to about 100. It wasn't long before the police located them and locked them inside, later escorting them to the ground. Blues won 1–0 and the lads invaded the pitch when the winning goal went in.

Afterwards they managed to mingle in amongst the crowds and slipped away up the road back towards the station. They walked along a main road and went under a flyover but soon became aware of activity behind them. It was a firm of Barnsley trying to catch them up, looking for some action. They carried on walking and pulled together in a tighter pack as Barnsley got closer. Then, when they thought they were close enough, the Zulus turned and charged. They went right into them and spread them out across the road, causing Barnsley to buckle and back off. The lads didn't let up and continued hitting them back until the police turned up. Skirmishes continued all the way to the station.

As several Blues had been arrested, the rest decided to wait for them in Sheffield. They were met by a large number of police who began shepherding them to a platform for the next train south. Morris, one of the main guys from Kings Norton, knew the train wouldn't be for another forty minutes, so he slipped away for a pint on the concourse.

There he was fronted by three Sheffield United lads. He told them the score but promised he would do what he could to get a team away from the "plod" to entertain them. He made a few calls and went outside the station, as they had told him they were in a pub down a side street nearby. After a few minutes, fifteen Blues had assembled outside and were waiting for more, when suddenly forty United came out of the side street.

Assuming control, Morris headed towards them, waving frantically and yelling that they should wait in case they brought it on top with the police. But United, sensing an easy victory, weren't going to wait and charged into them.

The fifteen stood their ground and advanced, with individual fights breaking out across the front line.

The lads in the station, just a few hundred yards away, must have heard the roar because they started disappearing over the track and walls, any way possible to escape the police and help their friends. Officers were soon on the scene to see fighting all over the place – small groups of Blues and United were rowing up side streets, on the nearby traffic island and outside the station entrance. By the time they got to grips with the situation, the next train south had been and gone, so Blues plotted up in the rail bar to wait for the next one.

Hungry for more, another United lad came in and suggested setting up another meet. But while he chatted to them, one of the Zulus, nicknamed "the Arsonist" [see page 136], hovered behind him and set fire to his coat. While not particularly fair, it was very funny. When the lad realised he was on fire he darted outside with plumes of smoke billowing behind him.

A trip to Barnsley also threw up an amusing incident involving Cud, who in the early 1990s was living in a flat rented from former TV chef Rusty Lee. Blues were away at Barnsley and Psycho and Big C came round early on the Saturday morning to collect him in a hire car. His girlfriend also lived there but had gone out and taken the keys, leaving Cud locked in, as the front door needed to be unlocked from the inside. After a brief discussion through the letterbox, the lads tried to break it open with drop kicks. A police car drove past and stopped to see what was going on. Cud shouted to the officers through the letterbox that he was locked in and was happy for them to kick the door off, so the police stood and watched. Eventually the lads forced it open and Cud wedged it shut before jumping in the car and heading off to the match, much to the amazement of the police.

When Blues played Hull at Boothferry Park in the same period, it was no surprise to see few turn out, but dismissing the opposition was sometimes unwise, as smaller clubs relished the chance to take on big names and could turn out in huge numbers, eager to prove their worth. Fifteen lads drove up and parked in a car park near the ground around lunchtime. The Zulus knew Hull would be in their Silver Cod pub near the ground, but as they made their way along the road, the Birmingham City players' coach passed by minus its back window. One of the players saw the group and shouted at them that a firm of Hull were up the road and had attacked the bus. This left the Zulus with no choice; they had to have a pop now, regardless of numbers.

They started to walk to where they thought they'd find Hull, but some got cold feet or "Millwall Flu" as it is sometimes known, reducing numbers to about ten, but all good lads. As they went under a bridge they saw sixty Hull coming across an island. The Zulus had a quick council of war to discuss tactics and decided to have a go. They waited until Hull were twenty yards away and then ran into them just as they started their charge. Hull stepped into the road, giving it large, and the Zulus ran forward. Morris scuffled with one lad and was put on the floor as more Hull waded in, but he scrambled back up, danced back about ten feet and regrouped with the others.

There then followed a game of hit and run, with Zulus darting forward, landing a few punches and kicks, then backing off. Inevitably the police soon appeared and calmed things down. Hull had scored a minor victory but didn't "smash the Zulus everywhere", as they later claimed.

When the Zulus got to the ground, about fifty more Blues lads were waiting and were told what had happened. Inside the ground, the Zulus sat in the seats and at half-time went to the buffet bar. As they stood around, one of the lads tried the door that led to the home seats. Much to everyone's enjoyment, it opened, so thirty of them piled through to give the natives a surprise. A few Hull were spotted further down the walkway and they flew into them and battered them without warning. Hull were chased down to the far end of the stand before the police intervened. The "disgusting behaviour" of the Zulus merited a mention on BRMB radio – a local station in Birmingham covering the game – because the match commentator was having a half time cup of tea when they kicked it off.

Chapter Sixteen

Moseley Road

BLUES PLAYING NOTTINGHAM Forest is a fixture both firms relish. Run-ins were fairly frequent, but during the 1997/98 season got especially heavy, with Forest trying to win the "Midlands crown".

A decade previously, in November 1988, Forest had come to St Andrew's for an FA Cup tie and won 1–0. A huge firm pulled into New Street Station on the train, and as they made their way up the Coventry Road, minor scuffles broke out, with more Forest arriving in vans. The fighting became intense and one Blues lad had a cider bottle bounced off his head. One of their main faces then was the late Paul Scarrott, the self-proclaimed "general of soccer yobs", who was a favourite of the national tabloids. Despite a long-standing feud between the two firms, some Zulus spent an entertaining few days with him in Paris when England played France in a friendly in the mid-1980s.

JJ, who joined the Zulus in 1982 at a pre-season friendly at Leamington Spa, recalls driving home from work when England were playing in Dusseldorf in the European Championship and listening to a BBC radio interview with a hooligan.

"Notting-um Forest are mag-ic," intoned the voice.

"I'm with Paul Scarrott who has 'Forest' tattooed on his lip," said the interviewer. "Why are you here?"

"Smash it up mate, smash it up."

"Are you serious?" The tone was one of disbelief.

"Yes mate. These Germans, they're dumkopfs. Smash it up."
That was Scarrott all over.

On the pitch, Blues got off to a bad start in the 1997/98
season, while Forest had been relegated to the Second Division
the previous season, bringing with them a reputation of being
"the boys" off the pitch. Some Zulus knew a few Forest lads
through the England scene and quite a bit of banter had been
going on during the summer building up to the match. About
thirty Zulus met in a pub in Beeston, just outside Nottingham, at
opening time on the Saturday morning. They had a pint and
began ringing around to see who else was about.

At midday they drove into Nottingham and plotted up in a
pub just off the ring road. It was far enough out of the centre of
town to dodge the attention of any police but near enough to
get into the main shopping area within a few minutes. About
100 lads gathered there and another 100 were drinking in a
pub by the train station. They had been spotted by the police,
who decided the best way to keep tabs on them was to lock
them in, but the lads had other ideas. A good number of them
ventured down into the cellar, escaped up the barrel-chute and
joined the rest of the lads at the other pub, leaving officers
guarding an empty boozer. When everyone was together they
had big numbers and the right people to do what they had
come for.

A couple of Forest's spotters clocked them as they began
walking into town and within minutes a small firm of Forest
appeared and fronted them, but quickly had it on their toes
when the Zulus went for them. That was enough to attract the
further attention of the police, who rounded nearly everyone
up.

Morris and a couple of others managed to slip away unnoticed
and went back to the pub. Eventually about forty managed to re-
group there and, deciding the city centre was now a no-no, they
went straight to the City Ground. As they walked down the road
they could see the floodlights in the distance. They crossed a

227

school playing field and climbed a fence, which put them on a path leading to a subway and shopping precinct.

As they got closer to the subway, they saw a load of lads hovering outside a pub on the other side of the road. They went under the subway and grouped up, knowing the Forest lads had spotted them and would no doubt be there to greet them when they emerged. As they began the ascent out of the subway the Zulus kept their heads and calmly walked into a hail of bricks and bottles from about 100 Forest lads, a move that one Zulu said was "one of the coolest things I've seen at football". They didn't roar or charge, just kept walking forward until they were within about ten yards of the Forest front line, then they let loose. The roar went up and they piled into them, taking on their line for about thirty seconds before it broke and Forest fled. The Zulus chased them over the road and back into the pub where the fighting continued in the doorway.

More Forest arrived in the side streets and joined in for a few minutes before the police arrived to restore order. When things had calmed down and the police sorted out an escort for Blues, Forest made a show of trying to attack them, but the "result" for the day was never in doubt. Blues had come to their manor and "taken the piss", and Forest knew it.

The gauntlet had been laid down for the return fixture at St Andrew's later on in the season. Some Zulus chatted to a few Forest after the game and they admitted they'd been done, though they said "fair play". They were clearly vexed, which was probably why so many of them went to St Andrew's later in the season.

Before that game, the phone lines between Blues and Forest were working overtime and it was widely known they were coming firm-handed, looking for revenge. On the day of the match the lads arranged for a bar in town to open up early so they could be ready for what lay ahead before the police had even got out of bed. A couple of Zulus then drove up to Nottingham to have a scout around and see what Forest were planning. It wasn't long before they found a group having breakfast in a café. They were sure they'd found Forest when more cars and a minivan arrived.

By nine o'clock, Blues had more than 100 lads together and all they had to do was wait. They got the call confirming Forest were on the move and that the two lads were in hot pursuit. While the Zulus waited to hear where they were meeting in Birmingham, more and more lads joined them in the boozer, bringing numbers up to about 300. Meanwhile, the two lads following Forest kept up all the way until they reached an island near St Andrew's, where they lost them in traffic on the far side of the ground. It could only mean one thing: Forest were not planning on going into town. They were going to meet over in Small Heath, "offside".

The 300 Zulus hit the road determined to find them. Ten lads who got to the area first went from pub to pub trying to locate them and eventually found them in the Marlborough, down a side street near to Small Heath train station. They flew into them straight away.

Cud and a couple of mates, Psycho and Mark, were playing football when they heard Forest had landed, so they made their way to the pub along with a few others. They didn't think there would be many but soon realised there were about 150. This was Mark's first major encounter with away fans and he was pretty scared. He knew he couldn't run but being with game lads like Cud, who could more than handle themselves, he knew he was in safe hands – although he was about to have a serious fighting experience.

As others arrived, they parked their cars and walked over the road to the pub, where they saw one Blues' lad, Bod, already attacking the pub door. Some Forest came out of the front door and started to chuck bricks and bottles from a bit of wasteland nearby. They were shouting, "Forest, Forest," and some ran down the road. More and more Zulus landed, bringing numbers up to twenty-five, and it well and truly went off. The Zulus did what they could to hold the road, with toe-to-toe battles spread over a wide area. People were going down and getting hurt.

All the time, the number of Zulus was growing, and by the time there were about fifty they had lost only twenty metres of road. Then the roar went up and every man flew into Forest's front line, adrenalin pumping, overtaking the fear. This proved to be too much for Forest and they buckled. With more Zulus arriving and joining in, Forest lost it. They fled in all directions, running through fences and over walls to escape as they realised they were getting spanked.

While the fighting was going on some Zulus had been busy setting about the Nottingham vans and cars, trashing them while some Forest stood up the road too scared to come down and kick it off again. After the main bulk of them split up, Cud charged at a splinter group, who didn't know what to do. A few Zulus were arrested and some Forest lads made statements to the police but most later retracted them. However, one did give evidence in court, which helped put three Blues away. That lad broke the unwritten rule – football lads are football lads and you don't grass, no matter what.

It was clear it had been a bad day for Forest. They had been well and truly turned over. They were attacked again coming out of the ground, with some Zulus waiting by their vans and cars to have another pop at them. They had seen a handful of lads stand against them at the start of the day and they lost it and never recovered.

———

After a Saturday night out in Whitley Bay, about 100 bleary-eyed Zulus met on a car park before driving south to the Stadium of Light for a match against Sunderland in the 1998/99 season. They parked a couple of miles from the ground and made their way there without encountering any local lads until they arrived. As there was only a handful of "Mackems", they stopped for a chat.

The locals told them to head up a road and over a bridge after the game, where they'd be waiting. The game ended and they started to walk away from the ground in search of their quarry. They were challenged by a few Sunderland leaving the car park outside the ground and some decided to stay and sort them out despite the majority wanting to stick together for the meet.

By the time the Zulus had chased the locals through the car park, the remaining sixty had arrived at the bridge. They could see a pub in the distance with lads outside and assumed that was the meeting place. The Blues mingled with normal supporters but some of their lads were also in amongst the crowds and they broke forward towards the pub.

Within seconds it emptied and there must have been another pub around the corner because their numbers filled the entire street and charged forward. The Zulus waded in as one and took out their frontline in seconds. Sunderland were charged back up the road, with their lads becoming easy pickings as they split up and scattered in the fracas. The police were not impressed and, determined to break it up, used their truncheons and dogs on anyone who came near them. One lad was grabbed by two officers and a third let his dog savage him. He fought back, sparked the dog handler, and was arrested. He would have seen prison time had it not been for some Sunderland lads who testified on his behalf when he claimed self defence.

Despite the relatively easy victory, many had memories of much tougher times in the North-east. "We respect Sunderland, although we have never really had any full-on battles with them," said Cud. "I remember we played them in a cup game in the Eighties and their ground was a moody place to go back then. We went up on two coaches and it was the first time a proper firm of us had gone there. We got dropped off on the wrong side of the ground and walked round the whole ground twice without any bother from Sunderland or the police, so we thought fair enough and went in. Blues were losing one-nil with two minutes to go, then we scored two goals and won the match. Some of our lads ran onto the pitch after we scored and got arrested. But, like I say, we respect them as a firm."

Not many football lads can say West Midlands Police have

come to their aid during a battle. Their reputation is as a fierce, no-nonsense force, so when one Kings Norton lad was getting a thumping from some Pompey lads, he was amazed to see that it wasn't a mate who rescued him but a Brummie copper.

Pompey's 6.57 Crew are a firm that Blues have a lot of history with. The 1980s saw the two groups take part in several memorable clashes [see Chapter 10] and the Zulus have much respect for them. For one match, around eighty Zulus hopped on a train and headed south. Pompey spotters were out in force when the lads arrived about midday, but were chased away as the Zulus walked through the town looking for a pub in which to settle down and wait. Nothing happened so they headed for Fratton Park at about two o'clock. They walked right around the ground in the hope of finding Pompey's lads but none were seen so they went in to watch the match.

As they were leaving after the game about ten Pompey fronted them up. They were chased down a road but kept stopping and turning around to call the Zulus on. The Zulus kept up the pursuit and engaged in some running battles. One Pompey lad had a golfing umbrella which attracted the attention of Morris, who got a bit too cocky, ran ahead of the rest of the Zulus and was whacked by several Pompey. He was cut off from the others as they circled him and the punches came raining down. But moments later he was aware that someone had come to his aid, was fending them off and causing Pompey to back off. He turned around to thank him but got a huge shock to see a policeman smiling smugly, with his truncheon drawn. Instead of nicking Morris, he winked and sent him on his way.

About twenty Zulus continued to follow Pompey until they reached a pub full of them, which signalled it was time for them to disappear. They walked away but after about 100 yards of checking their backs they thought, *fuck it*, turned around and spread out across the road. Pompey swarmed out of the pub but stopped short of running into them. Outnumbered but up for it, the Zulus waded in until the police again broke it up. If there had been more Zulus it would have been a proper victory but they were more than happy that twenty of them held their own against 100-plus Pompey lads.

Leicester's Baby Squad remained rivals into the 1990s and the two teams played each other at Filbert Street in the third round of the FA Cup in 1999. Around 150 Zulus met at midday in Nuneaton but the police were on to them pretty much straight away. Most got the train to Leicester but thirty drove to a pub they knew on the Narborough Road, where they waited about an hour then walked the mile or so to the ground.

Apart from chasing a few Leicester lads by the ground, it was uneventful before the match, and afterwards they were able to mingle amongst the crowds and walk straight out. They headed up a side street where they bumped into about twenty locals who were picking off small groups of Blues walking towards their cars. Twenty Blues flew straight into them and within a few minutes they were on their toes, with Blues in hot pursuit.

They chased them down a road and around a corner and straight into another Leicester firm numbering about sixty. Blues were spread out across the length of the road, with several finishing off the first lot they had chased. They now backed off around the corner and re-grouped. They were joined by others who had seen the fighting and numbered about forty. Leicester came charging down the road and it went off everywhere. No one backed down until the truncheon-wielding police turned up and prompted some to scatter.

Some Blues slid off up a side road on to a main road. They walked on to the junction where Leicester had come from and it went off again with Leicester on the run from the police. A series of hit-and-run fights lasted a few minutes until the police finally regained control and escorted Blues to the train station.

Ten other Zulus had taken a different route from the ground and ended up on the Narborough Road. As they passed a pub it emptied and about sixty blokes charged them. Psycho from Acocks Green held the firm together, and after the initial melee, some of the lads noticed a hardware store over the road and promptly crossed the street and emptied the front display of its contents. Spades, brooms, mops and the odd lump hammer were swiped and used on Leicester as they were chased up the road until the Old Bill arrived and Blues slipped off into the night, knowing they had done something special.

Confirmation of their exploits came later when one of them spoke to a Leicester lad on the phone, who said they were "erecting crosses on the Narborough Road for the fallen".

Glenroy: I fell asleep during most of the away game at Crystal Palace in 1999 after having a few drinks on the train down, then caught another train with the guys back to London Victoria. There we met a Chelsea fan who bravely said if we wanted it we were to do him there and then, but we didn't. He then said for us to go to the pub down the road called the Elusive Camel, so twenty-five of us went and the rest of our firm went to the Flying Scotsman for the strippers.

We were gagging for a row and we got it big time. As soon as I got served, the windows started breaking as the pub was attacked by 150 Chelsea. We threw chairs, tables, tills, spirit bottles and glass ashtrays in reply. Saten, Russell and a few guys even went out on the street and had it with them but there were too many. Saten got stabbed but didn't even notice. What a total nutter! But he is a pleasure to travel with.

By the time the police arrived we managed to hold the doors but the pub was trashed and thousands of pounds' worth of damage had been caused. I was arrested with a mate for violent disorder and held in Brixton Prison for a week, then convicted and sentenced to fifteen months. I served most of it in Wandsworth before Richard Burden, MP, kicked up a storm and they moved me to Stafford Prison, as I hadn't seen my kids for four months.

Overall, I wouldn't change a thing. I love it and I have been everywhere. I have also followed England and still do. I went to the Ireland game [in Dublin, halted by England fans throwing missiles] and it lasted twenty minutes before it kicked off. We took 200 to Scotland for England and rowed all day and night but I will finish after the World Cup in Germany in 2006.

———————————

Although Blues and Wolves had been rowing with each other since the 1970s, things came to a head with the now-infamous Moseley Road skirmish in April 2000. The days of the infamous Subway Army were long gone, and the Wolves firm was now fronted up by a well-known lad called Gilly Shaw. Several battles were fought between the two near-neighbours in the 1990s, then their firms didn't meet for a few years. However, Blues were ready, willing and able to take them on when the two teams next played each other. Wolves let it be known they were coming to Birmingham in numbers and Blues took it seriously, as there was a strong desire amongst the firm to put them in their place.

A massive mob assembled at the White Lion pub on the Bristol Road, as that was where Wolves were supposed to be heading. It was a "Who's Who" of Blues terrace culture going back to the late 1970s, with the kind of turnout normally only reserved for "payback" matches with Millwall and the like. Everyone was out, resulting in a firm of more than 300 eagerly awaiting news of their whereabouts.

A couple of lads had gone over to Wolverhampton earlier in the morning to try to pick them up there and follow them over to Birmingham, a tactic Blues had employed before, but the scouts didn't find them. However, the phones between the two firms were buzzing all morning: "We're coming, we'll tell you where soon . . ." This went on for hours, so there was a collective groan when Brains announced around one o'clock, "They're not coming, I just spoke to them."

But it wasn't more than ten minutes before new word came they were on Moseley Road in a pub called Breeze, towards Balsall Heath. That prompted another groan. The Blues lads knew that a huge march was taking place in the city, with thousands of Rover workers and their families protesting at

BMW's plans to sell its troubled subsidiary, the Longbridge car plant. Traffic would be brought to a standstill because of the thousands of trade unionists arriving from all over the country to join MPs, church leaders and pop stars in one of the biggest demonstrations of public support for a group of workers ever staged in Britain. Getting across the city or getting taxis would be virtually impossible once the march started and the banner-wielding protesters made their way to a park in Edgbaston for a rally. There was also the possibility that Wolves risked being picked up by the police.

But everyone wanted to try to get to them, so those with cars and vans nearby set off after it was decided they should meet at the New Inns pub. The first of the taxis came and Wally and a few others took the quickest route from the Bristol Road, left on to Highgate Middleway and straight into Moseley. But the worst thing that could happen did. When they got near the Birmingham Mosque, they became snarled up in the Rover march making its way to Cannon Hill Park, near Edgbaston Cricket Ground. Although it was just the start of the procession, there were thousands of people. The taxi driver was politely instructed to drive through, which he did.

One of the lads phoned the Wolves lot to let them know they had arrived, while explaining they were light in numbers because of people getting stuck in the march. As they had waited for Wolves all morning, they thought their rivals might wait for them, but that didn't happen.

Around thirty lads made it across around the same time and gathered in the chosen pub just along the road from Wolves' hideout. A game of pool got under way, while tickets for Robert McCracken's world title fight were traded and other lads arrived. Cud, Balla and Psycho pulled up near Breeze but then quickly reversed before Wolves noticed them. But when a couple more lads arrived and crossed the road to go into the New Inns, Wolves spotted them and decided it was time to strike. Blues realised they had been sussed as Breeze started emptying. They grabbed pool cues and the like from the pub and saw Wolves' numbers increasing as they came outside and headed in the direction of Blues.

Cud told everyone that they had to go for it and take it to them, and with that they charged outside, where Cud bumped into his brother, who was taking part in the Rover march, buying some food from a nearby shop.

"Watch this, this is the last big row you'll see," Cud told him as they ran towards Wolves's frontline, shouting "Zuluuuuu!"

Blues chased Wolves back to the club they had been in, where they were met with a barrage of bottles, bricks, pool cues, marine flares and even a couple of petrol bombs. The noise and intensity, coupled with the smell of burning petrol, added to the mayhem and as the police weren't around for a considerable time it was a free-for-all. Wolves, their line several deep, backed off, leaving their casualties on the floor to take a bad kicking. One was lying in the road with blood pouring out of his head for most of the battle. It was brutal and relentless.

Then they saw just how few Blues there were and moved forward again. Blues were then backed up and it didn't look good, until someone shouted to Cud, "Tell 'em to stand, they'll listen to you." He did and the line held.

It went toe-to-toe and one Wolves lad ran up the road with a big red and white plank from some roadworks, flinging it about like a giant sword. One of the bigger Zulus took it off him and bashed him with it. At some point two police officers, one a woman, pulled up nearby but there was no way they were going to get out and do anything and they remained safely ensconced in their patrol car, calling for back up.

Cud, who nursed a knee injury, was hobbling slightly and nearly fell over when he took a huge swipe at a guy with a pool cue but missed and spun round. Wally was carrying out his usual role of also keeping the line strong and together and became aware of a Wolves lad he knew who was doing the same. Another Blues firm of about a dozen, including Morris with some Mansfield friends, came from behind. At first Blues thought they were Wolves' reinforcements because they were so eager to join the fray. If they'd joined Blues' front line it might have helped matters, but they had a go at Wolves at their rear, without much success.

"It looked like a plan; in fact it was a total cock-up," said JJ. "They had been trying to get to the main fight but struggled so they parked near an island and were coming in behind Wolves just as the fight was about to kick off. They saw Wolves come flying out of their pub and then Blues appeared and one of the Mansfield guys went mad and went into Wolves. It got a bit hairy for them as things progressed but still the fighting went on. People were trying to bash each other with bricks and bats as the smoke from the petrol bombs billowed, making it resemble a riot in Belfast."

More police arrived just as one Wolves lad was bowling up the road with a brick in his hand, looking for someone to smack. Instead he copped it; a Blues lad, Mark, clocked the Wolves lad round the back of his head with another brick. The guy went rigid and fell flat on his back. It looked bad, and it was; he was in a coma.

Meanwhile, more Blues were gradually arriving and drove by or left again as they realized it was coming to an end because of the increased police presence.

JJ managed to jump in a cab and headed into the city centre with the aim of buying some new trousers as his Stone Island chinos were covered in claret. He found a shop, bought some and dumped the old ones in time to get back to the next meeting point before the game.

Cud: There were petrol bombs, flares and rockets going off around us, it was mad. It was one of the worst rows I've been in but they should have killed us, there were loads of them. Sometimes in a row you stop and say to your rivals, "C'mon," and it's up to them to do you, but sometimes you do want them to run. You always need the right people there to motivate others. Sometimes people won't do anything unless you have the right ones with you. I am in it for the knuckle and our lot make up a big firm of wreckers and fighters. It's like an army. Everyone has a role, a part to play.

The front line goes in but it's a combination of things that help you win rows.

You want your main guys at the front but it doesn't always happen like that. Sometimes they are at the back, as you can be walking down the road and it's put on you unexpectedly. People will wait for the generals to make the moves and they will stand back until they do. Blokes, some serious-looking geezers, can bounce up and down all day but cannot punch.

When the police arrived after this row I went off, as did a lot of people. I walked down the road and ended up in a Jamaican barbers and pretended I was there to have my hair cut. I sat and waited for a while, just trying to blend in and go unnoticed. The police stuck their heads round the door at one point to see if everything was alright and then went again and then I left.

Wally: I've read Bullshitter Gilly's version in *Terrace Legends* and I've been told about his version in his book [*Running With a Pack of Wolves*] and it's easy to see why he gets his nickname. He makes no comment about the numbers. They had 150 minimum, tooled up to fuck, they even threw petrol bombs. We were thirty and flew straight into them. Yes, Gilly you were right, there were bodies all over the place, but they were all Wolves.

Their frontline got well and truly wasted. They did back us off a couple of times but at no stage did we run. We backed up, re-grouped and went into them again. All that Gilly was doing was jumping up and down saying, "I'm Gilly, I'm Gilly." Whenever we went into them, he backed off. When the other little firm of Blues came from behind them it looked like panic set in amongst the Wolves lads and they didn't know where to turn. At no time did we run and neither did they, but they had the numbers.

Luckily for us, the thirty there first were top lads who could never run and leave people behind. I remember looking across our line knowing that everyone was giving it his best. Most battles usually only go on for a couple of minutes but this went on for about ten. Because of the Rover march, the Old Bill couldn't get there quick enough and, like us, they were probably waiting for Wolves to turn up in Brum city centre.

During rows like this, sometimes one person can save the day. That day for us I kept our line strong and together. I am not blowing my own trumpet but our lads will tell you that's always been my job, especially when the Bordesley firm was going strong. Anyone who didn't pull their weight would suffer a kangaroo court back in the Broadway pub after a row.

The saviour for Wolves that day was an Asian lad called Jo. I'd met him in Featherstone Prison. He was at the back of their firm, having it, when the other Blues firm came from behind. When he turned round he could see us clattering their frontline and backing them up. He had a clear view of what was going on. I watched him come from the back, arms going up and down, screaming at Wolves to stand. He got them going forward again and saved them from embarrassment. When he got to the front we came face to face with each other, smiled, then just side-stepped each other and carried on what we were doing.

After the game I met a few Wolves lads outside their end and walked into town with them. At the time I did say I'd give them the result that day because they did bring it to us and their organisation was first class. They'd hired a private club and got there undetected. Yes, they did back us up but we did the same to them even when they threw petrol bombs. We still went into them and all the bodies on the floor were theirs. It was touch and go for their lad who ended up in hospital after being hit with a brick. The Wolves lad didn't grass but he was in the newspapers in his hospital bed with his wife giving it the bullshit that he was an innocent bystander.

That's the truth of what happened with Wolves that day. Gilly has written his own version of events but just remember his nickname.

*   *   *

Mark G: I was at the White Lion pub about 10am and we were getting calls that Wolves were landing in town but then it was moved to Moseley, as they had hired a club for a supposed stag do. As soon as we heard that, we were off.

When it started, loads of them went down and after a few minutes a few more of us arrived. Bits and bobs were being thrown around and I picked up a brick and ran about twenty yards until I hit someone in the side of their face with it. He was out cold and dropped to the floor. The police arrived and they started to chase me. I ran down a side road, where they got me. The Old Bill told me they thought the guy I had hit was going to die. I heard he was in a coma for a month. I was charged with grievous bodily harm with intent and the guy kept coming to my court appearances. I was found guilty and got four-and-a-half years.

JJ: There's been a lot of rubbish spouted by Wolves about this event. They deserve their credit for organising themselves so well and getting offside. They backed off a good little mob of Blues on two occasions but were run twice by a much smaller and less well-armed firm. It was quite a spectacle, a *Mad Max* scenario, or as it was in medieval times with two warring tribes using everything and anything to get an advantage. They suffered nasty injuries and were left for dead in the road. Based on the experience of the ten per cent of Blues who actually engaged with them, they got off bloody lightly and should be grateful for it.

There were other Blues-Wolves moments after Moseley Road, but obviously the rivalry had got so bad that the law were all over it. We met Gilly at an England game and discussed some of these matters. He shared a balanced view in comparison to some of the rubbish that has been written. It's unfortunate that Wolves regard their greatest moments to be when they faced a small proportion of the Blues mob of the moment. "Never again in our lifetime" was how he described the scene at Moseley Road. He's probably right.

Chapter Seventeen

Rocky Lane

AFTER TWO DECADES of underachievement at St Andrew's, the club rose to the ranks of the Premiership in 2002, courtesy of the play-off system. It meant a huge amount to the club and its supporters, not least the chance to resume hostilities with their most despised rivals. The first time Blues and Aston Villa had met on the pitch in sixteen years was bound to be a fraught occasion off it.

It was a Monday night in September 2002, and on the evening before, half a dozen Blues lads were in a bar in the city centre discussing what might happen. Suggestions that small groups should attack Villa were dismissed in favour of one large onslaught. Because it was the first meeting in such a long time, it was inevitable that Villa would also have big numbers out.

On the day of the game, hooligans from both sides were out early in the afternoon. Around 200 Blues plotted up in the Crown pub in Balsall Heath. Villa's C-Crew – who had been their main firm in the early 1980s – were, unbeknown to Blues, meeting in Sensations on the Moseley Road, only five minutes away. Spotters were dispatched by Blues to check the lay of the land, but no Villa were seen out and about.

At around 4pm, Wally went out to have a look and saw Fowler, one of Villa's main faces, near O'Reilly's pub on Rocky Lane, along with 150 Villa. O'Reilly's, a popular Villa haunt, is at one end of Rocky Lane near a traffic island and the HP Sauce factory; Shanahan's, Blues' preferred watering hole, is a quarter of a mile away at the other end, on the right hand side. In between are industrial estates and wasteland on either side of the road, and a scrap yard near to Shanahan's. The road bends slightly near a bridge, about halfway between the two pubs.

When Wally returned, it was decided that Blues should make their way to Shanahan's via the White Tower pub, formerly called Moriarty's, on the edge of the Nechells area, because not everyone knew where Shanahan's was. As they pulled up at Moriarty's in several cars and vans, they noticed Pc Gant, a football surveillance officer, with several colleagues. Needless to say, this put some off, as it was now common practice for police to film incidents and use such evidence in court. Some returned to the Crown, leaving up to twenty Zulus, who made their way to Shanahan's.

Villa spotted the remaining Blues and were told more Zulus would be putting in an appearance in due course. Calls were put in to some of the others back at the Crown, urging them to return to help avoid any possibility of a victory for Villa. Although the lads were in a pub, it wasn't a big drinking occasion, as all minds were on what lay ahead. A few more Blues arrived, bringing numbers up to about twenty-five. As they waited for more, Villa started marching down from O'Reilly's just before 6pm.

The police presence and the time fighting started would prove crucial in the ensuing court cases. The surveillance team of no more than five officers saw how many Villa there were and were aware of the Zulus well before anything happened.

It must have been obvious to West Midlands Police that something was going to happen, but no calls alerting other units or requests for back-up were recorded on police radio logs until the moment it was about to kick off, leaving many thinking they just wanted to get it all on camera.

In court, Pc Gant said he called for back-up on his mobile phone before anything happened and couldn't explain why he didn't use his radio. Some even say Villa were heading in a different direction when they first left O'Reilly's, but were alerted to Blues' presence further up Rocky Lane by a handful of officers standing in the middle of the road preventing them from walking that way. Because of the bend in the road, the Zulus couldn't clearly see Villa coming towards them but they could hear them, due to their habit of chucking bottles. This signalled it was time for the Zulus to move.

The Zulu chant went up and everyone came out of the pub and turned left. The two firms clashed in the middle of the road. The Blues frontline numbered around thirty and stretched across Rocky Lane. Villa matched that but still it wasn't completely clear how many there were.

Bottles and bricks came raining down from both sides and it became apparent Villa were tooled up, as well as having CS gas, when Blues lad Jimmy Sherry was stabbed in the arm. The stabber was promptly punched by one of the Zulus, M. The thirty stood in the road as more and more Zulus frantically joined in after arriving just in time for the chance to give it to Villa. The industrial estates and scrap yard provided makeshift weapons, with one Villa lad wielding a drainpipe and Blues hurling part of a car engine in their direction. The mobs, some wearing scarves and hats to cover their faces, went back and forth across the road although according to the Zulus present, Villa never really brought it to Blues or managed to see them off, despite their numerical superiority. Blues, cautious about their numbers which had now reached fifty at most, charged into them with about thirty in the attack, got backed off, re-grouped and went into them again.

Wally called for the other Zulus who had arrived late to join them while still battling away on the front line. Police back-up arrived at 6.24pm, after the row had been going on for about four minutes. On the police tape, the officer who is filming the fight can be heard shouting the names of people he recognises from both firms as they wade in. But as soon as reinforcements arrived, everyone began to scatter, jumping into vans and cars to escape. Blues found out later in a conversation with some Villa lads that they expected the Zulus to run after they had hurled a volley of bottles.

As the sound of the numerous police sirens got louder, Wally, Ginger, Panda and two Villa lads they knew got into a van and drove off. As they fled, they passed a Villa C-Crew old-timer and pulled up and got out to talk to him about what had happened. He hadn't been involved but, as they chatted, a couple of officers pounced on them and took down their details. Wally engaged in a bit of verbal with one of them before they were told to leave. Meanwhile, as events were taking place on Rocky Lane, about twenty Zulus making their way there, believing it was still going off, bumped into 200 Villa who had been drinking in Sensations. Their paths crossed at an island by the Watering Hole pub and it kicked off. Blues stood and had it with them despite being massively outnumbered.

As kick-off neared, Wally and Co. continued into town and headed to St Andrew's. As they passed the McDonalds restaurant near the ground, they could see some Blues taking part in one of their favourite pastimes – fighting with the police. They went over and more Zulus turned up and got involved. Some Villa were also there but stood and watched, despite earlier claims they'd have it with Blues again and if the Old Bill were there then they'd fight them too. It eventually calmed down and everyone dispersed and went in to the ground to watch Blues win the derby 3–0.

The match wasn't short on incidents either. Robbie Savage and Gareth Barry engaged in a running feud for most of the first forty-five minutes. Blues scored first, then Villa nearly equalized five minutes before half-time. In the 77th minute, defender Olof Mellberg took a quick throw-in back to goalkeeper Peter Enckelman, who had taken his eyes off the ball. It slipped past him and into the net. Some Bluenoses invaded the pitch, Villa defender Steve Staunton was attacked and Enckelman was confronted and slapped round the ear. Villa then tried but failed to take control of the game. A shot by Vassell was ruled offside, prompting Villa manager Graham Taylor to go mad on the touchline. He ended up being ordered back to the dugout by the referee. A third goal by substitute Geoff Horsfield sealed the victory for Blues. It was a night every Villa fan would like to forget.

Despite the memorable win, those who had been involved in the off-pitch activities earlier on in the evening knew what was coming. They knew the police had captured it all on film from start to finish and could well have everyone bang to rights. After the game, the Villa firm disappeared, leaving in ones and twos and vanishing into the night. Some Zulus, including Wally, went to the away end, where they managed to find some Villa who had been involved in the shenanigans. They were waiting for a police escort and weren't moving till they got one. Wally complimented those that had performed well but slagged off the rest, saying they should have done Blues with the numbers they had, to which they replied, "Yeah, we know."

Soon after, around 100 police officers carried out a series of dawn raids at the homes of those they suspected of being involved in the disorder before the match. Eventually, police arrested and charged seventeen Birmingham fans and fifteen Villa. Most would be on bail for sixteen months before the case came to court. They were split into two groups, with each trial scheduled to last approximately one week.

When the police visited Wally at his home and he was read his rights, one officer said to him, "Remember me?" It was the copper he had abused minutes after the row when they were in the van, making their getaway. According to Wally, the officer then grabbed his testicles, looked him in the eye and said, "I am getting off on this." And with that Wally was carted off to the station.

Wally: Yet again Blues had to bring it to them despite the game being at St Andrew's. They were the ones who were tooled up. They had bottles, knives, gas, bricks and sticks and they go on because one of our lot had a piece of car engine. If you watch the video you can hear the bottles landing before you see any of them. The Old Bill weren't filming them, the camera was on the pub doors filming our lot coming out and running into them. It's obvious to a blind man that if there is going to be trouble between Zulus and Villa, who you film for evidence. There were thirty of us against 150 and they call it a result as we didn't turn them over – judge it for yourself.

A few Blues lads didn't get involved, and on the video you see me running back calling them on. I can see why they didn't, as we were heavily outnumbered, the Old Bill were filming it and so it was a nicking for sure. If it had been a half decent firm I might have had it up myself, but it was only Villa so to me it was get done on the spot and get nicked, running wasn't an option. I held our firm together that day.

Fowler had his one chance with his full firm and blew it. At least this time he didn't go in an ambulance. While we were making our way back to St Andrew's, about 200 of their other firm, the old C-Crew and Steamers, bumped into a firm of about twenty Blues by the ground. Blues had it with them and their claim to fame on that one is that one of them put a black lad in our firm on his arse. Wow.

I'd come up from the back and a firm of Blues had landed and was having it with the Old Bill at the front. Before the game they were saying they didn't care about the Old Bill and would have it. When it came to it and Blues steamed the Old Bill, they didn't even step off the pavement. They had their best firms out that day and couldn't do two little firms of twenty and thirty. Blues were out that night but not in big numbers. We had little firms plotted around, all capable of taking on anything Villa would come with. After the game they disappeared like rats into the night. We'd done them 3–0 and they knew Blues would be going mental afterwards.

The ones that were left pleaded with the Old Bill for an escort.

Cud: We were in the Crown and we knew Villa were going to be in O'Reilly's from about 1pm. All the pubs on Garrison Lane near St Andrew's were full of Blues lads just waiting. The plan was that we had to go in one big firm but we knew we couldn't take 200 blokes across town and we also knew that Villa don't travel. But we said, "Go for it," we'd go to Shanahan's and go for it.

The first lot at Shanahan's said there were Villa scouts there but they left as Blues arrived and went up the road and told everyone. We went in cars to Shanahan's, where we saw Wally, but we said let's leave because of Old Bill. A short time later we heard a mad roar and saw Villa at the top of the hill. Blues went running up to them and we parked our cars and went for it. Videos don't lie so there's no need to brag about numbers. We made the famous Zulu line which very rarely gets broken and it didn't this time. All the lads were having it, with the shout to "stand" going up while everyone was fighting in the road.

About ten lads had never been in anything like that before, it was their first major off and they were having the horrors because it all looked so daunting. Villa filled the whole road and we fought for about four minutes, which felt like a good half an hour in football fighting terms.

The next thing we knew, a big blue meat wagon came straight towards us and we could hear sirens so we scarpered, jumping into cars with people's legs hanging out of windows as they drove away. Some of our lot got caught but overall it was a result for us. We knew there were about 200 Blues lads trying to get over on foot and in taxis.

On the way back to the ground, Villa were sneaking through the back streets, tooled up. By the time twenty of us, some with their kids, arrived at the ground, Villa were at the entrance with the Old Bill. The lads with their kids saw some younger Blues lads and asked them to look after them and keep them out of the way. When they had done that, they went to tackle Villa and it went off with the Old Bill as they tried to get to them. It was a proper battle with the police and Villa just stood there in shock. If we'd got through to them it would have been the end of them.

A few lads grabbed a woman police officer and dragged her around the floor by her ankles. Bricks were also flying around but help soon came.

Villa are good when they have got numbers, they don't say a lot and I respect the old Villa C-Crew from the 1980s but their new lot ain't up to much.

With the police filming we were freaking out thinking could it be another operation. But after the game we went to a lap dancing club in Moseley, where some Villa had been earlier, and the word was some were in there again but we weren't sure. We met in a local pub, somewhere offside, put on our hats, hoods and balaclavas and walked up the road, eighty-handed, to where they were. We stormed the club but the front door was bolted shut from the inside. We tried to find a way to get in and I was watching and laughing when I heard a cry of "We're in!" from one of the lads. I went over to have a look and the lads ran out with loads of crates of drinks. They hadn't got into the club but they'd found the cellar and lots of Champagne. There was also a Porsche parked outside and someone smashed a window, let the handbrake off, pushed it into the road and left it there. It was a quick hit by us and then we were gone.

Wally: It was sixteen months before the case came to trial. Originally, all seventeen Blues and fifteen Villa pleaded not guilty. They kept us a couple of days apart each time we were up in court. Through a mutual friend, I agreed with Fowler it was no longer Blues v. Villa but us against the Old Bill. It grieved me to be civilised to him but I had to do it. During our many court appearances, they offered four of our lads a lesser charge to violent disorder of using threatening words and behaviour, for which the maximum sentence is six months. It's well known that if you plead guilty you get a third off, so they were looking at four months max with half remission, that's eight weeks. Now the criminal-minded know that's a fair deal, so all the Blues agreed that they should take the offer.

The brother of one of our lads, Keith Coley, is a Villa fan, and Keith went to see him one night and Fowler was in the pub. He was pissed up and badmouthing me, saying I was a cunt for letting our lot plead guilty and his boys were doing what he said and going not guilty all the way. He reckoned he had control of his boys.

At our first appearance at Birmingham Crown Court, like he said, he had control of his boys and they all went not guilty. The next time we went up, the judge was displeased when our barristers told him we intended to go not guilty and ordered us out of the courtroom, telling our barristers to warn us that if we carried on like this, anyone found guilty would start off on three years.

So off we went out of the court. None of us were budging and all went back in with not guilty pleas. Judge McCreath, who had specifically requested this trial, was not a happy man. When it was time for Fowler and Co. to go up, the judge gave them the same message and, with the exception of two of them, they all pleaded guilty. Bigmouth Mr Fowler had control of his boys alright; I wonder if he brought their nappies when the judge started talking about three years. Not guilty all the way, he said. Typical Villa, when it's on them they've no balls whatsoever. The two Villa lads got a retrial, but when they went back up the second time they went guilty as well. As usual, it was left to Blues to have it with the Old Bill.

When it came to putting us on trial, they split us into two groups. I was in the second. I sat through most of the first trial to see how things were going and to weigh up the prosecutor and I think he was doing the same with me. He mentioned my name so many times I thought I was in the dock and not the public gallery.

Day one got off to a good start for some of the lads but a bad one for Pc Gant. Three of the lads could only be identified as Mr A, Mr B and Mr C because of identification issues. Pc Gant had to admit that, although he had put names to the faces in the video, he couldn't testify in court how he knew who the three were, his knowledge was hearsay, that is, based on what other officers had told him. It went like this: he arrested Joe Bloggs and was asked how he knew he was Joe Bloggs. He said he knew because someone else had told him but he couldn't remember who that was, when they had told him, or why, so therefore he couldn't be sure it was Joe Bloggs.

Mr B denied being there. You couldn't see the face properly on the video and it was hard to work out who it was. His witness, the gaffer of the local pub, clearly remembered him being in the pub at six o'clock when she opened and she remembered the day well – September 16, 2002 – because the whole city was talking about it, and being a sports pub she had to keep up to date with football.

His two other witnesses had gone off travelling around the world but in the early stages had made a statement to his brief and they had let the courts know months beforehand that the longer the case dragged on, the less likely they would be to attend. So the statements were read out in court. The gaffer of the pub put up a good fight under intense pressure from the prosecutor, Mr Hegarty. He finished off by asking her what he thought would be a trick question.

"After the first Blues-Villa game, can you tell me the next time they met?"

"March 3, 2003," she replied.

That put him right in his place and he sat down shortly afterwards. I spoke to her about it outside the court and she said she remembered the second game better than the first as it was her daughter's birthday.

It was the same situation with Mr C. You couldn't see a face again, as it was covered up, and he denied it was him but didn't provide any witnesses. During the trial, Pc Gant was asked if he had any dealings with a person we shall call Mr Y. He said he didn't. This got everyone suspicious, as he and Mr Y used to talk to each other quite a lot at matches. Mr Y got into a lot of trouble over this, as a lot of the lads thought he was passing info to Pc Gant. No-one can say that he was but he didn't do himself any favours by talking to him all the time. Pc Gant saying under oath that he has had no dealings with Mr Y, when everyone used to see them talking, made things worse for both of them and I was to use this to my advantage when I was on trial.

Outside the courtroom we were all talking about what Gant had just said, and he or some other Old Bill must have heard what we were talking about, so obviously he wouldn't make the same mistake again – or so he thought.

The first trial lasted for a week. There were supposed to be seven up altogether but one didn't turn up and another, Nicky Fuller, pleaded guilty. Now Nicky had never been to a football match in his life and never been involved in violence. I don't even think he went to this game. One of the lads who lives by him showed Nicky a picture of himself that had been in the papers, so he handed himself in to police. They would probably never have got him otherwise but he wasn't to know. Before the trial started everyone's barrister was still trying to get them to go guilty but the lads stuck it out. Nicky turned up late and ended up pleading guilty. The only one who went guilty, Mr Fowler, was not one of us.

The jury found Mr B and Mr C not guilty but the other two were convicted. I was chuffed for the lads who got off on the first trial and I wasn't bothered if I was found guilty when I went up because this was already a result. It was to be another two weeks before I went on trial with the others and I was looking forward to it. I knew from the amount of times the prosecutor mentioned my name that they wanted me, and Pc Gant had said in his statement that the main instigator for Blues was me, and for Villa was Fowler. There were supposed to be six of us up in the second trial but Keith Coley didn't turn up as he was on his toes for another charge, GBH, for which he eventually got a life sentence. They decided not to go ahead with the charges against AS because of Pc Gant not being able to identify him properly.

That left Mr Casey, Mr Morris, Mr Morgan and Walton Wilkins. That's how the prosecutor introduced us. The others were called Mr and then there was a slight pause before he read out my full name. That was to try and make an impression with the jury and that's how it was all through the trial. Everyone was Mr, except me.

Before we went into court, our barristers were still trying to get us to plead guilty, saying we wouldn't get off with it. We were having none of it and going not guilty all the way. My barrister told me if I pleaded guilty I'd get eighteen months but if I got found guilty I'd get two years. Now a quick calculation makes six months difference, cut that in half and take your tagging into account and there is nothing in it. There was no deal to be had there as far as I was concerned. If they wanted my arse down the stairs then they would have to fight for it.

One of the others asked if we could try and get a lesser charge like the other four, but he was told it was violent disorder or nothing. In fact that charge should not have even been put to the others. The crafty fuckers had stitched them up. They had no evidence on them, but rather than let them off they dangled a carrot just so they could get a banning order on them. I didn't see that one coming.

Apparently the presiding judge, Judge McCreath, had a big drugs case due to start and if our trial dragged on it would fuck the other case up. But I'm not here to do the judge any favours, the same way he isn't going to do me any, so let's get on with it. I had another consultation with my barrister and he told me that someone had suggested that just before Blues ran out of the pub, a shout went up that the place was about to be petrol-bombed. All the time we were on bail we met up quite often to discuss what we were going to do but during that sixteen months, I never once heard that suggestion. Something told me not to go with it. I believed it was a trap set up to catch us out and could smell a rat.

I thought it over for a while and told my barrister that while it would be a good thing to say, I didn't hear anything like that and if I went into court and said that I did, I would be lying and I was not going in there to lie in case they had me out. That turned out to be a blessing in disguise. What also turned out to be a blessing was that my surname begins with a W, so I was the last one in the dock and could pick up on whatever mistakes others made. I had also sat through most of the first trial and knew what the prosecutor was up to.

The main Old Bill giving evidence were Pc Gant, Pc Kelly, Pc Peterson, Pc Allen and Pc Rentell from the British Transport Police. First up was Pc Gant. He has been a pain in the arse to me all the time he has been on the intelligence. During the four years he'd been doing it, I'd only been involved in any trouble once and he wasn't there. Every game I went to, I had my kids with me, yet he would follow me and my kids and film us. Wherever I went in the country with my kids, he would point us out to the local Old Bill and make sure they filmed us. I had no problem with him filming me on my own as I knew full well they knew who I was and I wouldn't try to hide my face. What I did have a problem with was him doing it to my kids – one as young as eleven. I caught him being sneaky about it a couple of times, hiding around corners, pointing a camera at us. When my barrister asked him about it, he didn't deny it, he just said, "If that's what he says," and shrugged his shoulders. In four years all he saw me do was go to a match with my kids and that warranted his attention.

He was also asked about his relationship with Mr Y but this time he said he did have dealings with him. In his statement, he said they drove past Shanahan's pub at 6pm and saw me and two others outside. They then drove 500 yards and saw 150 Villa outside O'Reilly's and then informed their control about the situation. We had a copy of radio logs and no calls went in until 6.19pm. He then said he made the call to control on his mobile. There were more than 400 Old Bill on duty that day on radios and he put in a call fearing that a major disturbance was about to take place, and he does it on his mobile so no one can hear it. Really? He said he did not inform the local station, Queen's Road, as he didn't think they could cope. This is the same police who cover crowds of 40,000 at Villa Park. The truth is they had no intention of stopping anything that night and were happy for it to go off so long as they could film it.

He was also asked whether, when he saw me outside the pub, anything was said about it and he replied that nothing was mentioned at all, they just carried on driving. A couple of times that the barristers had him in trouble, the judge stepped in to help him out. At one stage the judge nearly jumped out of his seat, gave one of the barristers the dirtiest looks and stopped him in his tracks.

Pcs Kelly and Allen gave evidence next but both pretty much stuck to their script. The one thing of importance, though, was that both agreed that when they saw me outside the pub, nothing was said about it. Pc Peterson went up next and it was going the same way, so I didn't take much notice, as he hadn't mentioned me in his statement. But one thing I did note was when he was asked if anything was said about me, he said he couldn't hear because he was in the back of the car. How would that stop him hearing anything?

Then came the biggest fuck-up yet. When he finished giving evidence, one of the barristers asked him if it was normal practice for officers to read their statements before they came into court and he said it was. The lawyer then asked him if he had read his and said he had. The barrister asked him again and, once more, he said yes.

The barrister passed the policeman a copy of his statement and asked him to read it out.

He started looking at it but wouldn't read it and started turning a few different colours and shaking. The barrister then said, "What you've said in your statement and what you've said in court today are two different things aren't they?" He didn't answer. Pressed again, he agreed it was a different story. He was asked which was the correct version of events and he said that the one he had told the court was accurate.

"So your statement is incorrect then?"

"Yes."

He was asked when he made his statement but he said he couldn't remember. "Let me remind you," said the barrister. "Your statement is dated September 16, 2002. Now, at twelve midnight it is no longer the sixteenth but the seventeenth, correct?" He agreed. "The incident took place at 6.20pm so in the five-and-a-half hours before midnight you made that statement?" He agreed. "Now you're telling the court you have a better memory sixteen months later than you did five-and-a-half hours after the incident?" He agreed. The barrister made a comment about getting some of the drugs he was on to make that happen to his memory.

Pc Peterson fucked up big time. You could see him sweating like a pig, pulling at his shirt collar to help him breathe. He couldn't drink enough water. Mind you he was under so much pressure he needed a hosepipe.

Next up was Pc Rentell from British Transport Police. He went the same way as Allen and Kelly, which was pretty straightforward but a bit too straight for the prosecution. When he was asked if anything was said about me when they drove past the pub, he said all five officers had a conversation about the fact I was outside the pub. Asked if this was a key moment in what was going to happen, he said it was the decisive moment. Although they couldn't see into the pub, they knew that if I was there then it was highly likely that there would be other Blues fans in the pub. He was asked if the conversation was loud and clear and he said it was and guess where he was sitting? In the back of the car. So now we have one police officer saying the other four are lying and Pc Peterson with his amazing memory. Things were starting to look good for all of us.

Casey and Morris did OK in the dock but what fucked it up for them was going for the petrol bomb story and saying when they came out of the pub the Old Bill had the road blocked off to the right, so they could only go left. The prosecutor had them out on both counts so things went against them. Morgan fell apart in the dock and ended up going guilty. After Casey had been up, I said to Morris and Morgan not to go into the dock, as I felt confident I had it sussed and didn't want the prosecutor gaining any more points with the jury. I was ready to go in and blow it wide open. But they both said they still wanted to go in, so that was that.

It was nearly the end of day four before I went into the dock. Before I went in, they read out my police interview. A DC Comely was in the dock reading the police part and the prosecutor read my part. What they did though was edit it and miss things out for the jury. I sussed it but wasn't sure what it was. What saved me was the judge deciding to finish for the day and make a fresh start the following morning. I was able to read my statement at home and I told the others what I had sussed and would reveal them in court the next day.

My barrister questioned me first, which was a pretty easy ride. The judge then called a break for lunch. On the way out of court, one of the lads' girlfriends saw DC Comely put his arm around the prosecutor and say, "Don't worry, you're going to bury him after." I was fuming and this made me even more determined to win this one. I went and had a couple of brandies and when I'm on the brandy that means only one thing, trouble.

I came back into court ready for a battle. It was shit or bust. I knew how I was going to play the prosecutor, as I had been studying him. I also had to play the jury; they are the ones you have to convince, as it's in their hands. When I got into the witness box, the first thing I did was to smile at the prosecutor and anyone who knows me will tell you this is something I don't do too often. People who have known me for thirty years can count on one hand the number of times they've seen me smile. I've got my own reasons for this, one of them being it can show a sign of weakness. When the prosecutor smiled back, I knew from that moment that I had him in the palm of my hand. Bury me? I don't think so.

The first thing he did was to pass me a photocopy of my interview. I had a quick glance and everything was there from what I could see; it wasn't the edited version. He was going on about it being a "no comment" statement, the same as the others, which he gave them a hard time about. It doesn't look good to a jury when you give a no comment statement. He started reading the first couple of pages, then he wanted to skip ahead a few, but I didn't. It turned into a bit of a pantomime, with him saying skip a page and me saying no and in the end the judge had to agree for me to read everything out.

In interview, the police had shown me a photo of myself taken from a still from the police video. I agreed the photo was me. They then started to talk about the video and I said I wanted to see it and I would talk about it, and they agreed to show me the tape. That was the deal, but they didn't do what they had agreed, so I went back to no comment. I turned to the jury and said the photo was evidence which I talked about. When they said they'd show me more evidence, but then didn't, I went "no comment". They backed out of the deal, not me. That's what the prosecutor and DC Comely hadn't revealed to the jury. Then I explained that another reason I went no comment was because I thought I'd have a better memory sixteen months later than I did then. That brought a bit of a smile to some of their faces.

The next part the prosecutor picked up on was that at one stage I said in interview that I was at O'Reilly's, when in fact it was Villa who were there. He then tried to make out that I went to O'Reilly's to organise things. I told him what I said had been a slip of the tongue but he wasn't having it, so I then took charge. I said, "Turn the page over, Mr Hegarty, and read what the police officer says." It read, "So, Walton, you were in O'Reilly's, sorry, I mean Shanahan's?" I pointed out that was a slip of the tongue by the police. I had made a slip and so did they. I took another look at the jury and could see a couple of them nodding in agreement with me. So now, as far as my statement goes, things were going my way.

The next thing Mr Hegarty said was, "Mr Wilkins, Pc Gant talks to Mr Y and Mr Y talks to Pc Gant. Yes?"

"So what if they do, what has it got to do with anything?"

At this point I froze on the spot. With that my barrister stood up and said, "Do what you've got to do." OK, Mr Hegarty, you know I sat through the first trial and was there when this was brought up then. When Pc Gant was asked about this connection he denied it, so I'm thinking why did he say no when hundreds of people have seen them speaking at matches? At this trial, when he was asked again he said, "Yes." I addressed Mr Hegarty and asked him why Pc Gant lied under oath in the first trial. There was no answer from him. This was the prosecutor who DC Comely said would bury me, but if the ground could have opened he would have buried himself on the spot. A quick shuffle of his papers and a big gulp of water and he moved on to the next subject, the story regarding the pub being bombed.

When the others went with this it fucked them up, because it just didn't happen. I then remembered when one of the others was in the dock he started saying things about what he said to his barrister and the judge stopped him and told him whatever had been said was confidential. So I used this line, "Can I mention something I said to my barrister in consultation?" The judge said the same thing to me, which I knew but it looked good before the jury. So I told them that when my barrister had asked me about the petrol bomb I told him I hadn't heard it and was not prepared to go into court and testify to it, as I would be lying, and I was not going to do that. My barrister stood up and nodded in agreement. More water for the prosecution! The only one getting buried here was him and I was glad I didn't go along with the petrol bomb story.

Now we started on the video. On the tape they think they have got me bang to rights, as there is no doubt it's me and I was not about to deny it. Another part of where the others went wrong was trying to say that when they came out of the pub, the Old Bill were to the right of them, blocking the road, so they could only go left. One by one, their stories were taken apart when the video was played and slowed down to show that, at the most, two Old Bill were there. My version of events was that when I came out of the pub I looked to my left and could see thirty of my mates being attacked by about 150 people. The prosecutor asked what was to my right and I said nothing, so he asked me why I didn't I go right. I said I saw that my friends were being attacked to my left and I made a conscious decision to go and help my friends. What type of friend would I be to go the other way?

I said I also knew that in amongst the attackers were members of Combat 18 [the violent neo-nazi group]. He asked me how I would know this and I replied, "Because they are Villa fans," pointed over to the Old Bill and suggested he ask them, as they are part of intelligence gathering and know that if you go onto Villa's website it's always full of racist stuff towards Blues fans, which they are known for. This was for the benefit of the two Asian members of the jury. The Old Bill knew this was true and I put them on the spot and they couldn't do anything about it, so you Villa twats who give it the racist shit helped me out a bit there. Nice one!

So now they've got me running forward on the video and ask me to explain myself. So I say I am running forward to help my friends and trying to contain the disorder. I could see the Old Bill and they weren't interested in stopping it, all they wanted to do was film it. Mr Hegarty, with a grin on his face as if to say, I've got to hear this, asked me how I thought I could contain the disorder. "Well," I said, "It's like this. For over fifteen years I worked the doors on the roughest pubs and clubs in Birmingham. I've been in some situations when there have been only four doormen and it's gone off with more than 150 people with tables, chairs, bottles, knives, baseball bats, the whole lot. As a doorman, four of us have had to get stuck in and sort it. We didn't run off, it was our job. So this time I haven't got four doormen, I've got thirty and I trust every single one of them to help me contain the disorder. I thought the best way to do that was to face it head-on, because if we turned and ran and we got caught from behind it would be worse for us."

Bury me? I'm bashing this prosecutor with his own shovel.

Right then, Mr Wilkins, there you are, running back, waving your arms, beckoning people on who haven't got involved, explain that then. He adjusted his wig and took another gulp of water but still gave me a little look to say, "I've got you now."

"Well Mr Hegarty, when I looked around I was disgusted that some people I knew were not helping, so I ran back down calling them on, saying. 'I'm in trouble, your friends are in

261

trouble, come and help.' I knew them as doormen and thought they were able to help me contain the disorder."

Mr Hegarty was in it up to his neck now and there was no way out. He still thought he'd got another couple of tricks up his sleeve, or should I say under his wig, because he kept lifting it up and down.

"Right then, Mr Wilkins, that chanting you can hear, 'Zulu,' what's that about?"

One of the others had said he had never heard of it before, which was the wrong thing to say to the jury, because even if you're not into football, everyone has heard of the Zulus. I just said every Blues fan is a Zulu and I've heard grannies, granddads, women and kids sing "Zulu Army". The whole ground sings it but it doesn't mean we're real Zulus. They call Spurs Yids and they're not Jews, and all the Arsenal Gooners and they're not German, and they call Blues Zulus, that's it, it's not a gang.

He was now up to his nose in it and all you could see was his eyes and wig moving. He said, "Mr Wilkins, that man there waving about part of a car engine, that's not normal behaviour is it?"

I just looked him straight in the eye and said, "Mr Hegarty, I totally agree that behaviour was disgraceful, sir."

No more questions for Mr Wilkins.

I froze on the spot again, not because I was stuck for words but because I was waiting for the bit that would fuck me up: my previous convictions. I'd seen Mr Hergarty give one of the others a hard time for his previous, a minor assault and a motoring offence. I had a twenty-year history of offending and at the time of my arrest I was still doing community service for a handling charge for a lorry load of computer stuff. I came out in 1999 for ten kilos of draw, there was my four years for football, a couple of detention centres, various other violence and theft charges going back to 1980. But it was never read out. Perhaps, because of the fun and games with the prosecution, they were too taken aback to remember.

Nice one Mr Hegarty.

When I came out the dock, DC Comely was still there and I

looked straight at him, pointed to my chest and said, "Bury me? Bury ME?" The whole court could hear it but I didn't realise at the time because the adrenalin was pumping. I knew I'd done the business. I celebrated that weekend even though we still had to go back for the verdict on the Monday. My barrister told me DC Comely had spoken to him about me making comments when I came out the dock, and if there was any more of it he would report me to the judge. Now I knew they were running scared.

When the judge started summing up, he admitted that he already had it worked out that he would sum up the same as he did in the first trial. But I had given him something else to think about. He still tried to put it to the jury in a way to make me look guilty, but it was a feeble attempt and he just blabbed on for ages about nothing.

When my barrister summed up on my behalf, he kept it short and sweet. The main thing he played on was that it was easy to see West Midlands Police were out to get me. With Gant filming me and my kids, and the point about the conversation in the car and how funny it was that four West Midlands Police officers either said there was nothing said or they didn't hear for whatever reason, but the British Transport Police officer said that they all had had a conversation about it, and that was the key moment they realised the potential for trouble.

There were also some key points put to the jury in writing that the prosecution had agreed to, including dismissing what Gant had said about seeing me kick and punch anyone, as it hadn't been seen on the video, and the person they did identify at one point as being me was in fact another defendant, Kenrick Stevens, one of those offered a lesser charge of making threatening words and behaviour.

Also there were the facts that the police did not call for back up at 6pm as they said, but at 6.19pm, the Blues fans were heavily outnumbered and all the weapons found, including CS gas, knives and snooker balls in socks, were discovered outside Villa's pub, O'Reilly's. And Villa say we were tooled up because one out of thirty of us had a bit of a car engine?

When the jury went out there were just three of us left – me, Casey and Morris. Morgan had buckled half way through and gone guilty. The jury came back in the afternoon with guilty verdicts on Casey and Morris and undecided on me. Everyone went over to the pub but I had to stay in the court. I thought it would be a while before the jury came back but they returned after about ten minutes. There was only Morris's girlfriend and my son Matthew in the courtroom when they told me I was not guilty. I didn't even smile then, once was enough in that courtroom.

The Old Bill were gutted. I was glad DC Comely was there to witness it but Pc Gant was missing. These two are stationed at my local police station at Stechford. I would have loved to have been a fly on the wall to see how the news was received.

Football lads will often say that, without doubt, the worst Old Bill for taking liberties with fans are West Midlands Police. People all over the country have had bad experiences with them and haven't forgotten them – and for most that's only been a couple of times a year for a few hours at a time. I've had that lot at Stechford on my case for more than twenty years, 24/7. That not guilty result was so fucking sweet.

The first game I went to after this was Bolton at home. I was stood up at the very back next to the wall, which everyone does at the back across the whole of the main stand as there is no one behind you, so you're not blocking anyone's view.

After a while me and a mate, Lenny, noticed a firm of stewards heading our way from the other side of the main stand. We soon found out who they were coming for. They were not the club's stewards but a private firm called Firewalker and they came straight up to me, saying I had to sit down for safety reasons. We watched them walk from one end of the stand down to me and no one else was told to sit down. I pointed this out to them and they said they were starting with me first. I asked them, to stop me being paranoid, to ask just one other person to sit down and then I would, but they insisted I was first and with that they left. There were two Old Bill at the entrance and the stewards walked past them, so I thought they were going to leave me alone, but I was wrong.

About five minutes later they came back with a heavy mob of Old Bill who came up saying I was being aggressive to the stewards, which was a load of bollocks. One of the club stewards stepped in and said I wasn't being aggressive at all. My son was with me but he was sitting four or five rows in front. He stood up to see what was happening and an Old Bill asked him what he was doing and he said nothing, he was looking to see what was happening because that was his dad. Straight away, the Old Bill grabbed him and started manhandling him. We were both thrown out of the ground. Now I understand their beef with me, but to do that to a fifteen-year-old kid who just wanted to see what was happening to his dad is out of order. When I go to home games now I don't sit with my kids, I move around the ground and meet them afterwards. This is a new tactic that West Midlands Police use to hassle you with your kids and they don't care how old they are.

It was a month later before the ones who got found guilty went back to court for sentencing. There were ten of them out of the original seventeen; five of us got not guilty and two others were still on their toes. At an earlier hearing, the judge had been talking about starting off at three years for anyone who went not guilty, but in the end the most he gave out was ten months and a ten-year ban.

They reckon if you plead guilty you get a better deal, but that is a load of bollocks because Nicky Fuller, the lad who had never been to a game in his life, had pleaded guilty and ended up getting more than some of the ones who went not guilty. The judge made some comment about not believing him, but he was the only one who told the truth. When it came to the four who had been offered lesser charges, three of them got community service and a four-year ban. Jimmy Sherry laughed out loud when he was sentenced to three months. He expected more, bearing in mind he had football convictions stretching back to the 1970s, and when they read them out it sounded like he was going for the record of being nicked at all ninety-two football grounds.

After the lads got their sentences it was in the local paper and was the top story on Central News. Nothing was ever mentioned about us getting a not guilty. I wonder why.

The next time the two teams met was in March at Villa Park. A mob of fifty Blues met in the Royal Oak on the corner of Lozells Road near the A34 at about 5pm. Villa were in the Adventurers pub, next door to a police station, and a Blues spotter confirmed that the cops were around. But some Villa, including Andy B, their main guy, pulled up in a black cab outside the Royal Oak and fronted up the Zulus. It didn't go their way and they got annihilated, with some ending up in hospital despite only fifteen or so Zulus taking part in proceedings. Squid, a Blues lad who probably isn't even five feet tall, did a memorable flying dropkick into Andy, putting him on his arse. After that, it became hard for Blues to drink in that pub.

About 200 Zulus made their way to Villa Park through Aston Park. Villa were on their way too but the police prevented any altercation by re-routing the Zulus. Villa seemed still to want some action and started going mad and attacking "shirts" and even did over one of their own – their Supporters' Club secretary – thinking he was from the Zulus because he was Asian.

Again, the match provided many talking points with Blues winning by two late goals from Stan Lazaridis and Geoff Horsfield, but most remember Dion Dublin being sent off for butting Robbie Savage after a late tackle and a bit of verbal. Graham Taylor resigned as Villa manager two months later.

Wally: Not a lot happened at the game at their place in March 2003. They met in a pub next door to one of the biggest police stations in Brum and told Blues to go there – lovely! Blues sent messages saying they wouldn't go, and I was still on bail for Rocky Lane.

During the game there were little fights in all parts of the ground so that can only mean Blues were everywhere, as I'm sure they weren't fighting each other. One Villa fan ran on the pitch and confronted Robbie Savage. A lot of Villa were running down the stands as if they were going on the pitch, but stopped when they got to the advertising boards. It looked good on television and people were surprised at Villa, but all they did was shape. Why not come on the pitch? How many times have you seen Blues on the pitch having it with other fans or Old Bill? Loads. How many times Villa? None.

Nothing happened after the game, and the next time the teams met, in October 2003 at St Andrew's, a few Zulus were unable to go due to bail conditions resulting from Rocky Lane. In fact, they had to go back to court because the police wanted to change their bail conditions. Originally, they had to stay two miles away from the grounds but the conditions were amended to keep them in their homes between 10am and 7pm on match days, with visits from police to check they were adhering to the new rules.

Wally: After we were promoted, all the derby games were on a Monday night.

But, for the first time in their history, Villa were playing on a Sunday morning on police advice. Until Blues and Albion came up, none of their games were ever classed as a risk. At the start of each season, every hooligan looks at the fixture list to see when the best rows are going to be and to check on the first and last games, and then their derby games. Can a hooligan honestly tell me they get excited when they are playing Villa? I doubt it. Obviously, when they play us and Albion there will be trouble but other than that it's bring the family and a packed lunch.

Anyway, nothing happened before the game that day as the Old Bill had got it sussed. A few hours after the game, almost 300 Villa marched towards town. I'll give them their dues on that one.

Before they got to the fire station, they got split into two firms of equal numbers. The one firm bumped into a firm of Blues in the subway and got run everywhere, running into the backs of shops. Some of them ran through the children's hospital and the Old Bill chased them and caved a few heads in with truncheons. There was sporadic fighting around town. I was getting commentary via mobile. The court had changed our bail conditions for this game and we had to stay indoors and the Old Bill went round to various homes to make sure we were in. Some people got no visits but I got two.

I was lucky that day, for some reason. At the time of my arrest I was living in Hollywood, on the outskirts of Brum. One of our bail conditions was that on match days we couldn't be within two miles of the ground, so I bought a new house and put myself in the radius. There wasn't a bail condition that said I couldn't go home. On the morning of the match, I just happened to read my letter from my solicitor and noticed my bail condition was for my old Hollywood address. I phoned the police station to let them know where I was, and they said I was lucky because they obviously had my old address and were going to check for me there.

By the way, Villa said they ran at the fire station because Blues had too many. It's OK when there are twenty or thirty of us but they class too many as seventy or so Blues to their 150. If we'd had another 20 at Rocky Lane we'd have done them proper.

I was able to go to the next game at Villa Park in February 2004. It was about two weeks after I was cleared over Rocky Lane, so the bail conditions had been removed. I had decided that the best thing for me to do was go on the corporate coaches from St Andrew's. I had to keep out of trouble, as the Old Bill were gutted I had got off. Me and a couple of others got whistled up, had breakfast at the ground and then got on the coaches with the prawn sandwich firm over to Villa Park. Villa yet again met in the Adventurers next to the police station. Blues had decided not to meet anywhere but just to get to New Street in time to get the train to Aston at about 11.20am. When Blues got off they were met by a load of Old Bill and escorted.

Only one of their lads was there, Andy B. He went over to one of our lot and said, "Do you know who I am? I'm Andy B ——." He was told fuck off. There were loads of Old Bill and he walked off with Pc Kelly, who is in football intelligence. I'd already sent word to Villa that due to me getting off I wouldn't be getting involved in anything and I'd be going on the corporate coaches, but when I came out of the ground all the Old Bill were lined up outside the away end. All the ones involved in the case were there. Then up popped Andy B a few yards ahead of me, in front of at least fifty officers, giving it the big one and trying to get me to kick off. I threw my hands in the air and the Old Bill let him carry on, waiting for me to react so they could nick me. When they saw I wasn't going to react, one of them pushed him away. He should buy himself a uniform because he is very good mates with them.

On the pitch Villa went two-up but Blues equalised in the last minute.

In December 2004, Blues won 2–1 at Villa Park. A pub in Perry Barr was the chosen meeting place for around 150 Zulus, but nothing much happened despite a call being put in to Villa. A Villa lad, DR, later told Wally that all they could muster was twenty-five lads. They knew Blues had sorted it offside but couldn't get any more than that, which they admitted was a bit of an embarrassment. Villa were again in the Adventurers pub.

Besides the 150 there was another firm of about sixty Blues who decided not to meet at the same place but to wait and see what happened. If the police sussed out one firm, the other could slip in. The cops did suss the 150 in Perry Barr and so the other firm met up somewhere and made their way to Villa Park. Villa knew what was going on but apparently would only say, "Come to the Adventurers."

The smaller firm of Blues was getting closer and closer to Villa Park and the police were going past them in cars and vans but didn't suss they were Zulus because they thought they had all the Blues in the pub in Perry Barr. This small firm got right next to Aston Park when two community support officers realised that this firm was Zulus; it was the black faces that gave it away. The two frantically called for back-up on their mobiles, which quickly arrived. The CSOs may have saved Villa's hooligans from more embarrassment that day, as that little firm was made up of "proper heads".

For the next game at St Andrew's, Villa sent messages that once and for all they were turning out for Blues and would do all sorts to them. Word came out that they were getting escorted from Aston. Wally was out and about when he saw this once-and-for-all best-ever firm, which reached a staggering total of ... fifty-four. He counted every one of them and ten were female.

Wally: This was the big surprise we were in for. They're running round the country at England games telling everyone bullshit that they're getting the upper hand and all they can pull is fifty-four and people believe them and put it in print. Nothing happened before or after the game but later that night a firm of young kids aged between sixteen and twenty went over to Aston. A few older heads told them not to go because if they got nicked they'd get the full blame. They weren't listening and their version is that Villa came out about 100-handed, throwing bottles as usual. The kids were having it with them until they saw the Old Bill and decided to have it up. Villa ran at them still, so they're saying they ran at Blues. Even if they did it was thirty young kids who went over to their manor outnumbered, as always. I'd like to see the day if any Villa would come to places like Bordesley Green, Acocks Green or Chelmsley Wood thirty-handed.

At Rocky Lane, Blues were outnumbered, yet more Blues got nicked than Villa. After their last two embarrassing turnouts, maybe now they'll go back to wherever they were hiding for twenty years and stop spreading bullshit. I know a few Villa lads who will freely admit that Blues are one of the top firms in the country and, don't get me wrong, they have got some good lads, but they are finished, overall. We've had our battles but there won't be any more Rocky Lanes.

That was the first time they had a lot of the older lot out but we've always had an active firm and they haven't. They don't know what it's about. They can remember when we used to terrorise them. The younger lot will still want to show them and do their thing but the scene is almost dead now. We had fewer than them at Rocky Lane but we had the right people there. Villa never brought it to us, we always had to come to them. I knew the Old Bill would be filming anything that happened but we knew we couldn't run from Villa.

Final Word

Wally: Football violence will never reach the heights it did in the 1980s. That's when the best times were had, not just for the fighting but for other things the hooligans set the standard for. Take fashion. Long before any overpaid, poncey footballers and so-called celebrities knew about designer clothing, the catwalk was on the terraces every Saturday afternoon. Whether it was the Scousers or the Cockneys that started it, there is no doubt that it was football hooligans that set a trend that still lasts to this day. If you wanted to see the latest clobber, you didn't buy some glossy magazine; you went to the match to see what other hoolies were wearing. Football hooligans set the standard, full stop.

Today's music scene is dominated by dance music. When the rave scene started in 1987 it was football lads who were doing the promoting. It was football lads who were doing the security at the illegal raves in fields and warehouses. It was them who were battling with the Old Bill so they didn't stop the parties. It was hoolies leading the convoys of people to the parties and outmanoeuvring the Old Bill to get the people in. We stood our ground until eventually they had to give us all night licences. Now that the music has gone mainstream and the designer wear is now on the local high street people tend to forget who was at the forefront of it all.

I personally don't have any regrets about my involvement in

football violence, even my four-year sentence. The crime is getting caught. I have been at the forefront of the Zulus from day one. Now, though, my hooligan days are behind me. After being cleared over the Rocky Lane incident with Villa, I'd be a fool to get involved again. That was my best battle by far and I know I put one up West Midlands Old Bill big time.

The Zulu name has been associated with Birmingham for nearly twenty-five years now and it will always remain with the club no matter what. But as a firm, I think it has come to an end. The same goes for the likes of West Ham and Millwall but the names live on and will be held in high esteem by any new hooligan firms. We will always be able to pull a firm together if we need to, but a lot of us have thrown in the towel. Though, as they say, you never know.

These are my top five firms based on my own experience. We can go on about it all day long but over the years there have been some good firms out there at different times.

1. West Ham

Without a doubt West Ham's ICF were the first organised firm to set the standard that many firms since have tried to achieve. The ICF name is legendary amongst older football firms. From the early to mid Eighties, when hooliganism was at its peak, West Ham led the way. I can honestly say that in our early days, first as the Apex, then the Zulus, the ICF were the ones we looked up to. The Scousers may claim to be the first clobbered-up firm in football but their style had no class. Going down to Arsenal put me wise, but the sight of the ICF in Farahs, Pringle jumpers and Burberry Macs is classic hooligan style. Even though they weren't really active from the mid Eighties, the ICF definitely set the benchmark.

2. Millwall

It was a close call for me between West Ham and Millwall, but the Hammers just about come in front on their organisation and tactics. Millwall's firm is awesome but what goes against them is other London firms join up with them for big games, so you can't say it's just their firm doing it. Still, anyone who goes to the Den has to take a serious firm or don't bother. You can go to certain places with small numbers and get a result but this is one place you won't get away with it.

3. Pompey

Even though we have had good results against Pompey, I rate them highly. You've got to give them credit for the way they used to go to London and give the Cockney firms major problems.

4. Cardiff

Although Cardiff didn't emerge with a serious firm until the Nineties, I think the Soul Crew would have put up a good show a decade earlier. They made their name in the lower divisions but when they have come across the big teams they have made their mark. I also admire them for their honesty. When I was down there for the Carling Cup against Liverpool, they made it clear they wanted it off with the Zulus; they didn't care if they won or lost, they just wanted it. Fair play to them.

5. Manchester United

In the Seventies, Man U rampaged their way to almost every ground they went to. Numbers-wise they can pull the biggest firm going but it's not about numbers. A lot of people say you never know when you're fighting Mancs if you're playing Man Utd, but when you have it with the Salford firm you know about it.

Other firms worth a mention are Chelsea, Leeds, Spurs and Man City, also the Wolves Subway firm from the early Eighties. But the worst firm out there? That has got to be Villa and I am not taking the piss, I'm being deadly serious. They come from the second biggest city in the country and class themselves as a big club. Yet their firm is a disgrace. How come a club that's so big has such a shit firm? You've read what they call a result – 150 of them tooled up and having it toe-to-toe with thirty at Rocky Lane. That's a result to them because they remember the days when twenty-odd of us would go up to Villa Park and slap them all over the place. This time they didn't run.

There is only one of them who I'll give any credit to over the last twenty years and that's Fowler. On a personal level I've got no time for him, but I'll credit where credit's due. In the early Eighties, Villa had a better firm than us but when the Zulus started up, their boys – the C-Crew and the Steamers – disappeared. They couldn't handle the Zulus and didn't even try, they just went missing. Whereas at least Fowler tried to do something about it, not that anything ever came of it. He still had a go and you have to acknowledge that.

Cud: The best days are gone that's for sure. Although, there seems to have been a bit of a resurgence of the older heads in other firms in the last few years, perhaps it's to settle old scores one last time. The lads that went down to the football back in the Seventies – the punks and skinheads – were part of a rebellion within society and I think if they didn't go to matches there would have been some serious crimes carried out, because there was nothing else to do.

There was a togetherness within the firm, like a family and every Saturday we were going to war. Others go to Iraq or wherever to fight for a cause they believe in, and defending our area was what we believed in. It's our turf and when others came to Birmingham we would protect it. When we went to other areas, the locals would protect their manor – it was even like that within Birmingham with all the different areas for a time. Every town is like it. It's the law of the jungle and it's been like that for hundreds of years: you land on us and we'll land on you. It might sound stupid but that is how it was and they were the best days of my life.

I'd like to set the record straight by saying the fact West Ham claim they have never been done really pisses everyone off. They were a major firm but we got results against them. Many firms I've mentioned in this book, and even some not mentioned, on any given day get a result against anyone, home or away. Whether you're Grimsby – no disrespect – or you're Millwall, everyone gets turned over and most people get a result from time to time. If not, you must be shit. As for Stoke saying they got on the pitch at the match in 1992, that's rubbish. They never got on and were just throwing rabbit punches from the fence. If they'd have made the same efforts to get on the pitch, who knows what would have happened?

After reading the book *Top Boys* and the part from Spenna from Villa, he mentions two rows and they were in the last few years – 150 against thirty at Rocky Lane and Villa stood and had it with Blues. Well, if they class that as a result they really are a top five firm. All I can say with those kinds of numbers you would stand wouldn't you! Work it out for yourself.

As for the last stand they made at McDonalds on the Coventry Road before the match – for fuck's sake, some faces were with their kids and were going to their first Villa–Blues game and still Villa didn't get a result. Fifteen noses against 80-100 Villa. Where's all his fucking stories from the late Seventies and early Eighties, which in my view were the real times? I don't hate Villa, I just think they're shit, but I thank the old C-Crew for many battles.

In the day, 1980/82, the Acocks Green lads were the best firm for numbers in my opinion. We were between fifteen and twenty-strong down the games and we were outnumbered many times but fuck numbers, some you win, some you lose. You can say we did not have it all our own way, not just with other firms but because of the in-house fighting in our firm as well, but once that was sorted we had the run of the manor.

Don't get me wrong, when the C-Crew were out, before the Zulus, they were proper. Black Danny gets a big mention as he was the only cunt who had the balls to front me in the day, and if it wasn't for him I would not be the person I am today, because I knew if we did not crush them we would have major problems – and not long after '82 season, the C-Crew disbanded.

For me, Wolves are the same stamp as Villa. In the day their Subway Army were a good firm, on a par with if not better than the C-Crew. We had many battles with them, mostly victorious but we lost a few as well. I don't need to bullshit; I liked Wolves because in them days my cousin was Wolves hardcore and tried to arrange many kick-offs. But as for today, their geezer – who looks like one of the hillbillies out of that '70s film *The Hills Have Eyes* – I don't think he's had a proper scrap in his life.

When we had it off with them for a good ten minutes on Moseley Road, you ask any proper lad down the footy this: if you row for that long, someone is going to get seriously hurt, especially when you have got over 100 lads tooled up with bats, petrol bombs and a so-called rocket launcher, which Wolves had. Zulus made a line, outnumbered to fuck and took it to them with one not serious casualty. Wolves, eleven seriously hurt and one in a coma. It's not rocket science lads, come on!

I'm quite definitely retired today; the scene is dead for me and will remain so. No comebacks. But I can still look back to the heyday and select who I think were the top firms of the Eighties.

WEST HAM and MILLWALL

Sorry, but I find it hard to separate the two. West Ham were proper organised, cool, smart, could do the biz week in and week out and were never known for just smashing things up. They are a firm many Blues looked up to and were in awe of until the Zulus formed. Millwall were not as organised but fucking mental on their day. We had many good battles with them. Nuff respect.

CARDIFF

They were always performing over the years and were very consistent (a bit like us) and their big numbers give any firm a run for their money.

TOTTENHAM

They were the firm we had more fun and games with than anyone – a proper outfit.

MAN UNITED

It was a numbers game with this lot. They were like Vikings descending on a town and were known for smashing everywhere up, but their hardcore were tops from my encounters.

PORTSMOUTH

For me Pompey could easily make my top three for the havoc they caused everywhere but for some reason they never got major results on us.

Other firms worth a mention are Chelsea, Leeds, Forest, Middlesbrough, Stoke and Man City.

As for us, where do I think we come? Well, that's not for me to

Final Word

say. All I can say is that when the Zulus went to town in the Eighties, we left our stamp . . .